Social Media in Southeast Italy

WHY WE POST

PUBLISHED AND FORTHCOMING TITLES:

Social Media in Southeast Turkey
Elisabetta Costa

Social Media in Southeast Italy
Razvan Nicolescu

Social Media in Northern Chile
Nell Haynes

Social Media in Trinidad
Jolynna Sinanan

Social Media in Rural China
Tom McDonald

Social Media in Emergent Brazil
Juliano Spyer

Social Media in an English Village
Daniel Miller

Social Media in South India
Shriram Venkatraman

Visualizing Facebook
Daniel Miller and Jolynna Sinanan

Social Media in Industrial China
Xinyuan Wang

How the World Changed Social Media
Daniel Miller et al

Download free: www.ucl.ac.uk/ucl-press

Why We Post

Social Media in Southeast Italy

Crafting Ideals

Razvan Nicolescu

First published in 2016 by
UCL Press
University College London
Gower Street
London WC1E 6BT

Available to download free: www.ucl.ac.uk/ucl-press

ISBN: 978–1–910634–72–1 (Hbk.)
ISBN: 978–1–910634–73–8 (Pbk.)
ISBN: 978–1–910634–74–5 (PDF)
ISBN: 978–1–910634–75–2 (epub)
ISBN: 978–1–910634–76–9 (mobi)
ISBN: 978–1–911307–69–3 (html)
DOI: 10.14324/111.9781910634745

To my parents, Alexandru and Doina Dorina

Introduction to the series Why We Post

This book is one of a series of 11 titles. Nine are monographs devoted to specific field sites in Brazil, Chile, China, England, India, Trinidad, Turkey and this one in Italy – they will be published in 2016–17. The series also includes a comparative book about all of our findings, published to accompany the other titles, as well as a book which contrasts the visuals that people post on Facebook in the English field site, with those on the Trinidadian field site.

When we tell people that we have written nine monographs about social media around the world, and that they all have the same chapter headings (apart from Chapter 5), they are concerned about potential repetition. However, if you decide to read several of these books (which we very much hope you do), you will see that this device has been helpful in showing the precise opposite. Each book is as individual and distinct as if it were on an entirely different topic.

This is perhaps our single most important finding. Most studies of the internet and social media are based on research methods that assume we can generalise across different groups. We tend to look at tweets in one place and write about 'Twitter'. We conduct tests about social media and friendship in one population, and then write on this topic as if friendship means the same thing for all populations. By presenting nine books with the same chapter headings, you can judge for yourselves what kinds of generalisations are, or are not, possible.

Our intention is not to evaluate social media either positively or negatively. The purpose is educational, providing detailed evidence of what social media has become in each place and the local consequences, including local evaluations.

Each book is based on 15 months of research during which time most of the anthropologists lived, worked and interacted with people, always in the local language. Yet they differ from the dominant tradition of writing social science books. Firstly, they do not engage with the academic literatures on social media. It would be highly repetitive to have the same discussions in all nine books. Instead discussions of these literatures are to be found in our comparative book, *How the World Changed Social Media*. Secondly, these monographs are not comparative, which again is the primary function of this other volume. Thirdly, given the immense interest in social media from the general public, we have tried to write in an accessible and open style. This means we have adopted a mode more common in historical writing of keeping all citations and the discussion of all wider academic issues to endnotes. If you prefer to read above the line, each text offers a simple narrative about our findings. If you want to read a more conventional academic book that relates the material to its academic context, this can be done through engaging with the endnotes.

We hope you enjoy the results, and we hope you will also read our comparative book – and perhaps some of the other monographs – in addition to this one.

Acknowledgements

My wholehearted thanks go first to the wonderful people from Grano and the surrounding area for their generosity in accepting me as part of their lives and also for sharing time, thoughts and expertise with me. This book is just a small part of what I have learned from them and, while some may disagree with parts of it, I hope that overall they will find it truthful and insightful. As promised during field work, I have taken care to protect the identities of those who preferred to remain anonymous. I also changed the name of the town to *Grano*, which in Italian means 'grain' or 'wheat' – an everyday element, and essential source, of life. For everything that I did not do well enough in this book, I sincerely ask them to forgive me.

Secondly, I wish to thank the amazing team of the 'Why We Post' project: Daniel Miller, Elisabetta Costa, Nell Haines, Tom McDonald, Juliano Spier, Jolynna Sinanan, Shriram Venkrataman and Xinyuan Wang, who were joined later by Sheba Mohammed, Cassie Quarless and Laura Haapio-Kirk. They were, and will continue to be, a constant source of inspiration and motivation. We all have learned from each other what collaborative and comparative anthropology can mean and what spectacular results it brings. The merit is primarily due to Professor Daniel Miller who astutely mobilised us to think and act in a way that was beneficial and rewarding to us and to the discipline.

I would now like to name those who helped me most during the field research, with work as research assistants, by offering constant advice and directions or by treating me with hospitality and generosity: Marina De Giorgi, Raffaella Quaranta, Gabriele Quaranta, Manuela Baglivo, Ornella Ricchiuto, Giuseppe Ricchiuto, Anna Lena Manca, Maria Grazia Bello, Anna Rita Aniceto, Santo De Giorgi, Maria Luisa Planteda, Mary Cortese, Cosimo Cortese, Alfredo Elia, Luana Morciano, Agnese Branca, Agostino and Lina, Pina Scarcella, Agnese Dell'Abate, Biagino Bleve, Barbara Maisto and family, Rolando Civilla and family, Alfredo De Giuseppe and so many dear friends I gained while staying in Grano.

I also wish to thank Ugo Fabietti and University Milano-Bicocca for granting me the ethical permit to research in Italy; to Elisabetta Costa for easing this process; and to Roberta Sassatelli for her valuable comments on my preliminary field report. For the elaboration of this book I am indebted to all my colleagues in the 'Why We Post' project for commenting on different sections; to Daniel Miller for reviewing an earlier draft; to Joy Kirk, Chris Penfold from UCL Press and an anonymous reviewer for reviewing the entire manuscript; and to Oana Michael, Gabriela Nicolescu, David Ferguson and Trevor Williams for revising different chapters. Shriram Venkatraman helped me with statistical data and graphs, and Bogdan Maran and Gabriela Nicolescu helped with visual materials. As always, I am indebted to the virtuosity of Professor Vintilă Mihăilescu for inspiring me in how to look at the world and anthropology.

This research was equally the product of the attentiveness and scholarship of anthropologist Gabriela Nicolescu, my wife, who postponed her own work for more than a year to accompany me in the field. She ended up making many more friends than I did; helping me significantly during research, including with filmmaking; starting her own research project; and also reviewing this manuscript. To her, this book goes with love.

The research was funded by the European Research Council (grant ERC-2011-AdG-295486 Socnet).

Contents

List of figures

1
Introduction: Grano, an average place in southeast Italy

The book series 'Why We Post' brings an anthropological perspective to the study of social media, and this study of Grano,[1] a small town in southeast Italy, demonstrates how essential that perspective is in interpreting and understanding the evidence about the use of social media. One of the values of this field site is that the Italians studied here are arguably more concerned with issues of personal appearance and how they look in public than the people living in any of the other eight sites in the 'Why We Post' series.[2] As we will see throughout the book, public appearance and, in particular, the cultivation of beauty in relation to morality is absolutely fundamental to who they are and is something on which they spend much of their resources and time. In the standard discussion of social media, such activities are immediately assumed to represent the growth of individualism and even narcissism. This book reveals the diametrically opposite view. Actually beauty and personal appearance turn out to be collective and highly burdensome expectations imposed on individuals, and represent the obligation of each citizen to contribute to regional and national projects that make them live up to certain ideals. There are very clear constraints on exactly which people may or may not post pictures of themselves on Facebook, and these are clearly intended to ensure that this cult of beauty remains a collective project and does not descend into individual self-interest.

Although we are in a thoroughly modern European town, this constraint with regard to crafting a public image permeates almost every aspect of what does or does not go on to Facebook. Merely to live a day in Grano, where for three hours in the afternoon one can hear a pin drop because it is siesta time, is to appreciate just how much conformity and normativity dominate the lives of its people. As a result, the way a married woman uses Facebook will be entirely different from the way that an unmarried woman does. A man with a university degree belongs to a different category from a man without such a qualification. This means the former may well be unemployed because the expectation is that he should not accept most of the conventional work available locally. This makes him part of a group that has a special relationship to Facebook as it is one of the few places where he can express the skill and status of his education, which has in other respects turned out to be more of a liability than an asset.

Grano is a place that has relatively little use for social media, has largely rejected Instagram and Twitter so far, and keeps Facebook constrained to very particular uses. The reason for this is that people are already and very effectively doing the things that Facebook is supposed to be able to provide for them. So most people do not really need this new technology. The irony is that those who do use it are not in the vanguard of some modernity, as is often claimed for social media, but rather retain many traditions about community and sociality. Indeed this case is good evidence for the argument that social media itself has flourished in many other places because of its conservatism. Facebook brings many people back to community and the intense sociality they have lost, even though you might think that in a place such as Grano this sociality has never disappeared. The main beneficiaries of social media in the region are people who have had their lives disrupted in different ways, such as by modern transnational labour migration or the lack of a current workplace, and need a technology to help them rebuild communications that have become more difficult or recuperate social status they have lost.

We will explain how all these needs relate to the touchstone of social relations in Grano, which is to maintain a strict and often tense separation between the exterior and interior life of each person. The exterior is represented by the individual's relationship to the local community, the region and his or her attitude towards the state, and it is reflected in what people wear, how they look after themselves, how they raise their children and sometimes what car they drive. The interior is typically represented by the individual's relationship to their nuclear and extended family and their relationship with close friends. Social media follows this basic dualism: Facebook is responsible for reflecting the exterior, in daily status messages and visual materials shared online, while the interior is usually expedited on WhatsApp, in tense phone calls with your father, or in personal photos taken with your mobile phone or personal camera which are not shared publicly. In short, Facebook is for *gli altri* (the others) and WhatsApp is for *io stesso* (myself). It is this dual nature of relationships, and the capacity of each individual to master and decipher their meanings in different contexts, which defines the person and structures social relations.

In this context, most people in the region use social media not to challenge norms or propose new ways of doing things, but to strengthen and scale social relations. On the one hand, public-facing media, represented by Facebook, are rather restrained and normative, and most people in Grano try to be consistent online with the way they are seen offline. There is much in this region's history that accounts for why people are very concerned with the way social visibility reflects their social status. One result is that most people in Grano feel they should friend on Facebook all the other people they know, while most of their online interactions are not with family members, close friends or romantic partners.

On the other hand, people use more private and personal media, in the form of phone calls, text messages and, more recently, WhatsApp to express and build personal relations, centred on the individual and their nuclear family. The enhanced visibility brought by social media and digital technology helps people attentively to construct different layers of intimacy. For example, young people might mostly use WhatsApp with their partners, set up WhatsApp groups for the different social circles they want to be part of, and also constantly share personal thoughts and feelings with best friends and parents. People use social media to be more nuanced in expressing personal relationships and to demonstrate the relationship between the external appearance and the interior qualities.

In a larger perspective, we suggest that social media constitutes just another environment where people work out and reflect their respective roles in society. Conventionally, people in Grano have always found subtle ways to express social differentiation on an everyday basis. In particular, what drives most people in Grano to use public-facing social media at all is the need to replicate, defend and sometimes restore their respective social positions. Many sense that social media should be like an ordinary place where they go constantly, in the same way that they go into the streets, to the numerous local festivals or the workplace. This is why Facebook is neither a reflection of relationships nor of a person in his or her totality, but rather of one core element of what a person decides to be. It is the permanent crafting of this personal element in relation to collective ideas and values and social position that is seen as a new kind of social responsibility.

The second argument of the book is that social media allows for multiple versions of individualism to be seen as an expression of social conformity. This means that people craft themselves online in relation not to individual ideals, but rather to social ones. Individualism is accepted when it points to collective values, which relate to gender, class, social status and religion. Thus, many teenage *fidanzate* (fiancées) see their online photos as paving an essential step towards their future life; young working-class men use WhatsApp much more intensively than Facebook because here they can be much freer; married women show online their individual skills in caring for their families; and local intellectuals and artisans constantly display their respective work. These social solidarities contradict the grand theories in social sciences which argue that the rise in information technology and social networking indicates a fall from communities, kinship and intense sociality and an increase in personal autonomy and fragmented individualism.[3]

In conclusion, this book demonstrates that in Grano social media is not essentially something new and innovative in itself. Rather, it allows people to be creative and inventive in order to map out their various social relations in new environments and sometimes to articulate complex ideas about the society in which they are living. Most people see social media as just another place where they can delegate and work out different parts of their sociality. This suggests that in southeast Italy social media is not perceived as liberating or as making people more individualistic and narcissistic – although people might sometimes indicate such ideas online because they wish to differentiate themselves within what is perceived to be a very public environment – but, most of the time, social media is seen as a really good gadget to express that which is already known. What is really new is the capacity of social media to scale relationships and to allow more people to demonstrate an attachment to particular ideals present in their society.

The setting

Travelling by train from Rome to the heel of the Italian boot, the landscape changes dramatically. In a little more than five hours you pass from the smooth damp hills covered with thick woods that surround Rome to the regular agricultural fields and large vineyards of Abruzzo, and then to the dry land dominated by olive trees in the region of Puglia. Vegetation changes from different shades of bright green to much paler green. In the city of Lecce you change trains and get on the regional and much slower one that arrives in Grano after cutting through the region of Salento, the southernmost part of Puglia. Here smaller plantations of olive trees alternate with large stretches of abandoned land and wild vegetation. Every now and then small cultivated plots reveal the dry red soil and colour the landscape. It takes some time to understand why Puglia is often referred to as 'le Puglie' in the plural. It derives from the region's rich cultural diversity and the numerous rules imposed here over the centuries, and from its relatively isolated position at the bottom of the Italian heel, far from main commercial routes, and the numerous local dialects which differ completely from one town to the next.[4]

The town of Grano, surrounded by endless plantations of olive trees, is situated south of the city of Lecce and just a few kilometres from the rocky and spectacular coast of the Adriatic Sea. It is the administrative, economic and political centre of a *commune* (bigger administrative unit) with the same name. More than three-quarters of the 20,000 inhabitants of the *commune* live in the town of Grano and the rest in a cluster of eight small *frazioni* (villages) scattered on a territory of 48 square km.[5] Between these villages there are kilometres of walls, built and re-built numerous times over hundreds of years. They are built from stones extracted from the enclosed ground which has been turned into small parcels of cultivable land, and they border narrow twisting and turning lanes known only by the locals. These walls run through countless private properties guarded by a handful of traditional *pajare* (stone shelters), leafy fig trees and gigantic *fichi d'india* (prickly pears). Modern fences and gates enclose tidy rural houses with generous gardens and small orchards with olive, orange and lemon trees.

The town lies around the fortified *palazzo* erected by the first baron of the region at the end of the sixteenth century on a small slope next to the *Chiesa Madre* (mother church). Small eighteenth-century houses, whitewashed, with shuttered windows and flat roofs, line the narrow and semicircular streets of the old centre, paved with large granite flagstones. Only about one-quarter of these houses are permanently inhabited because the area is seen by the locals as old and impractical and, until recent environmental improvements, large parts of it were dumps. In the surrounding areas the local aristocracy and the emerging bourgeoisie built imposing two-storey houses throughout the nineteenth and early twentieth centuries; these are painted in lively pale colours such as carmine, light pink and tea green, with large semi-circular wooden gates leading to spacious inner courtyards. Prestigious architects were commissioned to deliver original and individual designs with fine stone adornments and, in Grano Porto situated on the coast of the Adriatic Sea, large and

(a)

(b)

Fig. 1.1 Map of Italy highlighting Puglia and the region of Salento (a) and an overview of Grano (b)[6]

Fig. 1.2 Everyday Grano showing, respectively, the old town, newer and modern parts of the town and a wealthy house (photos by the author)

luxuriant gardens, all of which completely changed the style and look of the old city.[7]

Although I lived and conducted most of the research in the town of Grano, it was not possible to confine the current book to Grano alone. The life of the town is constituted by an intense and permanent social, economic and cultural exchange with the entire region. Grano acts as an important social and economic hub for a territory about 20–25 kilometres wide, and social media increases the visibility of the entire area – not only people, but also services, businesses and local initiatives. Many people commute to and from Grano for work on a daily basis. For example, about three-quarters of the 300 staff at the three local high schools are not from Grano and, in 2013, 214 students from Grano were studying at the university of Salento in Lecce.

During the active periods of the day, the central areas of Grano where the commercial spaces, food shops, cafés and the main public institutions are located are busy and lively. Most people jump in their cars for the smallest job they have to do: they rush for appointments and errands, shop at ease, meet friends for a coffee, or simple hang out for a while in the main square and use their smartphones to call somebody. As many have to move between villages in the region, and the local public transport is considered impractical, Grano is packed during the peak periods of the day with small and noisy vehicles rushing adroitly through its narrow twisting streets.[8] The street railings at the main intersections are covered in local advertisements, and huge public notice boards display the latest decisions of the municipality, names of the recently deceased and special offers from local businesses.

The old square of the town is bordered by the massive castle that currently hosts the town hall and faces an array of elegant aristocratic buildings built over different historical periods. Under their slim balconies and svelte, round-shaped vaults, a few bars and food places are open until midnight during the summer. The imposing *Chiesa Madre* closes the rectangle of the piazza which, as in many Italian cities, is also known as *il salotto* (the sitting room). A row of massive wooden benches, shaded by thin local trees, completes the setting. Here old people gather in the late afternoon, and during the summer there is a swarm of children playing football, their parents, and people of all ages who come for a walk or an ice-cream. Groups of teenagers check their messages and the latest football results on their smartphones at the foot of the bronze equestrian statue or on the wide steps of the church. The square is also a main intersection for other villages in the *commune*, so rushing cars and noisy motorcycles and *ape* (commercial three-wheel vehicles) come and go until late evening. It is during the evening that the cafés and food shops in the area are really busy. In summer, the municipality turns the square into a large pedestrian space where most of the cultural events in the town take place.

The other social and economic centre of the town is *Piazza dei Domenicani*. Initially erected in the 1920s and 1930s near the old cemetery as part of a modern overhaul of the entire area, it went through several successive makeovers during the last century. The most recent one was in the 1990s when the local authorities decided to demolish the commercial centre, erected only 30 years previously, and create instead a modern esplanade bordered by white marble benches and metallic streetlamps. Nearby, a line of tall palm trees planted along the relatively new three-storey blocks of flats shadows the busiest commercial part of the town. Four cafés, two bars, two ice-cream shops, two traditional *osterie* (clubs), one of the three pharmacies of the town and half a dozen retail shops are located in this square, while some three dozen other retail shops, several banks and estate agents are situated on the sinuous streets that converge into it. Expensive local shops and franchises of big brands such as United Colors of Benetton, Versace, Antares and GRS mix with butchers, general food shops, a couple of

Fig. 1.3 Teenagers texting in the modern square (photo by Gabriela Nicolescu)

travel agencies and a driving school. Old people from the surrounding neighbourhoods gather where the main street divides around a branchless ancient olive tree that hunches in front of the newspaper kiosk, and hundreds of children and parents from across the region take to the esplanade each afternoon.

The two main squares of the town correspond to very different lifestyles and ideas that co-exist in Grano. The aristocratic old square is related to what is locally considered 'high-culture', but also history and tradition, and to more sophisticated needs for visibility. It is also the site of the local administration and the first place you would show to a hurried tourist. In contrast, the large modern square is more popular because it is more oriented towards the internal life of the town and region, and is considered much less pretentious and demanding.

Throughout this book we will see how this separation characterises the social life of Grano and the use of social media. People tend to have clear preferences either for the popular politics, flea markets and sports shows that take place in the modern square, or for the 'high' politics, classical music, book launches, traditional fairs and expensive food that are usually organised in the old square.[9] These are not two distinct models of society. Rather, most people navigate between these two dispositions in an attempt to understand the different ideas present in their society. In this context, social media constitutes a safe kind of environment that can be both public and private, and where people practice their everyday engagement with bigger social ideals. In this book, we will see why an aristocrat would always hang around the old square, have a reduced online presence and post more theoretical ideas on Facebook, while an average middle-class person would spend most of their free time in the modern square, be more expansive online, post more photos and share popular memes. The norm is to craft that particular online presence which relates to established ideals and reflects the individual's position in society.

The rhythms of Grano

Grano is a small place where everybody knows everybody. It is not uncommon for eight or ten cousins of the same family to live in the same village or for some areas to have several inhabitants with the same surname. The population is extremely homogeneous in many aspects: 99 per cent of the residents declare themselves to be Italian and almost 80 per cent are Catholic.[10]

The first evening I arrived in Grano, my landlord took me for a walk through the town. Angelo is a strong man in his late sixties, of average-height and grey-haired. He is a father of three, with one son living in Grano, the other in Milano, and the youngest child, a daughter, in Rome. He walks slowly, somewhat hesitatingly, but in general he is never in a hurry to talk or do things. Walking with him on a warm April evening on the crowded streets of Grano, I could not help noticing that he seemed to know almost everyone in the town. From time to time we stopped for a while to exchange a few words with someone he knew and he introduced me as a foreign student and friend. He told me slowly the history of the town, insisting on how different it was when he was young. After walking for more than an hour, we stopped to buy a few take-away pizzas from the local pizzeria where he has been a regular client for at least 20 years. Back home, his wife was expecting us, and I exercised my poor Italian at the time while eating the hot pizzas.

Later on, I realised that what we had done during my first day of field work was in fact a *giro* (literally 'tour'), and it was an extremely important part of the town's culture. It is perhaps related to the strong tradition of popular *sagre* or *feste popolari* (festivals), when the entire community dresses in their best outfits and strolls around the centre of the town greeting passers-by, eating and observing the different attractions. There is currently a stream of such festivals in Grano throughout the year which celebrate traditional cuisine, agricultural products and crafts. To these we should add the religious festivals dedicated to the patron saints of each town, its *frazioni* and some of the neighbourhoods. As recently as for the month of August 2014 alone, the local administration counted more than 40 popular festivals held in Grano and the surrounding area. The most important ones are organised for Christmas, for the patron saint of Grano, and for *Ferragosto* (the Assumption of the Virgin Mary). Each combines popular attractions with religious festivities lasting several days, during which the streets and main areas of the town are decorated with tens of thousands of *luminarie* (coloured lights arranged in huge arcs) and garlands. The festivals open with three cannon fusillades and marching brass bands during the day, while evenings are even more frenetic with several events going on at the same time and people strolling endlessly between colourful stalls, which sell bric-a-brac, handcrafts, sweets, nuts and crêpes, and the various different attractions. Women display elegant accessories such as special earrings, expensive necklaces and designer bags while groups of acquiescent parents try to manage their children's attraction to the mobile amusement parks. All the shops in the town prepare traditional foods and display special

Fig. 1.4 Photo from a *festa* shared on Facebook

seasonal offers and, during this period, the hair and beauty salons are overwhelmed with appointments made months in advance. The festivals always end well after midnight with spectacular fireworks in the old square of the town.

What the *giro* preserves throughout the year is a sense of shared intimacy as locals stroll through the town in search of something that catches their eye. It also represents an everyday technique to navigate not only between different places of the town, but also to see and engage with ideas and ways of being in Grano. In summer, numerous groups of teenagers and young couples start their regular tours after dinner, taking in popular spots of the town, such as the self-service shop, the cheap *panini* (sandwich) bar, the ice cream shops or the Juventus Torino football club. These long walks, the numerous encounters, the afternoon siesta and the several hours a day dedicated to children are part of what people jokingly call *ritmi salentini* ('Salentine rhythms'). This refers to the propensity of locals for doing one thing at a time, in no rush, *a passo d'uomo* ('at the pace of a walking man'), in contrast to the rapid flows of life in the big urban centres in northern Italy and the sense of anxiety they can create. This is one reason why the use of social media in Grano could be very different from the use of social media in other parts of Italy. *Il giro* and the requirements for constant social visibility are essential parts of a lifestyle that combines austerity and self-restriction within the household with conspicuous consumption and demands for a neat personal appearance in public.

On a typical workday the town is quite busy.[11] The morning rush starts after 7:30 when food shops open, hasty parents drop off their children at school on their way to work and police officers control the heavy traffic at the crossings. This is followed by the time when people, mainly women, go shopping for the day, the weekly market becomes crowded, and many civil servants take their second coffee of the day. The coffee places start to be really busy: highly skilled bartenders who start work at 6:00 in the morning serve hot coffees in spotless white settings promptly and with great expertise. Anywhere in Grano a normal coffee costs 80 cents. Even if people are in a hurry, it takes a lot to refuse a coffee offered by someone you have not seen for some time. Accepting is a sign of friendship and appreciation, but could also represent paying back some debt or sealing a deal. Consequently, one of my main challenges during field work was how to drink less than three or four coffees a day while constantly begging people to make them less strong.

By midday, the town quickly empties as people rush home for lunch. Heavy metallic grates are pulled down everywhere over commercial spaces and the town remains deserted for a few hours. Only the railway station, the hospital, the post office and a few other places like the two self-service laundries, one kebab restaurant and a handful of bars, specialising in selling traditional snacks and *panini* for professionals, remain open.

If most of the town seems to stop, life continues to bustle inside houses. For many, the moment when the family reunites for lunch represents the pivotal moment of the day. It is the point, for example, between the intense work of the morning and a relatively relaxed schedule in the afternoon; or between a morning focus on professional work and an afternoon focus on the children. Maybe this is why most of the families are strict about respecting lunchtime. The meal itself is substantial but simple, and rather inexpensive for most of the week. It typically consists of two dishes, the first one being based on some sort of pasta served piping hot directly from the oven. The second dish might, for example, be roasted or cooked meat with boiled vegetables or lentils in the winter and salads in the summer. Fresh bread, small handmade pizzas or a large bottle of local red wine might be also present on the table. A small dessert consisting of fruit, fresh fennel, nuts and a cup of coffee usually follows, with the television on most of the time relaying the national news.

After a few hours during which the town can be as quiet as in the middle of the night, it suddenly awakens around five o'clock in the afternoon. Cars start to rush through the streets again and, as many mothers confirmed, 'the madness starts': most children in Grano have several extra-curricular activities, typically private tuition in English language and some sport such as swimming, Taekwondo or football. When there are two or three children in the family, this schedule becomes quite demanding. Therefore, in an afternoon slot of just over two hours, parents have to balance their children's activities, their own jobs and the domestic chores. It is mainly mothers who take on this role, as many have more time to do so than the fathers and are considered to have the main responsibility for the children's education. When I first took my son to swimming lessons I realised that important service areas of the swimming pool were designed for mothers rather than fathers accompanying their children.

Summers are pivotal to the entire year in the way that lunches are pivotal to the day. From the first days of June, when school approaches the end of term, people spend more time outside their homes and many start to make frequent trips to the seaside. By the end of July, when temperatures during the day are constantly close to 40°C, the tourist season has started. Grano is not a tourist destination as such, mainly because of the wild steep coast of the Adriatic Sea and the lack of dedicated infra-structure. In this context most people who come here in the summer were born in the region. They *scendono* ('come down') from the north of Italy and central Europe, bringing their families and friends. They usually spend several weeks in Grano, visit family scattered across the region, and take part in the local festivals. It is a time when the wider family reunites: grandparents take their grandchildren to the seaside and playgrounds, cook for everyone and usually complain that this part of the year is too hectic and tiring. Summer evenings are packed with people enjoying a few hours of fresh air and attending the numerous public events.

It is estimated that, during the two central months of summer (July and August), the population of Grano increases by around one-third. The absolute peak is reached in the second week of August, which culminates with in the major festival of *Ferragosto* on the 15th of the month. The ancient festivals of the season are combined with the Catholic celebration of the Assumption of the St. Virgin Mary into one week of continuous festivities. Throughout the region of Salento even the larger back-office businesses may close down completely for several days, while for retailers, food shops, accommodation units and restau-rants this is the busiest period when they make the highest profits of the entire year. Grano Porto, the small village on the Adriatic coast that is part of the commune of Grano, becomes a popular destination for the local population, and the 20 or so B&Bs, four small hotels, two camp-ing sites and several restaurants are finally busy. Summer bars open up all along the coast and organise parties with DJs and live concerts. Teenagers and young people from all around the area prolong their eve-ning walks along the spectacular coastal road. The three families of fish-ermen strive to fulfil the never-ending flow of demand from local fish shops, supermarkets and restaurants.

The summer provides not only a major economic boost, creating a plethora of temporary jobs for people with no formal employment, but is also the stage for an effervescent cultural life. The brochure published by the local council listed 125 cultural events in the summer of 2013 and 140 events in the same period of 2014. Moreover, it is estimated that the actual quantity of events is two or three times this because many are organised at short notice. At weekends people have to navigate between multiple events happening at the same time. The biggest performances have an audience of a few hundred people and are preceded by public speeches delivered by the organisers, the host of the show and some-times the mayor or the director of the local Department of Culture and

Arts. These performances often imitate major Italian shows, such as the San Remo song contest, the Venice Film Festival, or thematic television shows. A huge industry dedicated to promoting and preparing materials for these events has flourished on Facebook in recent years.

The life of the town is characterised by the startling contrast between the flamboyant and intense summers and the rather dispiriting colder seasons. After school starts on 15 September, Grano seems empty and dull. From then until Christmas the days shorten and the *tramontana* (chilly and dry northern winds) replace the warmer and humid winds coming from North Africa (*scirocco*). People do not find many reasons to leave their homes, with the noticeable exception of the few old men who continue to meet outside and diligently stroll across the town squares from one end to the other in a bid to warm up. Some prefer to light their fires in the evenings and receive visits at home. The town erupts briefly for Christmas when there are brightly lit street decorations, shops are adorned with seasonal colours and gifts and, in their houses, people build traditional miniature scenes of the nativity (*presepe*) using paper, glue, wood and cloth. After New Year the life of the town falls once more into an apparent inertia that continues throughout the freezing months of January and February. The temperature does not fall below 2–3°C, but the freezing northerly winds whip through the town most of the time, and the large stone houses feel cold and oversized.

The carnival is the second biggest event of the winter, and parties are organised by public institutions, especially nurseries and schools. In Grano the carnival seems to be dedicated to children: with the exception of a few eccentrics and sporadic themed parties in the region, children are the only ones who dress-up in costumes and for a few days excitedly handle a small arsenal of confetti, coloured foam, sticks and trumpets. For the last few years, however, despite the efforts of some enthusiasts, there has been no street parade in Grano during the carnival, and so people have to attend the parades in neighbouring towns where the tradition is stronger.

Social and economic background

Grano's society is highly hierarchical, which has important consequences for communication and the use of social media. It is not only that different layers in the hierarchy have slightly different lifestyles, but also that social relations, norms and routines are structured hierarchically. In particular this means that people tend to communicate and establish relationships with those from the same social level. People define themselves within the social hierarchy and create group solidarities based on work, education, personal appearance and tastes. These are existential issues, that is, they are part of attaining a sense of where one belongs in life, rather than vehicles to move up the social hierarchy. Public-facing social media grants users permanent visibility outside the conventional public spaces and this works towards enforcing, rather than challenging, the existing social hierarchy. But let us take a look back in history to see how this sense of hierarchy started.

The first *signori* (noblemen) of Grano can be traced back to the early thirteenth century.[12] A long array of noblemen passed down the right to rule the fiefdom of Grano until the end of the sixteenth century when this right was bought by a rich family who ruled it until the end of the feudal period.[13] For most of this time Salento was part of the Kingdom of the Two Sicilies which ruled the southern provinces of present-day Italy. Throughout this period noblemen worked constantly to increase their powers and privileges from the different kings that succeeded to the throne, exploiting the fact that the region of southern Salento was relatively distant from the main centres of the kingdom and yet it had a major economic and military role. This resulted in most of the political, economic and social life of the region being controlled by noblemen and princes who had absolute power over significant parts of the population.[14]

Maybe the most striking feature of this region's history is the contrast between feudal *baroni* (noblemen) and *contadini* (peasantry). When feudality was abolished in 1806, although the barons were stripped of their juridical powers they kept most of their privileges, including the ownership of the land.[15] However, this abolition marked a decisive step towards the emergence of a thin layer of local middle-class that consolidated itself throughout the nineteenth century.[16] This layer of society was formed from better-off peasants who gained autonomy in working their small properties and managed to buy land from the aristocracy and the Church, as well as from *artigiani* (artisans), functionaries, townsmen and a series of merchants and traders who took over certain services from landowners, such as transportation and milling. While the relative success of the better-off farmers was related to their propensity to work hard and to take command over a cheap workforce, represented partly by their family groups but mainly by landless peasants,[17] the artisans constituted a special category; their craft represented a sure way out of agricultural labour and was now subject to increasing demand. They acquired specialist skills as builders, pavers, stone carvers, house painters, carpenters, iron and leather workers, and potters. Women started to be renowned for the quality and diligence of their work, and gathered a clientele interested in tailoring, lace and leather making.

At the same time the reforms introduced by the French, and built upon in different ways throughout the nineteenth century, gave rise to the new category of public servants. Each province had to appoint its land agents, tax inspectors, local and provincial counsellors, magistrates and a small army of other civil servants. They benefited from fixed and more predictable incomes, which represented a revolution for the local population. Work in the public sector became an irresistible aspiration for the local middle class who started to invest in higher education, which was seen as mandatory to achieve these positions. The highly educated young people formed the local elite during the late nineteenth and early twentieth centuries: teachers, public servants and a few *professionisti*, that is, accountants, notaries, lawyers and doctors.

However, up to the end of the Second World War, most of the local population were *contadini* (peasants) living in rough conditions. Up to 80 per cent were *braccianti* (wage workers) who had no possessions: no animals, no agricultural tools and, most importantly, no agricultural land. Their lives have been described as being characterised by exploitation, misery and enduring famine.[18] This led to important class struggles and violent clashes throughout southern Italy, the most recent of which began in 1943–4 and ended a few years after the Second World War.[19] Therefore, when compared to present society, we may appreciate that one of the most dramatic changes in the second half of the twentieth century was the quasi-disappearance of the Italian agricultural worker working for others as well as working outside their own household.[20] In Puglia this happened against a setting of mass education, emigration in order to find work and most importantly, social mobility.

In the first two decades after the Second World War, Grano was affected by mass work migration. This phenomenon characterised the entire south of Italy and was caused, on the one hand, by massive unemployment, the collapse of agriculture and an acute crisis in work relations in Italy and, on the other hand, by the relaunch of industrial production in post-war Europe. It is estimated that between 1958 and 1963 more than one and a half million people from the southern provinces of Italy emigrated to work in the 'industrial triangle' of Torino-Milano-Genova and to more affluent Central European countries, such as Switzerland, France, Germany and Belgium.[21] In Salento, between 40 and 60 per cent of the population aged 20 to 30 years old emigrated to find work.[22] Most of these were men who had to turn overnight (the duration of the trip by train from southern Italy to Switzerland) from farmers into construction workers, builders or carpenters. But, in many cases, this was a temporary migration with individuals still being strongly anchored in their place of origin.[23] At the same time many women became permanent breadwinners as they worked in the local tobacco industry and also raised their children.

The relative growth in wealth during these decades was reflected in the built environment, which expanded rapidly. The city grew to three times its original size by the early 1980s, when the local authorities had to intervene in order to regulate its urban development. People used to invest most of their cash capital in building new houses or extending the existing ones, because the tradition was that newly weds should start married life in a new house. A common practice was that men worked during most of the year *fuori* (outside) and with the cash gained in the summer they purchased materials and worked on building their houses in Salento in the winter.[24] In earlier times, starting married life without a house was unimaginable. As a friend put it: 'for us marriage is not a beginning, but an end.' She was referring to the fact that the young couple is expected to form a family only when they have a house and most domestic possessions, so they do not really struggle as a family with major economic shortcomings.

By 2014, 82 per cent of the local population lived in their own houses and there was an average of 2.6 people in each household. Apart from the demands of the physical construction of the house, living inside it as a family was also a large and demanding undertaking. The home is basically built on the Catholic tradition of the *famiglia Cristiana* (Christian family) living life in order and virtue. Nowadays domestic roles are often not as separated into gender roles as they used to be, but there are domains where this separation still operates. Women, for example, are generally in charge of the internal matters of the home and take responsibility for raising children, including their religious education. Men have relatively more autonomy in forming social relationships outside the household. We will see that women use social media much more than men do. They are responsible for maintaining social relations on private media, but also feel a responsibility to reflect their families on public-facing social media. For example, the fact that women have always demonstrated that they adhere to core values by keeping a clean and tidy home and following strict dress codes outside the house is now reflected in their tendency to use Facebook as a window into their families.

A particular rise in preoccupation with style and consumption started in the 1980s when southern Salento had an unprecedented economic boom. For nearly two decades, hundreds of workshops and medium-sized business in the area produced different sorts of textiles and leather products for the upmarket Italian industry and for leading Italian high-fashion brands such as Armani, Dolce & Gabbana and Versace.[25] The main reasons were twofold: the relatively low production costs compared with the north of Italy and the tradition and high quality of the manual work available in this area.[26] More than 3,000 people from across the region were employed in Grano in this light industry. According to the director of the economic department of the town hall, in the 1990s Grano produced almost half of all the ties manufactured in Europe and, for a brief period in the early 2000s, it attained the second highest GDP per capita in the region after Bari.

People remember that period as a golden age for Grano. For the first time ever work was plenty and relatively easy; both men and women could work if they wanted to and were well remunerated. Many emigrants returned home, the bars and restaurants were full, and people had to make business trip and meeting reservations weeks in advance for the only hotel in the town. Domestic consumption increased spectacularly: the first supermarket that was part of a national chain, owned by the former prime minister Silvio Berlusconi, opened in 1992 and was seen by both the young and the adult population as the ultimate sign of modernity and prosperity. Teenagers used its large parking space as the main place to gather. For the first time people shopped for more than few days' supplies at a time and started to face difficulties in storing the large amounts of goods they had purchased. Today traces of this consumption fever can be seen in the many houses in Grano that have a television in each room.

However, this economic prosperity ended in the early 2000s mainly due to the strong competition that the Italian fashion industry faced from Asian producers. Crushed within the supplier chain, and without having diversified its products and markets, by 2003 only three textile workshops were left in Grano and there were less than 40 employees. In 2005 the local population, which had been constantly increasing until then, started a steady annual decrease which is still continuing. For many this was just the recurrence of a situation which the Salento region has found itself in throughout history: being frustratingly bypassed by big capital and the main flow of commerce.

People in Grano started once more to look up to the much wealthier north of Italy in almost every domain: for fashion and style to Milan; for education to Milan, Rome and Bologna; for political stability and a powerful state to Britain; and for organisation and structure to

Germany and Switzerland. This might be related to the fact that popular culture in the south of Italy was described by major Italian scholars as the combination of three factors: a particular sense of marginality; an attraction to modernity; and the existence of major economic, social and cultural differences between the unequal levels of society.[27] We will see how these elements are synthesised into a particular attention to present online 'good' and moral values, including a persistent reference to the uniqueness of local territory.

The current life of Grano

At the time of my field work there was a general sense that work was not available in the area and the Italian government had to do something. This was amplified not only by constant negative reports in the mainstream media about internal politics and economic shortages, but also by the sharpening of the political discourse and frequent criticisms from the business sector and public commentators. In Grano only about 70 per cent of the total active population was employed officially, while the rest was split between informal labour and unemployment.[28] With an average monthly salary of €1,300[29] and more than 100 families dependent on regular help from the Church, most of the population considered they were seriously affected by the economic crisis that had affected Italy since 2008.[30]

However, if you walked along the streets of Grano you would certainly not see this: you would probably be stunned by the number of upmarket shops, cafés and restaurants, most of them stylishly renovated and decorated by professionals on a monthly basis. You would see people wearing expensive clothes and purchasing pricey goods. For example, it is not unusual for a loving middle-class husband to give his wife a €300 designer bag twice a year or for a working-class father to buy his daughter expensive Armani sunglasses on her graduation from vocational school.

The main employer in Grano is the state: around 1,800 people from across the region work in the local administration and public services. About 600 work in education alone, while the local hospital employs almost 400 people. At the time of my field work, the most desired work was in public administration (*funzionario*). Thus many of the reasons which persuaded the emerging middle-class to invest massively in the education of their children remain valid to the present day: first, this

(a)

(b)

Fig. 1.5 Window of a hairdressing salon (a) and flea market
(b) (photos by the author)

kind of job offered a fixed and relatively good salary and a great deal of autonomy to fit working life around domestic chores. For example, in a family the spouse who worked locally in the public sector was usually in charge of preparing lunch and had prime responsibilities for looking after the children. Secondly, a decent position in administration required only a medium-level education, which was a standard for most middle-class families. Finally, the public sector offered a greater social flexibility than any other occupation, including the opportunity to network efficiently and secure jobs for other members of the family.

The second most important area of employment in Grano is in agriculture, with over 1,800 registered farms working 2,600 hectares of agricultural land.[31] The land is almost entirely private and among the most fertile in the region, largely because groundwater is situated at a relatively high level. It is cultivated with olive trees (60 per cent) and cereals, especially wheat, barley and oats, while there are only 18 hectares of vineyards.[32] However, only 25 of these farms are *imprese agricole* (larger units) generating an average yearly revenue of more than €15,000. The rest are small family entreprises which assure a relative autonomy to many households.[33]

The most visible sector by far is commerce: in the entire *comune* there are more than 700 active commercial activities, including 97 clothes, shoes and accessories shops, 70 cafés and bars, 33 restaurants and trattorias and more than 30 hairdressing and beauty salons. The four supermarkets, eight petrol stations, four used-car businesses, 21 automatic machines and almost 40 mobile vendors indicate that there is quite a lively commercial sector concentrated in the town of Grano. While many of the small businesses rely on established networks and popularity, newcomers tend to compensate for the lack of local connections and visibility by investing regularly in their online presence.

At the same time businesses often act as true repositories of social status: it is, for example, considered prestigious to own a shop, regardless of whether or not it makes much profit. In most cases the entire family works to move the business forward. To give other examples, many people who work in advertising take on work for free on a regular basis and owners of B&Bs are happy with just a few tens of clients a year. In the context of difficult economic times, the owner of a struggling business may be quite popular as a person. The way this connects strongly to a study of social media is that these activities promote and depend on social networking.

In particular, many of the 534 artisans registered in Grano have started to rely heavily on social media to promote their work: carpenters, painters, potters, hairdressers, beauticians and sweet makers now use Facebook to display their products and link these to their personal lives.[34] In Chapter 6 we will see how this is also true for other social categories, such as the highly educated unemployed, who need Facebook to present their particular expertise and possibly bring together their formal education and their practical skills.

Family life and relationships

My ethnographic material suggests that much of the social life in Grano is centred on the nuclear family and household.[35] In Grano it is said that women *portano avanti* (take forward) the family. Married women have a central position in their families and manage most of the economic resources of the household.[36] The customary practice that the husband, as the main breadwinner, hands over all the money he earns to his wife is still respected in many families. However, as many women now also work outside the domestic sphere, they actually have a far greater workload than their husbands: they do paid work, cook, clean and purchase basic goods on an everyday basis, and are also responsible for the increasing number of tasks required to provide the 'right' education for their children. Even where both parents perceive the education of their children to be crucial, the responsibility falls as a moral duty to the mother. This value system is reflected in the public sphere, for example in nurseries and primary schools, where most of the staff are female.

On the whole women are responsible for constancy and care in the smallest everyday details, while men are in charge of bigger projects, such as building a house or planning a holiday. This kind of separation corresponds to a particular division of labour and balance between spouses which has been always considered essential for a good and respected family. At the same time this complementarity of domestic roles extends over two or three generations. For example, the family acts as a reliable safety net for children long after they find stable jobs and move into their own houses: it is normal for parents to help their children with money or for grandparents to bring fresh vegetables from their gardens, cook and look after their grand-children.

In terms of this research, it is crucial to understand the family in Grano as the pivotal unit in both public and personal life. This can be seen not only in the strong tradition of *'I panni sporchi si lavano in famiglia'* (keeping one's 'dirty washing' inside the family),[37] but also of only expressing more intense feelings at an intimate level. The internal mechanism of each family decides what can go public and what should remain private and safe.[38] When the widow of a much-loved school teacher in Grano was asked to share some happy moments with the readers of a volume dedicated to him, she refused to do so, preferring to keep these memories for herself and her family. At every turn people take decisions as to what can be shared, and with whom, and what cannot be shared.

We will see that the ideal of the nuclear family is fundamental in the use of social media. At first people in Grano were very alert to the hugely increased social visibility that this environment presented. They managed the unpredictability of social media by fiercely monitoring the extremely public domain represented by Facebook's News Feed and keeping it separate from everything else. Beyond this demarcation, people have employed a whole range of techniques, genres and media, from telephone and text messages to WhatsApp and Instagram, to express different kinds of relationships and to build different corresponding layers of intimacy.

Media ecology in Grano

We have seen that in Grano people define themselves by insisting on internal (intellectual, moral, cultural) and external (clothing, expression, attitude) aspects of their personality, which are always considered in relation to the values they are expected to uphold. This results in people communicating in several concentric groups, such as the nuclear family, the extended family and the local community. At the same time care is taken that this does not contradict norms in the social hierarchy. In this context, social media plays a critical role in ensuring that these different requirements are given a type and level of visibility that can be recognised and approved by the different segments of the community.

Let us start with the most popular media by far: television. My household survey shows an average of 2.3 television sets per household, which can be correlated to an average of 2.5 beds per household. The best television is usually placed in the *salone* (sitting room), but the most used is often the one in the kitchen. Television watching follows people's daily rhythms and reflects the structure of the society: housewives follow the more practical television programmes before and after lunch as a background to domestic work; teenagers watch television in the early afternoon; professionals enjoy watching political shows in the late evening; unemployed people may watch television late into the night; and almost everybody watches the news during lunchtime.[39] Some business owners and newspaper reporters watch television programmes on portable computers during work hours via online streaming.

In contrast, radio is much less used in most households. Some intellectuals and professionals may listen to the early morning news before leaving for work or while having their coffee. People who commute by car do listen to the radio intensely, for example on their short journey to Lecce. Radio is, however, widely heard in public spaces, such as shops, cafés and restaurants, where it is usually tuned to regional stations specialising in Italian music. A local radio station based in a nearby town broadcasts three channels across the entire region and a local entrepreneur has invested in a private small television station, but is waiting for the advertising rates to go back up to the levels they were at before the economic crisis.

Newspapers have a distinguished place in local culture that goes back to the beginning of the nineteenth century when the first local and regional journals were established. Currently there is a thirst for information and a true culture across the social spectrum of following the news. The two weekly journals published in Grano are distributed in all public spaces and sometimes even delivered door-to-door. Most devout families subscribe to the weekly *famiglia Cristiana* (Christian family), half of the parishes in Grano publish their own monthly journals and most schools have their own regular publication. Basically, in any house in Grano you will at any time find a few different journals. The biggest local journal encourages ordinary people to write articles or contribute to its content in other ways: in 2013 it had more than 40 contributors over and above the editorial staff. Even though it is available online, everybody reads the printed version.

The newspapers' local news items are popular; they are continually discussed on the streets and inside households and compared to the television reports. Most people agree that the local press always reflects the reality better than the national media, even though they realise it is sometimes biased by political views. The argument is that, unlike national television channels, it does not favour the bigger economic and political interests.[40] At the same time the local press never publishes any negative news regarding individuals in the community. For example, incidents such as domestic violence, drug addiction, or small criminal activities by local residents are only discussed face-to-face in conventional social settings. There is simply no tradition of making something public, even if everybody in the town already knows about it. There is no correlation between news discussed innumerable times in innumerable private spaces and the making public of negative news. In this context Facebook is seen as an environment that brings together concomitantly many different sources of information: local, regional, national and global, but it still follows clear norms regarding their distribution and interpretation.

The matters which are deemed worthy of public visibility can also be seen in the numerous public announcements or in the constant investments shop owners make in decorating their shop windows and refurbishing the interior of their commercial spaces. Whereas the taxes imposed by the administration for public advertising are considered affordable, the costs of the advertising agencies are prohibitive. It costs €600 to advertise one medium-sized poster for two weeks, so small businesses use Facebook intensively for advertising. One co-owner of a hairdressing salon estimated that her promotions on Facebook generate a customer increase of less than 5 per cent, while outdoor advertising brings an increase of 10 per cent in customers who also spend more money inside the salon. Most business owners prefer to have a Facebook page for their business and invest only from time to time in expensive outdoor publicity because it adds prestige and an additional note of reliability to the business. But on most occasions business owners print out posters and leaflets and ask retailers to display these for free.[41]

In the context of a rather poor internet provision locally, young people in Grano are pleased with the advent of mobile internet, which has taken off since 2010. There are only two public spaces left that offer free internet access, for a maximum period of one hour a day: the public library and the job centre. Just three public spaces offer free wi-fi services to their clients and one café offers fixed internet access at €2 for half an hour, which is considered quite expensive. At the same time, the cost of internet broadband is fairly high – between €19 and €40 a month which may include free landline minutes – and many families cannot afford it. Internet access in schools is limited to the classes on Information Technology, but both professors and students find that connections are much too slow. School students and those in higher education use the internet mainly as a search tool: they *fare ricerca* (do research) for their homework, look up information on their preferred celebrity or read news. There is a general sense that the internet is a place to go when you need to find something particular, and this is similar to how television is perceived.

Email is virtually unknown among teenagers and not very popular among the rest of the population, except for those who use it at work. In my household survey just one-fifth of respondents declared they used email on a daily basis. People with a higher education tend to use email and LinkedIn more, but even so these tools are not really perceived as responding to their personal needs. If we add in that only 3 per cent of the households owned an e-reading device we can see that what people are really passionate about is owning electronic devices such as computers, video consoles and smartphones that allow them to play and relate more informally. For example, 64 per cent of the households surveyed had at least one home video game device (PlayStation, Xbox, Wii), which was often used by several members of the family. Typically it is the young father who acquires the gaming platform for himself (sometimes offered as a present by his spouse), and then invests regularly in games encouraging his children to play together. Even if today's teenagers prefer playing games on their personal electronic devices, we may say that home gaming is still seen as a social activity in most families in Grano.

A similarly strong emphasis on socialisation can be seen from the social media survey, which showed that 70 per cent of the respondents never clicked the 'like' button for a local business, and many who did were families or friends of that particular business.[42] A common explanation was that physical presence and permanent interaction are important and people did not see any reason to follow online a local commercial activity they had known personally for many years. However, online shopping from international networks (Amazon, eBay, Groupon) was quite popular among young people because they could access products faster and at cheaper prices than through local businesses.[43] At the time of my field work there were two businesses in Grano offering electronic marketing services and, in 2014, around one-third of their revenue was assured by a handful of clients. The general director of one of these companies confirmed that this was simply because his customers had pushed him in this direction, so a couple of years ago he and his small team decided to make a considerable investment in hardware, training and employing a professional web designer. They had not really thought that internet-based services would be so successful.

Texting is hugely popular among teenagers who can easily send several hundred text messages a month, and, with the advent of WhatsApp, the older population are texting much more than before. If in the summer of 2013 WhatsApp was considered a somewhat pretentious or little-known service, in less than a year it became the most used mobile application because people see it as complementing voice calls and Facebook, providing increased intimacy between mothers and children, between *fidanzati* or between best friends. This is reflected in most adults having a relatively small number of WhatsApp contacts

(20–25 on average) and being part of just a couple of groups on this platform. Mobile phones can also represent a major source of anxiety, such as when a young woman hears her partner's phone buzzing at one o'clock in the morning.

In the light of my research I understand social media as being any media that enables some sort of communication within a group. In scope this could be a direct, indirect or broadcast communication, and in terms of time it could be either synchronous or asynchronous. While public-facing media resembles traditional broadcast media, though to much smaller groups, the more private media looks more like traditional dyadic communication but may extend to groups, which is what makes both social media. Mobile devices such as smartphones invite a fast reaction time, while most of the people I talked to preferred to sit at computers inside their homes and revise the photos they have uploaded when they were outside, search for a specific song or film, or simply look at the perfect photo of their classmate in higher resolution. For most people the use of Facebook on the street is considered 'too much' because it denotes inattention and possibly self-promotion. Therefore, using the public Facebook in the intimacy of the home represents the proper way to act. This is what most people recognise as being the pleasure and gratification of social media.

Why Grano?

At one level, Grano is not that different from most other similar-sized towns in the province of Salento. This becomes evident when we contrast the descriptions in this book with other sites examined in the 'Why We Post' project or when looking at the local answers to general questions about the impact of social media on the world in which we live. On such occasions all the smaller and larger towns in Salento, or the larger region of Puglia, unite in a solemn solidarity and seem incredibly similar in contrast to other parts of southern Italy, such as the region of Naples which is on the western coast of the peninsula at a distance of five hours drive and eight hours by bus or train.[44]

I lived in Grano for 15 months during 2013 and 2014. My wife Gabriela, who is also an anthropologist, and our two children joined me for almost a year. My son went to a local nursery and had to learn Italian. We left our daughter with different babysitters and friends and, later on, in a nursery as well, while my wife worked in the local library or from home. This opened many doors that otherwise would have been simply inaccessible. Grano is a gendered society and being married is the central position from which you are allowed to cross all sorts of social borders. As a single man I could have never reached the levels of intimacy and friendship that nurseries and playgrounds have to offer. People simply trusted me more perhaps because I complied with what they would expect from somebody like me: commitment to family and work.

I had the privilege of getting to know hundreds of people and sharing innumerable personal stories and experiences. I ended up knowing well over 80 people living in 30 households, including local officials and public figures. I conducted formal in-depth interviews with 91 people, most of them recorded, and had several hundred formal and informal conversations on different aspects of the project. When you live in the field for this amount of time, any minor job turns out to be an opportunity to learn something about the society around you.

I also conducted three types of questionnaire: an exploratory one, which included a detailed household survey and individual data on the use of electronic media and was conducted with 106 respondents at the beginning of the research; a second questionnaire, which focused on the use of Facebook and was conducted with 109 respondents; a third questionnaire with 539 school students, who were mostly in the last two years of secondary schools in Grano, which focused on teenagers' use of social media.[45] I also recorded several hours of film documenting people, customs and places and co-edited ten short clips that were used in teaching at UCL and in producing the free e-learning course called *The Anthropology of Social Media*.[46]

However, what was probably the most fascinating element of this research was the online component. I opened a personal Facebook profile dedicated to my research. It was a public profile and I set the privacy settings so that friends and followers could not see each other. In the 'About me' section I detailed my role as a researcher and the scope of the project. The profile name was Razvan Nicolescu Ucl, the profile photo showed me somewhat younger and the background photo showed me together with my wife. In total I friended 210 people on this profile, most of whom participated in the research. I found it particularly difficult because this research profile soon became a personal one, for example many Facebook friends became really close friends. I was careful to explain the nature of my research in every context, even though many people were not too concerned with their Facebook presence because this was seen as a public platform. I decided to follow 20 Instagram profiles and 12 Twitter accounts, because the usage of these two services in

Grano was scarce. As I was writing this book all these profiles were still active and constantly growing in usage.

I gathered extensive ethnographic materials, which included the records of local, regional and national censuses; read volumes about social history and the local economy; and became acquainted with the current political scene. Actually it was a challenge keeping pace with the wealth of available material: local press, brochures, art catalogues, professional and amateur videos, and official local data. In good Italian tradition, many people in the region were involved in different kinds of editorial activities and several published volumes on various aspects of Grano and its surroundings: a teacher and publicist wrote a few books on the history of the place and its institutions; a publisher edited a couple of anthologies on the local folk traditions; one successful entrepreneur wrote four books and produced several short documentaries on the social history of Grano; and a few cultural associations organised events, exhibitions and talks several times a year. The local library kept the full collection of all major journals that were published locally throughout the last century.[47] Italy is also thorough about compiling statistics and making these available online as the state encourages complete transparency in governance (for example, in Grano the council meetings were public and streamed live on the internet).

To me Grano no longer looks like an average town in Italy with around 20,000 inhabitants, which was the required criteria of the project. The process of ethnographic field work and anthropological writing has distinguished it for me from other towns. The next chapter will give a general sense of how people in Grano use social media. Then Chapter 3 will focus in and take a closer look at what people post on Facebook and formulate a few preliminary suggestions about how these postings reflect the way people see their society and social relations. We will take this visibility down one level in Chapter 4, where we discuss how people use social media in relation to their more intimate and private relationships. Chapters 5 and 6 will widen the lens and explain how both public displays and private relations are two sides of the very specific sociality of Grano. Chapter 5 discusses the critical importance of public visibility and the social requirement to craft it. Chapter 6 describes how people use social media in relation to the fundamental issues of work and education. Finally the conclusion of this book will put all these into an even larger perspective, and explain why understanding the use of social media in an average corner of the world such as Grano is essential to appreciating the world we live in.

2
The social media landscape

The small, quiet square of Santa Eufemia is overflowing today. Anxious, dressed-up parents welcome groups of grandparents, cousins and close friends as they arrive with bunches of flowers and small gifts wrapped in shiny paper. They kiss each other with affection, laugh loudly, congratulate each other on their looks and ask where the children are. Everybody is well-dressed: many mothers wear high heels, elegant dresses or blouses and black sunglasses, while fathers wear light white shirts with the first one or two buttons undone, comfortable low shoes and even black shades. After a few minutes' talk and joyful greetings across the crowd, people hasten to the cars parked on the narrow streets that lead to the square, or they start to find their places on the white plastic chairs arranged meticulously in front of a small stage on one side of the church. Each family has a half-row reserved for them in the audience.

It is *cresima*, definitely the most important event in the community at the beginning of summer. This is the ceremony of confirmation celebrated by the Western Catholic Church in the presence of a bishop, when the Holy Spirit is believed to descend on those believers who have vowed to be good Christians. In Italy *cresima* takes place when children are 12 or 13 years old, after a few years of learning the catechism,[1] by which time it is believed that the young person knows enough about the Catholic faith and precepts to consent to a way of life that pleases God.

The thrilled young people who are to receive confirmation are dressed in new and adult clothes, have fresh haircuts and are expected to participate in the ceremony with humility and obedience. The service has been prepared months in advance by each parish. Everybody who has participated in these preparations is a little nervous for the young children because of their roles in front of the high clerics and such a large audience. In the end 20 young people and a few adults who have been recently baptised form two lines between the seats and wait to be called to the altar table on the small stage. Once at the altar, they bow their heads slowly and receive their blessing and the sign of the cross from the bishop. Then, relieved and happy, they take the microphone in turn to recite a verse from the Holy Scripture. The entire audience stands up and responds with a short prayer. The ceremony ends with a homily from the bishop and applause from the emotional congregation.

The ceremony is followed by a big celebration within the family where the newly confirmed young person is the centre of attention: they receive expensive presents from different family members and godparents and small, symbolic mementos from distant relatives and friends. These gifts have evolved considerably in recent years. Traditionally parents used to give their daughters new or family jewels, such as rings, necklaces and pendant crosses, while boys would receive grown-up clothes and elegant wristwatches. There used to be immense social pressure to take particular and lifelong care of these gifts. If tempted after several years to sell some of their golden necklaces received at the *cresima*, people would resist this, fearing that, for example, the old and dear auntie might someday ask if they still had the gift given many years before. *Cresima* gifts were therefore seen by the entire family as repositories of respect and precious memories, and constituted subjects for recurrent discussion throughout their life.

In the 1980s the most common gift for *cresima* was a scooter, which might have cost the equivalent of as much as €2–3,000, but those were the years of economic boom for Grano when people could afford such presents. Ten years later parents started to give their children personal computers and later on laptops and game consoles for this occasion. Many parents were quite happy with this change as they considered these devices useful, less dangerous and much cheaper than a good scooter. At the time I was carrying out my field work in Grano the most prestigious gifts for *cresima* by far were tablets and smartphones. Parents had mixed feelings about this, as many thought that the new mobile devices increased their children's autonomy while having an unclear role in assisting them in getting a good education. Nevertheless, *cresima* is regarded as the kind of occasion when children are allowed to receive what they most want to make them truly happy.

However, the age at which most children received their first smartphone was around 10 years old, with many parents trying hard to resist reducing it further. This is the age when many children start to use social media, including many controversial platforms such as Ask.fm,[2] despite most parents voicing a preference for their children

Mobile Phone Types Among Teenagers

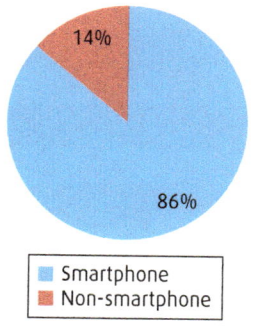

14%

86%

- ■ Smartphone
- ■ Non-smartphone

Type of Computer Use Among Teenagers

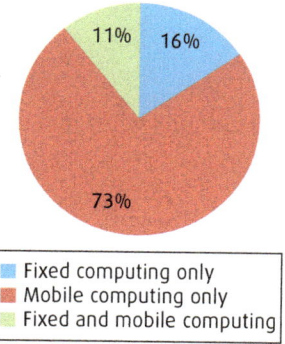

11%   16%

73%

- ■ Fixed computing only
- ■ Mobile computing only
- ■ Fixed and mobile computing

Fig. 2.1 Use of digital technology among teenagers (data from the students' questionnaire, n=539)

to wait and only start using social media after the age of 14.[3] Throughout adolescence young people's mobile and online presence is constantly updated as their world continuously expands: many receive their secondary education outside their hometown, they start romantic relationships and they gain increased autonomy from their families.

My school questionnaire revealed that 86 per cent of students aged 17–19 owned a smartphone and 99 per cent owned or shared at least one computer in their family. The importance of mobility is also shown by the fact that 83 per cent owned some sort of mobile computer and only 16 per cent owned a desktop computer. In addition, 45 per cent of the households had at least one gaming platform that was often used by two or more members of the family, typically the father and children. Other individual electronic devices, such as iPods, iPads and MP3 players, were present in 40 per cent of the households. In Chapter 6 we will

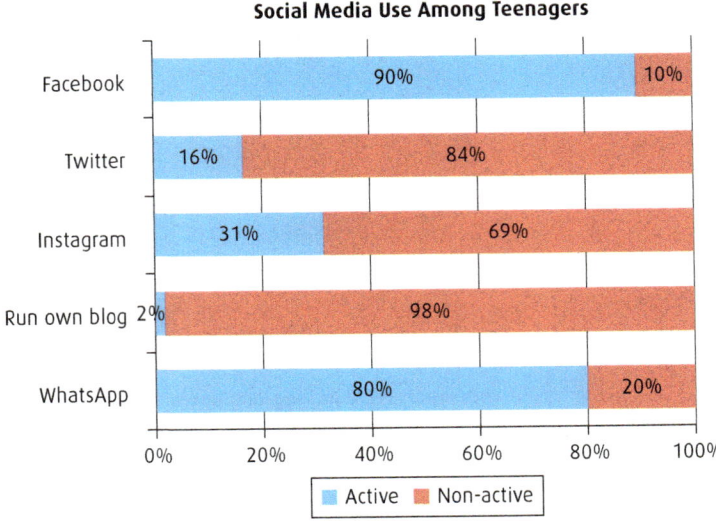

Social Media Use Among Teenagers

	Active	Non-active
Facebook	90%	10%
Twitter	16%	84%
Instagram	31%	69%
Run own blog	2%	98%
WhatsApp	80%	20%

Fig. 2.2 Social media use among teenagers (data from the students' questionnaire, n=539)

see that this relative affluence in terms of technological devices within households reflects the particular importance placed on home education in Grano.

Fig. 2.2 shows that more than 90 per cent of students were actively using Facebook and 80 per cent were using WhatsApp. These impressive numbers reflect that in Grano the two services were seen as complementary facets of sociality: Facebook was seen as the public face and WhatsApp as the private and personal face.

In contrast, students did not have a consistent opinion about the use of Instagram and Twitter. Relatively more students used Twitter to be in contact with friends than to follow celebrities (45 as opposed to 30 per cent) and many used it mainly to stay in contact with colleagues, family members and partners (22 per cent). Instagram was used more clearly to establish relationships based on shared interests, but many also used it to stay in contact with school colleagues (18 per cent) and friends from their hometown (14 per cent). For example, those who were commuting to study in Grano used Instagram to share images from their hometown with school colleagues, and to share images from school and Grano with friends from home. Most of the parents or older relatives did not even bother to ask their children what they did on Twitter or Instagram, even less actually to try and log on to these sites.

At the time of my field work, the use of digital technology was seen as a mark of the social coming-of-age of a young person, as the scooter had been three decades before. This wealth in mobile communication and computing was related to the adults' sense that digital devices were important in giving their children a good start in life. We will explore this further in Chapter 6, but for now it is important to note that both scooters and digital technology were used to mark an explicit change of life patterns and rhythm: scooters were used to move around town independently, start intimate relations and exchange goods and small favours with their peers, while computers and laptops represented a partial return to the home. However, the mobility and multimedia capacities gained through digital devices allowed teenagers to express their autonomy in even more sophisticated ways: they could text love messages as they got up from the lunch table or engage in several simultaneous mobile discussions as they met their friends in the town square. What is underlying this change in technology over recent years is the increasing options teenagers have to connect with peers, find information, play and generally present themselves to others.[4] We will look at the relationships between all these aspects and note how women dominate in the use of social media. Indeed, if social media had a gender, in Grano it would definitely be female.

One reason for starting with a ceremony that marks a shift in one's perceived age is that this is a highly significant factor in understanding social media in Grano. The next sections will focus in turn on young people, the elderly and the in-between working population of the town, and examine why the use of social media varies significantly with age. We will see that if younger generations tend to use social media in a more uniform way, the adult and older generations do so in ways that reflect the social categories to which they belong.

The youngest people on social media

Raffaella is a 14-year-old student at the local high school. She is of medium height, thin, with long, straight dark hair and big black eyes. She has had a Facebook account for two years now. Her profile is public as she has never thought this could be a problem. She has 840 Facebook friends, mainly school colleagues. Usually each day after lunch she turns on her family's laptop, arranged in a corner of the sitting room, and clicks on to her Facebook account, which is usually already logged on. For two or three hours Raffaella does 'everything she needs to do': homework, which usually involves chatting with different people in her class; listening to music on YouTube; checking out the official website of One Direction, her favourite band; leaving comments and a few 'likes' on Facebook; and following a few conversations on WhatsApp. Sometimes, especially during the long winter evenings, she goes online again after returning from her piano lessons or after dinner. Raffaella knows she should post more statuses and be quicker when replying online if she wants her own thoughts 'to count'. But she feels she does not really want to make an impression (*postare per farmi vedere*). Last time she changed her profile picture was more than three months ago.

Raffaella's mother is quite reluctant for her daughter to use Facebook. She created her own Facebook profile when she decided a few years ago that she had to see what Anna Maria, Raffaella's older sister, 'was doing there'. So she friended her online, and now has herself gained almost 80 online friends, most of them women: mothers, relatives and more than a dozen friends of her two daughters. The mother often wonders how her daughters can post just 'everything' on Facebook. When I talked to the family, the mother was quite confused by how Raffaella seemed not to make any choices about what she should and should not post online, or to differentiate among her online friends when posting on private issues. She remembers being horrified when Raffaella announced excitedly on Facebook that she was in love, or when she posted a few photos of herself wearing professional make-up.

The first shock had been when Anna Maria posted photos from her 18th birthday. Her mother described how uneasy she had felt when going through the photos uploaded by her daughter online. She opened them slowly, in sequence, examining details and nervously waiting to see what the next photo in the group would be. She sat by herself, at the desk, not knowing what to expect. She remembers that all she felt were thousands of curious eyes scrutinising her daughter and leaving comments that sometimes had an insolence she simply could not bear. The photos were not even taken at home, but in a restaurant, and she and her husband were not in the photos. The parents do take photos occasionally, but they always keep them private, stored on the camera or the family computer, and rarely look at them or show them to others outside the family. As a parent, she knew that turning 18 was extremely important for her daughter, but she, nevertheless, felt invaded and increasingly sad when going through the photos. She kept thinking how the photos were simply out there, available for anyone to see them whenever they felt like it. After a while she stopped reading the comments, which were mainly saying how beautiful Anna Maria looked and sending her love: *'Belllaaaa!'* (Beautiful!), *'Sei bellissima come sempre'* (You are beautiful as always), or simply '♡♡♡'.

In contrast, Raffaella's father has quite a different attitude to being online: from time to time he shares slightly inappropriate videos on WhatsApp with his daughters and never really looks at what they do online. Because of his more demanding work schedule as a teaching assistant, he spends less time at home with his family. In contrast, like many of her female friends, Raffaella's mother feels directly responsible for her daughters' behaviour. Many mothers feel they have strong reasons to be nervous, for example, when looking at the immense number of online friends their children have, while they themselves and most people they know have far fewer such contacts.

Referring to the way teenagers use Facebook, another young mother told me bluntly: 'They don't know how to use it', and continued, irritated: 'Because they put everything there!' The mother was annoyed by the amount of information that left her house through her 15-year-old daughter's Facebook page and, more generally, by the fact that her daughter's Facebook friends also seem not to filter out or edit anything when posting. In contrast, whenever she herself posted something online, she tried to think of her Facebook friends as a collection of distinct social categories, such as family, friends, simple acquaintances or work colleagues. She then tried to give to each category something that would be meaningful for them. Indeed, most adults in Grano think of their online audience as a collection of different groups of friends. It is within each of these groups that the visual postings are decoded and recognised.

Most teenagers, however, have just one way of posting on Facebook, which is for all their contacts to see their posts. If they want to enter a specific discussion, they use Facebook chat or WhatsApp messages instead. Teenagers' undifferentiated postings on Facebook were seen by parents as too open, direct and annoying. Teenagers also seemed not to draw a clear distinction between online and offline. For example, unlike adults, teenage couples expected each other to 'like' each other's posts, hug, smile, send purple hearts and continuous appreciations to each other as a clear signal to others of their relationship.

Thus social media provides the setting where teenagers learn and practice sociability inside their various peer groups, with no significant help or guidance from adults, just as was the case when they were playing in the town square. Psychologists have famously shown how, between the ages of 11 and 15, children begin their evolution from an egocentric to a wider understanding of the world.[5] This means that children start at this age to realise they are not in fact the 'centre of the world' and start to look at the world from multiple angles. In social terms, this process corresponds to a movement from a concrete to a more abstract understanding of relationships. For the present discussion it is important that teenagers now enter into a vast system of communication and relations with a large number of peers in a relatively short period of time. There seems to be little time and space for them to learn to filter out ideas or be very strict in following pre-defined rules for communicating in the way that adults do. Instead teenagers attempt to sort out these rules through experience, that is, on the go, which actually means while being active on social media.

Many young people argued that they did not need a smartphone because they could meet their friends in person if they wanted to. Nevertheless most of them actually had a smartphone and used it to expand these offline encounters in spaces and at times that were conventionally related to other activities. Perhaps the most important shift caused by new technology in the last decades was the shift from the *predictability* of everyday face-to-face encounters to the ever-expanding *possibilities* generated by the newly mediated encounters. For teenagers, exploring these possibilities was seen as essential in establishing social relationships and crafting their personhood, while many parents saw the media as uncontrollable and potentially dangerous.

My student survey showed that 72 per cent of respondents had more than 500 Facebook friends and 18 per cent more than 2,000. But teenagers knew far fewer people personally. The tension between the confined space of physical encounters and the expanded space of possible interactions opened up by the online environment was expressed in an obligation to show a relative consistency between offline and online interactions. For example, many young people promptly sanctioned those who pretended or demonstrated online that they were different there than they were offline: 'Some [colleagues] do not even greet you on the street and at home [on Facebook] they talk to everyone, they comment, ...' So, for example, a girl who regularly uploads lots of selfies taken at home, dressed and made-up provocatively, is then obliged to adopt an equally extrovert attitude at school. The fact that young people will criticise this kind of inconsistency in what they call 'reality' and 'Facebook' suggests that social media does not give them a sense of 'unreality' or 'mystification', but rather that they generally expect to find online what they already know from the offline environment. Consistency between online and offline is seen as 'truth', while repeated variations are sanctioned as inappropriate and disappointing.

The quantitative data shows that what teenagers most disliked about Facebook was the lack of privacy (20 per cent), inappropriate behaviour, which included self-promotion (19 per cent) and fake profiles (10 per cent). Subsequent interviews with students confirmed that, for most, Facebook was about being true to oneself and not transgressing boundaries. For example, the aversion to fake profiles was related to the fact that offline your friends simply cannot be fake. Indeed, most teenagers do not assume different roles in different social contexts as adults can do. Therefore, if being truthful is an essential quality offline, most teenagers do not see any reason why this should not also be the case online.

The opportunity for extreme visibility is exploited by the few teenagers who for different reasons use Facebook in order to *mettersi in mostra* (put themselves on display). This is perhaps best exemplified by the category of *bimbiminchia* – relatively young children who behave online and on social media as if they are much older, or who adopt different, narcissistic or annoying stances. Every school has a few students who are accused of falling into this category: 'people who don't ever have their own identity and depend on their own idol, posting embarrassing photos and publishing insignificant thoughts enriched with stupid words like 'I roll over', 'I cry', 'I burst', 'aww'' (Laura, 19 years old). This definition also suggests that intimate and intense feelings are to be kept private and not trumpeted in the face of unknown people. At the same time, a tolerant opinion regarding excessive self-promotion online was: 'This is simply what he's doing [showing off on Facebook], he just thinks he is good looking' (Antonio, 18 years old). As we will see later in the book, these two judgements set limits for normative behaviour online.

At the same time, the concept of privacy is not simply related to the ego. Many teenagers condemn an indolent attitude in those peers who do not protect their privacy online. Inappropriate photos are not only seen as a possible embarrassment to those who have posted them – some teenagers said that they themselves did not want to see other people's overly explicit photos. These considerations are essential because Facebook is associated with relationships. What teenagers liked most about Facebook was the ability to stay in contact with friends and family (34 per cent), to see or post photos (20 per cent), to chat (10 per cent) and to get to know new people (6 per cent). Only 2 per cent appreciated Facebook as a source of information and updates, compared to 41 per cent who appreciated the internet primarily as providing a source of information, news and research.

As the story of Raffaella and Anna Maria suggests, at the time of my field work there was a general unease regarding the use of social media by teenagers in Grano. Parents were anxious because they did not really know what their children did online. They were annoyed when they saw their children nonchalantly contravening the limits they themselves had prescribed for public media.[6] In turn teachers scolded students and some parents because mobile phones frequently interrupted classes and some students filmed them while they were teaching. On the other hand, most students saw mobile phones and social media as educationally useful in allowing them to exchange homework via WhatsApp or because, in a handful of cases, they could be in the same online group with their favourite teacher. But otherwise the vast majority agreed that the last thing they used social media for was actually to study.

There were important differences in social media use across social groups. In the poorest neighbourhoods in Grano, where the school drop-off rate was highest, young people start using Facebook a few years later than their wealthier peers, typically at 14–16 years old. Until this age, for many, social media and digital technology were less accessible: they could not afford a new smartphone, a personal computer, mobile internet subscription or broadband internet connection at home. Teenagers from lower social and economic backgrounds also sensed an important lag in appropriating the language and genres used online. For example, one student told me she sometimes does not feel like going online where many of her better-off colleagues dominate the discussions. She may also feel embarrassed that she cannot upload photos wearing new clothes on Facebook, and is disheartened when looking at photos from birthday parties to which she has not been invited. Many teenagers confirmed that the school does very little to introduce them to the use of new media, which might reduce the gaps between students. The few IT classes focus on a rather theoretical curriculum so it is up to the parents to transmit technology and computing skills to their children.[7]

The world of adults

My research shows that it is the nuclear family that supports and attempts to even out the various differences in the use of media: parents encourage their children to use smartphones and laptops in order to be 'like everyone else', teenagers introduce their parents to Facebook and young adults introduce their parents to computers and Skype.

Angela, a 72-year-old widow and mother of four, remembers how happy she was when, together with six other trainees who were over 60, she first learned to switch on a PC by herself and could connect with her family over the internet. Angela had enrolled on one of the numerous courses to improve computer literacy offered by local schools with funding from the European Union.[8] Angela is a very energetic woman who rides a bicycle every day, works regularly in her enormous garden at Grano Porto, bathes in the sea until late November and, on occasion, takes care of her three grandchildren. Angela's children have set up a private group on Facebook called *Bucarello Family* (using their surname), where they discuss anything from everyday matters and political news to preparing for major events, such as refurbishment works at their coast house or the wedding ceremony of Angela's second youngest son who lives in Rome. One of the reasons they needed a Facebook group was to reunite the family: two of Angela's children live in Grano, one in Rome and another one in Milan. Like many people of her age who are on Facebook, Angela is most grateful that she is able to 'see' her beloved children in a medium that is not too technologically demanding and also to retain a memory of all their past encounters. She often finds herself browsing the group's past conversations and photos posted by her family. Sometimes Angela feels that online she is better able to understand some aspects of her children that she had not noticed before; for example, how tough life in Rome can be or how much her grandchildren had grown.

If social media can expand the space of possibilities for young people, the actual online encounters remain quite constant over time for most people in Grano. My household survey showed that for the majority of the respondents (68 per cent), more than 50 per cent of their connections were from their home town.[9] While this is definitely due to Grano being a small town, the chances to connect with people from outside a person's hometown increase as the person raises their level of education and social capital: for example, people with university degrees have numerous online connections with ex-colleagues from university and friends made during their years of study. In the next chapter we will see how the content that circulates on Facebook reflects these relationships.

Fig. 2.3b shows that, after a frenzy of online activity during teenage years, the adoption of smartphones and the use of Facebook drops off dramatically in successive age groups. A common practice for many young people a few years after graduating from high school is to 'clean' their Facebook account: they effectively sit down at their computer and in a couple of hours go through the entire list of Facebook friends

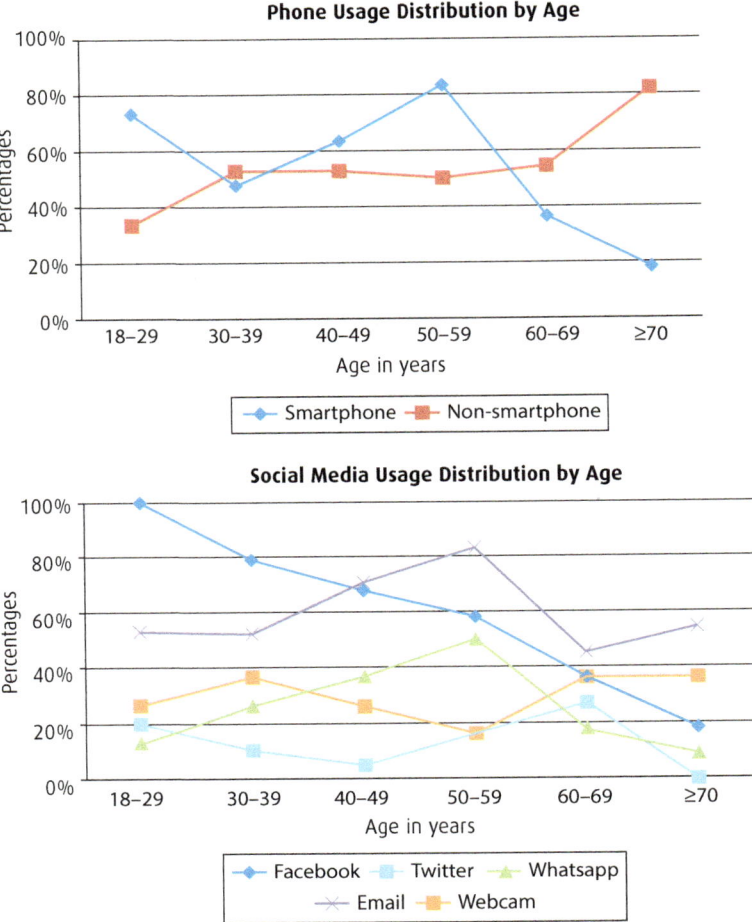

Fig. 2.3 Variation of age of mobile phone use (a) and social media use (b) (data from the household survey, n=106)

and unfriend anybody they do not know personally or have any doubts about. Thus, many end up restricting themselves to just 300–400 online friends and feel relieved that they actually do know all of these people.

The other public-facing social media services were far less popular: my household survey showed that only 11 per cent of the respondents had a Twitter account; seven per cent used Instagram; six per cent used LinkedIn; and five per cent used Google+.[10] Usually these platforms were thought to express individualism and social difference, and most people do not want to stand out from their peers, whether online or offline. As we will see in the next chapter, most Facebook postings are about issues that everybody agrees on or that are already known. In contrast, people use Twitter and Instagram to depart from this kind of predictability. For example, Twitter is used mostly to engage with the outer world and to make friends that are very different from those in Grano, while Instagram is used to demonstrate through photography one's special skills or sensibility. In this context, teenagers stand out because they also use Twitter and Instagram to strengthen relationships. This partially explains the relatively higher success of these two services among teenagers as opposed to the older population.

Although based on a relatively small sample, Fig. 2.3 is an expression of how diverse and unpredictable the use of social media is. It shows that people in their fifties have a pivotal position: they represent the peak in smartphone adoption, the use of WhatsApp and email, but are the least likely to use a webcam. They also follow the trend of decreasing Facebook use with age. Their uses of social media correspond to a rewarding balance between work, economic comfort and the need to negotiate changing relations in their nuclear families. Their children turn into young adults and this is reflected in a more intensive use of WhatsApp. Most older people do not see a need for Facebook in terms of expressing their social relations or presenting themselves to the community.

Facebook is seen as eminently public and subject to social norms, whereas people use WhatsApp to express the more personal and intimate aspects of their lives: fathers can spend a few hours' arguing with their adult sons on the mobile phone; lovers can exchange hundreds of WhatsApp messages, emoticons and photos a day; colleagues can coordinate everyday activities; and families and friends can schedule *serate* (evenings) to spend together. WhatsApp represents a relative indicator of economic and social success: owning a proper smartphone and being in constant contact with a large family and a great number of friends.

Fig. 2.4 shows the frequency in use of different media. We can observe that only half of those who are always connected on WhatsApp are also always connected on Facebook. This is due to the higher complexity of using Facebook on smartphones and the association of WhatsApp with mobile phone calls and texting. The adult population is by far the most eclectic from the point of view of media use: they range from enthusiastic adopters of technology to more reticent individuals who have a minimal presence online, while an important sector refuses to adopt smartphones and social media at all.

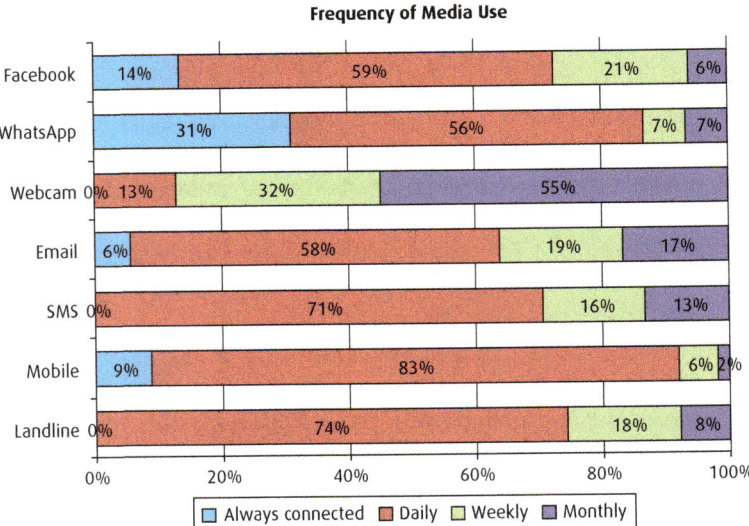

Fig. 2.4 The frequency of use of different media in Grano (data from the household survey, n=106)

Fig. 2.5 shows an inventory of electronic devices within households and puts these into perspective alongside other domestic possessions. We can see that it is not unusual for houses with three bedrooms and more to have three television sets, while it is much rarer to have more than one computer device per household. Households which are connected to the internet via broadband roughly correspond to the sector of the population which considers itself to be economically comfortable.

Constants and variations in social media use

As in the English language, Italians use the same word for all friends – in general life and on Facebook: *amici*. In the household survey respondents had difficulty in assigning their Facebook friends to the different categories suggested by the questionnaire: friends from the workplace, friends from the neighbourhood or colleagues from school. People could assign many of their Facebook friends to all of these categories at once, and they could define levels of friendship that were different from those suggested by the questionnaire. In this rather small settlement with important regional mobility, most people think they have known

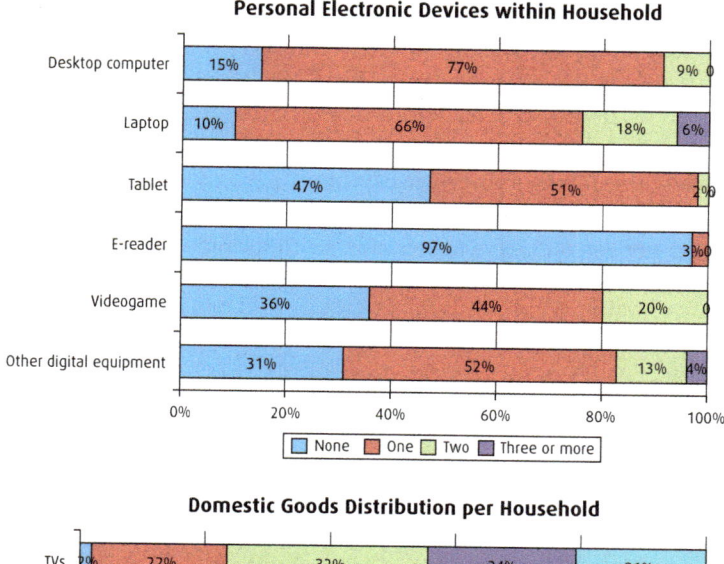

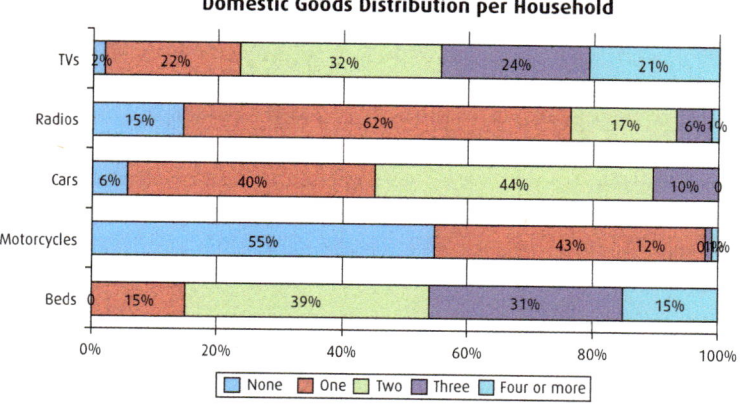

Fig. 2.5 Inventory of electronic devices (a) and household possessions (b) (data from the household survey, n=106)

each other forever. In many cases this is true, as they might have gone to nursery and to school together, played in the same neighbourhood or at least have a common distant relative or, indeed, friend. Their paths may have diverged at some point in their lives, but after having their first child they would tend to rediscover their friendships, maybe because once again their schedule and interests had become similar. Therefore the term *amici* includes all these subtleties in a rather self-explanatory and inclusive way. The way people separate their *amici* is through giving them differentiated access to their own lives, be that via Facebook, WhatsApp or face-to-face encounters.

At the same time, social media does not usually enhance sociality. For example, Alfredo is known to be a rather secluded person. He follows quite a predictable daily rhythm as he moves between the apartment he shares with his fiancée, his parents' house, the nearest food shops and his workplace (he is a part-time physiotherapist). He rarely talks on his mobile phone, almost never uses text messages and his online presence is confined to his professional Facebook page, which is managed by his fiancée. But Alfredo has a big passion for films and the Italian mafia. He could spend hours watching films on television or downloaded from the internet, and talk with his friends about his collection of Scotch whiskey and the latest article or book on the Italian mafia that he has read. However, Alfredo comments that showing all this on Facebook would be simply too much.

This is related to the fact that most Facebook postings in Grano are related to work activity and cultural capital.[11] I will define my use of the latter term. In any community, there are a myriad reasons why people may either look up to or down on other people: these could be disagreements over the best way to raise a child; a sense of superiority because of having greater wealth; or because a person holds a degree or has a vocational talent. Sometimes these differences are expressed in more subtle ways. For example, some people talk in a certain way or they express their liking of a particular art object in a way that intimidates those who do not. By doing this, people show they are different. Often this difference does not translate into money, but into another sort of capital that is cultural.[12]

I need to define another key term. Sociologist Erving Goffman famously showed that the way we behave in the world is similar to acting in a theatre play.[13] We are not only conscious of our role in society, but we also want to deliver to the audience the best performance we can, given a specific role. This includes trying to manage what other people, as the audience, think of us. In this situation the self is not just one rigid and autonomous entity. Rather it is an intrinsic part of the multiple plays in which it acts. Therefore the self varies according to which social role a person is playing in their daily lives.

My research shows that in Grano the use of social media relates to notions of selfhood within social relations. With the exception of teenagers, intense social media use does not create cultural capital. Rather, it is the other way around: people who consider they possess some sort of higher cultural capital feel obliged to show this on social media. They also tend to use the media in general more extensively. For example, many lawyers, doctors, accountants and teachers read daily newspapers, listen to the morning news on the radio and watch the evening news on television; they talk endlessly on their mobile phone in their free periods and they text in their busier periods. They update their Facebook page when coming back from work and Skype their relatives and old university colleagues at weekends. They actually use a vast range of media products in order to keep pace with their professional and domestic duties, and also to reflect their particular position in society.

In contrast, people with a lower social and economic background tend to use Facebook much more than email or Skype. They tend to have busier work schedules and they watch television and talk on their mobile phone much more than they use other media. Farmers and small professionals, such as plumbers, builders and painters, scarcely use social media at all. A typical example would be a self-employed man in his mid-forties who works by the day in construction and has an old dusty Nokia phone and no Facebook account. He does not have an internet connection at home, but every now and then uses his sister's, who lives on the floor below in the same house. Most people from lower social and economic backgrounds use mobile phones more rarely than their wealthier peers. They barely send more than a few text messages a week and use the phone just a few times a day, usually to the same group of people. As we will see in Chapter 6, this reticence in using social media is related to an educational background that did not support computer literacy, and the complete disconnection between work and electronic media.

The reason why stone carvers, potters and artists actively use Facebook is to increase the visibility of their work. Their online activity is very much centred on their work. Because they produce objects that are highly appreciated and prized by people with high cultural capital, they themselves come to be very prestigious in the community. In this case, their higher social status boosts their online presence. It implies appreciating the aesthetic and moral qualities of their work. Friending them on Facebook and constantly validating their activity online has become a common way to borrow something from their distinguished standing.

People with similar social and economic backgrounds and professions can have very different ideas of how social media should be used. For example, the dynamic head teacher of the vocational high school in Grano accepts friendship requests on Facebook only after her students graduate from school. She thinks that this distance is mandatory for delivering a good education to her students. In contrast, some teachers do not hesitate to mix the seriousness of their work with the ambiguity of Facebook. They actively encourage students to set up Facebook pages and WhatsApp groups for the various activities they are involved in, in an attempt to help their students to bond better and to collaborate when doing homework. This reflects the different ways in which people in Grano use public-facing social media to reflect what they see as their social role.

A further variation is in how occupations determine the uses of media. For example, shop assistants with less demanding jobs and many state employees connect to the internet through mobile devices during periods of inactivity at work, much more than they do in their free time. Then, while most people in Grano have just one mobile phone and are quite discreet on social media, many entrepreneurs have two smartphones and, like teenagers, could have more than 1,000 online connections. They regularly update their personal Facebook profile and the Facebook page of their business, and spend hundreds of euros on communication each month. At the same time they rarely use email and Skype, and have little time to watch television. Housewives are more active online during the early afternoons when they are less busy. These variations again express people's dispositions in using social media.

The rhythms of social media

With the notable exceptions of entrepreneurs and teenagers, most people in Grano use public-facing social media in a rather reserved way. Very little of their lives actually goes on Facebook: they are typically online for 10–20 minutes a day or less, mainly in order to update and respond to different requests from friends. The main place they visit is Facebook News Feed where, in a short amount of time, people are able to find both information on their loved ones and general news. Most people in Grano seem to be attached only to one or two technologies at a time: teenagers prefer smartphones and Facebook; adults prefer television and the mobile phone; and old people prefer television and visits from the younger family. Social relations are so close-knit that people do not normally feel the need to rely too much on any particular technology.

A married couple sleepily checking Facebook each evening in bed after putting their three children to sleep is a typical example of online behaviour. During the day these people have so many things to do that they simply could not care less about being online. Giuseppe, for example, wakes up just after 6:00 in the morning, goes directly to the warehouse to check for merchandise and then opens his food shop at 7:00. His wife Analisa prepares breakfast for her two older children and breastfeeds her new baby, then drops her children at nursery and drives to the shop with her baby to help her husband with new orders and suppliers. If her work requires more effort, she might ask a woman who lives close to the shop to look after her baby for a couple of hours. After a full day of work, Giuseppe is exhausted; he brings home any fresh bread and pizzas that are left over, or sometimes gives them away for free and joins his family for dinner. Both Giuseppe and Analisa climb wearily into bed after 22:00 and open their Facebook accounts – Analisa much more often than Giuseppe. They catch up with their friends, messages and what has happened in Grano. Sometimes Analisa informs Giuseppe about a news item or news from a friend, and they discuss it briefly. They do not have the energy to spend more than 20 minutes or so on the platform, but they insist on logging in regularly as they feel it is their duty to respond to the people they care for. This huge imbalance between time dedicated to work and time dedicated to the use of social media suggests that Giuseppe and Analisa use social media mainly to compensate for the fact that their busy work and family life does not leave enough space for social relations.

Indeed, most people in Grano see public-facing social media as a sort of hobby or nice-to-have add-on that is used in relation to some ideal they have: married women post about their children; professionals post their work accomplishments and share advertisements related to their work; intellectuals read, watch, post and dream of debates and critical comments; activists share humanitarian, ecological and moralistic articles; good-looking teenage girls and young women post relatively more selfies; and so on. This focus on a personal ideal or passion can be seen more clearly on Twitter and Instagram, but then they are followed or commented on mostly by people from outside the community.

Simona, a separated mother of two, wakes up between 7:30 and 8:00. She works in a pastry shop that opens later in the morning. Her two daughters are old enough to walk by themselves to school. She enjoys having a longer breakfast and coffee, and also doing a few domestic chores before work. Simona may work for as much as 10 or 12 hours a day, depending on the orders her boss has received from his clients. Inside the pastry shop there is not good connectivity and so the only period when she can be on social media is in the late evening. She normally spends 30–40 minutes on both Facebook and Twitter. She prefers Twitter to communicate intensively with people she does not know on subjects that she is really passionate about, such as painting, art and films. Twitter represents a place where she feels really free and fulfilled. Sometimes she spends two hours chatting on Twitter, but she knows she can catch up on sleep in the morning because her schedule allows this.

As in the case of the couple presented above, Simona does not feel the need to make constant use of Facebook, but she associates this service with the obligation to respect her online commitments and interests, even if she is online at a later time of day than others. However, Simona feels that her use of Facebook implies a series of limitations. As a single mother, she feels she cannot upload too many photos of herself, and she cannot discuss many topics because Facebook is too public.

If Simona does not feel a need to use Facebook constantly, her day is filled with an interminable stream of WhatsApp messages. In any given day about 80 per cent of her WhatsApp messages are those exchanged with her family: her parents, her two daughters, her older brother and a few cousins. She enjoys feeling that all these people she loves are close in many ways: from simple 'Good morning' messages to entertaining clips and works from art exhibitions in Rome. Indeed, as WhatsApp is particularly easy to use, Simona can keep an eye on these particularly enjoyable messages during her laborious and repetitive work.

At the same time, Grano is a quite sociable place and people constantly move around the region, so they really do not need Facebook to co-ordinate or stay in contact with friends and acquaintances. Therefore many feel that Facebook simply represents an acceptable way to be in touch with people, including staying in contact with friends and relatives who live in other parts of Italy or abroad. Several people are actually more active online with people who live up north than with their closest friends in town. This suggests that in a way local sociality does not leave much space for online sociality.

Anthropologists Madianou and Miller gave the name 'polymedia' to the complex mechanism by which people decide which communication media they should engage with in any given situation.[14] The authors show that people's decision to follow one type of media as opposed to another is becoming less economically or technologically driven, and this enables technology to reflect social relationships. My research suggests that social media provides people with the opportunity to choose from among different ways in which to present themselves to society. It is because of social media that Simona finds it easier to show she is a successful mother, worker, member of the community and to express subtle artistic tastes at the same time. She finds different channels to take on each of these roles without one contradicting another. Later in the book we will see how people also use social media to relate to the upper layers of Italian society.

So far we have seen that it is normal for people to use a mix of communications in relation to what they want to be. The following sections will discuss different attitudes and viewpoints to social media that are essential in understanding the way society in Grano works.

Refusing Facebook

Sandra graduated in modern languages in Venice and then lived for a few years in Lecce. When she recently became pregnant she did not want to tell the baby's father about her pregnancy because they did not have a 'real' relationship. She decided to leave her small, part-time job, return to Grano and give birth there. At 34 years old, Sandra installed herself in her teenage room at the home of her parents, who were very happy with her decision. She tore the old posters of rock musicians from the walls, hung up instead a few scarfs and one big textile that she had brought from Venice, emptied her backpack on to the side table and the small desk in front of the bed and waited for the baby to arrive. For the next six months Sandra rarely left the house. She went for a coffee early in the morning in a café outside the central area where she lived, read the newspapers and then took a long walk home where she would immerse herself in volumes of literature and history until lunch. In the evening she would put on her unlaced black boots and corduroy dress and go and visit her grandmother or meet some of her few friends in Grano.

The first thing Sandra did when she decided to return to Grano to give birth was to close down her Facebook account. She just wanted to be by herself and avoid any scrutiny from her online contacts. Now she sensed that her life was so different from the one she had had before that she did not see any reason to be active on Facebook anymore. She talks on her standard feature mobile phone a few times a week with her two close friends, who do not live in Grano, and calls anybody else only when she has something to say. She has decided that she may let the father of her child assume the role of a father at some point if he wants to, but, for now, Sandra just wants to be at home where she feels safe and to enjoy her pregnancy. Sandra always had a rebellious nature and, as her two brothers also moved away to university, her parents had started to feel in recent years that they had lost a vital link with their children. They repainted a bigger bedroom and decorated it for Sandra to move into with her baby after the birth. By the time I left Grano, Sandra's baby was eight months old and she still had not re-joined Facebook. She had a new life and could not care less about the online world.

This kind of retreat from public social media can also be seen in the gesture made by many young people in closing their Facebook accounts after getting married. This is seen as a sign of their strongest commitment being to their new relationship.[15] As several local lawyers confirmed, the main reasons for divorce in Grano used to be *pettegolezi* (gossip), but are now the uses made of Facebook and the mobile phone. New media offer opportunities for cheating on your partner, but also for being discovered. It is not uncommon for men to ask women to friend them on Facebook because of their beautiful profile picture. This, and commenting on posts made by those of the opposite gender, can be extremely annoying to the partners of those in couples. Instead of closing down their accounts, some may choose to run jointly one single Facebook account as a sign that their actual relationship is much more important than any other one and is based on reciprocal trust.

In general, the attitude towards Facebook ranges from 'I don't like it, it's just gossip' to 'I enjoy Facebook, but don't take it too seriously'. This is related to the tradition of an intense social life outside the confines of technology and to what defines a respectable person and family. Respectability implies a particular rigorousness and predictability in everyday practices: in respecting dress codes; knowing when to go out and when to stay in the house; how to care for the family; and how to show commitment to work. Most women do not go out to buy bread or to take their children to school before having dressed themselves meticulously; parents do not feed their babies outside their homes; houses are flawlessly clean at all times; and, for most men, work days include chatting during several coffee breaks. In this setting, Facebook represents the media where the conventional order of things could be bluntly exposed to public scrutiny.

The fact that almost half (48 per cent) of the respondents in my household survey had a public Facebook profile is an expression of how people in Grano see the public sphere. Society is simply not structured to think about something that is so evidently public in terms of private spaces. Public-facing social media, and Facebook in particular, are seen as inherently public because they are free and open to all. Many people told me they never changed their privacy settings because they did not care if anyone looked at them online. Indeed, quite a few would be happy if many people did check their online profile. One young woman, for example, runs a personal blog on her daily life in order to let other people know her deeper emotions. She uses Facebook to publicise her blog and to make her numerous online friends actually read her blog, as otherwise they would not.

This suggests that social media consolidates normative social relations. Many of those who refuse to use Facebook sense that, for different reasons, they are outside this normativity. People who are not on Facebook or WhatsApp face serious challenges in proving their attachment to social values. If the entire family is texting a distant sibling via WhatsApp, or the majority of parents post on Facebook about their children's accomplishments in or outside school, people who refuse to buy a smartphone or to be on Facebook then have to try much harder to find other ways to demonstrate that they are by no means less sensitive or involved.

Good and bad Facebook

Maybe the most common response to questions regarding how people felt about social media was that, like anything in this world, social media could be either good or bad depending on how people used it. This means that social media does not have any intrinsic worth, but rather that it acquires different qualities in the hands and eyes of its users. The biggest task for most people is therefore to manage the unprecedented visibility and closeness public-facing social media brings. Failure to manage these properly leads to different instances of bad use of social media, which were mainly sexual harassment, jealousy and other sorts of unsolicited interferences with personal life (advertising was often placed in this category).

In this context, what teenagers and some highly educated individuals in Grano challenge online are the categories adults or 'society' in general have established. But there are ways to control this: for example, a 13-year-old girl in Grano is friends with her mother on Facebook and with her father on Twitter. Each time her parents see that she has posted something they consider to be inappropriate, they send her a private message, for example: 'Why do you act stupid?' She then normally does not edit or repost the initial message, but keeps in mind that her online behaviour should not be a certain way, and also feels happier than ever that her parents cannot see her private messages. Like many teenagers, she thinks that 'real relations' are neither in the private nor in the public domain – you just express them as you feel it is appropriate. We suggest that it is this sense of appropriateness that defines the middle ground between good and bad on public social media.

A couple's decision to share a single Facebook account can be seen as another way to navigate between good and bad. For example, a few days after deciding to get married, Giovanna and Marco decided also to share a single Facebook account. They saw this as a critical commitment to their relationship. Marco closed down his own Facebook account and started to use the Facebook account of his future wife. They had a common list of friends, but each used Facebook for quite different things: Giovanna more for chatting to her friends online and Marco for finding and sharing news items. Even if each of them explores the same Facebook News Feed, most of the time they are interested in very different issues. The two of them took particular care not to be too radical or extravagant online and not to get too close to people they knew could harm their unity as a couple. Therefore they would probably 'like' or comment less than they would have done when they had separate Facebook accounts. Both Giovanna and Marco argue that the joint Facebook account brings excitement into the relationship. Each of them finds out nice things about the other, including enjoying the constant attention needed to adopt a particular attitude online that reflects their strong romantic relationship.

Giovanna and Marco almost never make reference in their postings to their actual relationship. This is implicit and they have no need to confirm it any more. Family life is usually perceived as being essentially intimate and a given – by God – and therefore showing or even alluding to it on Facebook is not only dangerous but also pointless. This suggests that having a joint Facebook profile could be seen as an objectification of a couple's relationship. It is this unexpected intimacy found in an essentially public space and the permanent discovery of new common passions that makes Facebook exciting and consolidates them as a couple.

People keep any non-conforming or slightly disturbing issue for private media. For example, many gay people who had not migrated north to the big cities where they could be open about their orientation chose to marry locally and have children. Some engaged in extra-marital gay relationships, but they kept this strictly private; one could not detect the smallest suggestion that somebody was gay simply by viewing their public Facebook profile.

This example confirms how public life in Grano is characterised by social conformity and how there is a strong consistency between online and offline practices. This is very different from findings in all other countries so far in the 'Why We Post' project, apart from northern Chile. Most of the time Facebook is not perceived as a medium where people can behave differently from the way they do offline, nor as a place to draw attention to individual interests that are not shared by other people. We have seen that, even if many people in Grano do not spend too much time on Facebook, it is actually an essential part of their social presence. This also means that Facebook, as the most important public-facing social media, is not seen simply as another medium, but as an essential part of social life.

In this context, much effort is put into integrating what could be a potentially subversive realm into the rather predictable social life of Grano. People normally act on Facebook in the way the rest of their community expect them to because they know that a person's integrity requires that they continue to be the same person online that they are offline. Conversely services that are far easier to use on smartphones and work much faster on the slow mobile networks, such as Twitter, Instagram and Snapchat, are seen as being too innovative and their potential for being subversive is still high. This suggests that Facebook domesticates the subversive potential of social media and allows people to render their lives acceptable to the local community.

From Grano to Italian society in general

We should recognise that the way people in Grano use social media is not typical of general Italian society, or even that of southern Italy. Every time I started to explain findings from my field work to Italian friends and colleagues, anthropologists who work and live elsewhere in Italy, they would comment immediately that behaviours were very different in Milan, Rome or in other parts of the south of Itay. I would then have to give a detailed description of Grano society and explain its particular relationship to the regional and national setting. In this section, we will lay out this explanation which is essential for understanding the rest of the book.

In the introduction we saw that people in Grano are aware of their marginal position and look up to the wealthier north of Italy and Central Europe in almost every domain, from the economy to fashion. People often compensate for this by networking locally, which has major social and economic implications. Facebook works to reinforce, rather than to challenge, this mechanism. In Grano Facebook does not bring globalisation, inclusiveness and equality, but rather it brings a clear mirror which reflects the local society.[16] For example, Facebook is dominated by endless appreciations of the local environment and products, be these the beauty of the local landscape, the quality of the food, the aesthetics of *artigianato* ('artisanship') or the exceptional nature of the music and traditions. The permanent emphasis on summer as opposed to other seasons on Facebook, as in the entire cultural life of Grano, is part of a tendency to distinguish this region of southern Salento from the rest of Italy and to create a local narrative of the sublime.[17] However, at the same time people in Grano suggest that even these qualities miss out on the management and organisation available *fuori* (in other places). Therefore they use Facebook to attach themselves to different versions of the 'superlative' that come from higher levels of Italian society, and to work out their respective roles as guardians of these values.

The synthesis of the two concomitant forces that come, on the one hand, from higher society and, on the other, from local tradition is done through a concern and ability to craft the self, which is clearly meant for public admiration. This is now seen as a major reason to use Facebook, because this environment is seen to complement and validate offline public visibility, and it is also situated halfway between the local and the higher levels of society. As we will see later in the book, this is mediated by a small but highly visible cultural vanguard, which is influential in promoting both local exceptionalism and attachment to national and international values. The vanguard is composed not only of local intellectuals, politicians and artists, but also of local celebrities, fashion houses, beauty salons and some *artigiani*. They are seen as holding the highest cultural capital in Grano. Usually these individuals are well connected outside the town and have prime access to critical information and resources. Therefore they act as true gatekeepers to the higher levels of Italian society. We will see that these people, who represent perhaps less than 5 per cent of the local population, have found in social media a promising environment where they can take over some critical features from conventional media channels, such as the television, the printed press and advertising, and turn them into supplementary sources of cultural capital.

A typical example of how social media brings or consolidates social prestige to those who think are they are entitled to it is that of people with a higher education in Grano. In Chapter 6 we will discuss why, during their period of under-employment, people with a higher educational background sense an acute need to have somewhere where they can register their special knowledge, thoughts and skills that are not currently demanded by the local job market. With time on their hands, many love to stress in subtle ways on social media different aspects of their knowledge. Here they specialise in different, non-lucrative genres, such as commentating wittily on current Italian politics, sharing more pretentions, ideas and skills, or participating regularly in different social and cultural events in the region. Some become enthusiastic environmental activists, set up small vocational groups or specialise in various digital projects, such as the design and maintenance of an online presence for a variety of local institutions and businesses. As many commented, if they were not active on Facebook they sensed they would feel left behind in their society. Facebook allows for this kind of self-expression in the absence of a work environment suited to their training and knowledge.

By being active online many highly educated people work at restoring the social prestige to which they think they are entitled. They often feel conflicted in their personal use of Facebook as they have both to address the local norms of posting, which many might find restricting and limiting, and still to display their more glittering cosmopolitan interests and views that reflect the social life of the university cities where they used to live. Many have more Facebook contacts from those metropolitan places than from their home region. One woman who had accepted almost nobody from Grano as a Facebook contact commented: 'I prefer to meet them [local friends] and talk in person. I find it strange to friend [on Facebook] people who pass in front of my door.'

Now, if many of those highly educated individuals enjoy positioning themselves as partially outside the all-too-constraining local expectations between offline and online behaviours, this is not true for those who have already consolidated their higher capital. For example, the local aristocracy, intellectuals and politicians hardly ever adopt alternative identities online or play with the local norms. Their Facebook postings are a permanent compromise between the presentation of their family and interventions related to their work. So these individuals are relatively less witty and relaxed online, and their postings tend to be more focused and applied: politicians can exhaustively comment only on mainstream political news items or local initiatives; most authors cannot depart from their lyrical style when posting; and aristocrats restrict their online presence to family and close friends.

The higher strata of people in Grano put constant effort into public appearance. They see Facebook both as an enabler of social visibility and as a potential danger because it can reveal unwanted aspects of individuals and their personalities. So they are extremely attentive to controlling their online presence. This is true for most people in Grano and results, as we will see in the next chapter, in the majority of Facebook postings being about issues everybody agrees on. This suggests that innovation and change reside in the medium itself and not necessarily in what people do on that particular medium.

In contrast, most people from the lower levels of the local economic and social hierarchy view Facebook with relatively more reluctance, as many are not very sure how they can contribute to the values expressed in this environment. In particular, young people often see social media as representing promising tools to reduce the gaps with their peers and to demonstrate their attachment to collectively shared values. Although this chapter has shown the diversity of such media and the choices people now have, it is already clear that they rarely use this new opportunity to do anything that would not be approved of by their peers, even if they do not particularly agree with some of those peers. Almost nobody in Grano ignores or unfriends their Facebook connections. In my survey on social media use, just 4 per cent of the respondents declared that they had ever 'de-friended' somebody on Facebook because of their political views, even though this is perhaps the major source of public dispute among the adult population.

This completes the image of a highly conventional use of social media in Grano. We suggest that social media are not seen as bringing something particularly new because most people use them in a manner that coincides with the existing norms of their society.[18] As a result, Facebook rarely allows space for people to reinvent themselves and be creative, if this is not in keeping with how they are offline, and so this particular use of Facebook is only achieved by some teenagers and very few liberal cultural elites and artists. As we will see in the next chapter, conformity with the offline persona is usually expressed by manipulating a handful of online methods and genres that may seem quite varied at first glance, but which all point to the recurrent themes of the importance of social visibility in relation to personal values.

The ages of social media

This chapter has shown that there is no simple way to generalise about the use of social media, even for a population that is relatively reserved in using it or when compared to other countries in the 'Why We Post' project, such as Brazil and China. But the chapter has identified an overall structure of social media use that does vary across age groups and as people age, in which the adult population and the elderly attempt to maintain online the existing offline social structures of Grano society.

We have seen that teenagers are by far the most dynamic and relaxed users of social media, mainly because many sense a great opportunity in this environment to explore and affirm themselves in varied ways. This opportunity is usually the result of indirect contributions from their families: most children receive, in the few years before they turn into teenagers and during their early teens, a small avalanche of technological gadgets with permission to use them, particularly in the form of the *cresima* gifts. These gifts have always had the role of representing an act of not only turning children into good Christians, but also of preparing them for adult life – and it was parents and families who saw this need being met in more recent years by the various communication technologies now available.

Teenagers can use social media to explore the world with an unprecedented level of autonomy and can establish their first long-distance relations to an extent that was more difficult to achieve in the past. Interestingly, Twitter and Instagram have contributed to this more than Facebook because they combine access to information and a much clearer perception of life outside Grano with an almost complete absence of parental control. Thus, when turning into young adults, people have already had several years of experience on social media. As they grow older young people start to respect the existing stricter rules for communication and public appearance that correspond to their social status. A typical example would be women who, as young teenagers, might have spent hours preparing themselves for a selfie to upload on Facebook; as they grow older and, for example, get engaged, the emphasis on representing themselves visually shifts to a greater focus on showing their relationship to other people in their offline society. They post fewer selfies and more group photos. Married women rarely post selfies and instead focus on showing what they do well, such as teaching, crafting and looking after their families.

Many young people introduce their parents to Facebook – if they were not really using the platform before – and help them connect with other relatives and family friends who are online. Most adults try to occupy the kinds of places online that parallel those they inhabit in their offline society. Failure to do this is deemed inappropriate and is sanctioned by peers. As we have discussed, one exception is seen in some of those with higher cultural capital who may venture to transgress the conventional norms in Grano for use of social media, but they would usually do so in a manner consistent with their role as public figures.

Chapter 5 shows that there is continuity between the care and attention teenagers pay to their selfies, the care young adults will put into choosing their outfits for posting online and the concern married women have about how Facebook posts will reflect on their families. We will see that much of the burden of social visibility falls on women. Buying, washing and ironing clothes, and making sure their families are impeccably dressed to go out, has the double value of ensuring that they look perfect offline when they go into town as well as online if anyone should take a photo and post it on their Facebook page. As such, Facebook demonstrates a capacity to constantly open a window on to domestic life.

A particular position is assumed by the elderly in relation to social media. They intervene online much less than the younger population, relatively speaking, and instead prefer simply to act as onlookers to the online environment. Almost all younger people they know are there, but the elderly feel it is safer to communicate with them using more private media and face-to-face. They are interested in viewing photographs more than text, and let younger online friends initiate any contact with them. This is similar to life offline, when they are more likely to receive than to make regular visits to young relatives.

This discussion suggests that, rather than being innovative and challenging, Facebook simply acts to reinforce the strong existing conformity within Grano society. It is said that the internet revolution was deemed a revolution because so many people and key players adopted the technology that the world could never be same again. Similarly, most literature and social interventions have seen social media as representing a new and unprecedented potential for creativity and social equality. However, as we will continue to see outlined in this book, compared to the contrast between, for example, the rather turbulent national Italian political world, the difficult local economic situation and the seldom tumultuous private life, public social media in Grano seem to represent very stable and predictable spheres. Let us now turn our attention to how just a handful of genres of online material can articulate this kind of stability.

3
Visual postings: looking for 'the good'

This chapter examines the main genres of visual postings on Facebook, which is by far the most used public-facing social media in Grano. It shows why, by simply looking and interpreting public postings, we cannot tell much about individual people, but we can understand how they see the society they live in. Facebook postings work towards reinforcing conventional values, such as those represented by Catholicism, family life, tradition and social norms. This contrasts somewhat to the use of other public-facing social media, such as Twitter and Instagram, where people express more individual passions and skills. In this context, what really brings society together is Facebook as a platform and as a practice.

We can divide public postings into three widely accepted themes which stand out: relationships, personal appearance and moral sense. The most visible relationships by far on Facebook are those with peers, rather than those with family members and very close friends, which are discussed in the next chapter. This makes many Facebook postings subtle and intended for a specific audience. Public appearance, and in particular the idea of beauty, is something that cuts through most genres of Facebook postings, as we see in Chapter 5. Finally, an acute sense of appropriate behaviour distinguishes Facebook's use in Grano and surrounding areas from its use elsewhere in the world. This could come from many sources: an intimate relationship with God, a moral sense or a strong drive to promote progressive ideas. In postings such as those condemning poverty, intolerance or a corrupt political system, it could come out of a desire to emphasise the highest achievement of the human spirit, a common heritage or current social issues. This chapter focuses on the acute sense of moral judgement and a striving to express 'good' values in popular visual forms that are represented by most Facebook postings.

Sharing the meme

By far the most popular Facebook posting genre among those of the adult and elderly population is the meme. Memes are usually not produced by people in Grano, but rather shared from popular internet sites. Most are received in daily newsfeeds or from popular Facebook pages, such as *Caffeina Event*,[1] *fanpage.it*,[2] *Travel Fanpage*,[3] *Il Pellegrino di Padre Pio*,[4] *direttanews.it*[5] and some smaller ones. Nevertheless, once shared on Facebook, memes seem to have a life of their own: people share memes when they feel they touch on some aspects of their own personality. Most memes shared on Facebook do not stand for: 'Hey, look, this is something I find interesting!' but rather: 'Hey, look, this is what I really believe in!'. Therefore these memes stand for absolute personal truths, in striking contrast to most of the news items or photographs shared on the internet that are simply seen as interesting or aesthetically agreeable.

(a)

Fig. 3.1 Moral memes. The first meme (a) reads: 'Each evening put your shoes under the bed, as far as possible, so that in the morning in order to get to them you have to kneel down...And once you find yourself on your knees thank God for His grace, for His mercy and for his understanding.' Denzel Washington. The second meme (b) reads: 'I always thought that those who talk little have eyes which make a tremendous noise.' The last meme in the group (c) reads: 'Those who look only at the ephemeral beauty of the body ignore the eternal wonder of the soul.'

(b)

" *Ho sempre pensato che chi parla poco ha gli occhi che fanno un rumore tremendo* "

fanpage.it

(c)

Chi sa scrutare
solo
l'effimera bellezza del corpo
ignora
l'eterna meraviglia dell'anima.

Fig. 3.1 (*continued*)

Indeed, memes are read not as standalone pieces, but as the intimate thoughts of the people who have shared them. Their interpretation and online appreciations through 'likes' and comments are also very personal most of the time. Let us take a closer look: the last meme in the figure above was posted in the summer of 2014 by a women in her late twenties, with the intention of drawing attention to the inner beauty that exists in each person, as opposed to the exterior and more visible beauty that is presented in the media and on the internet. In this meme the interior beauty is mirrored by an exterior one, as exemplified by the perfectly still surface of the water, the warm colours and the delicate body of the swan, which are all appreciated as being essentially universal qualities. We call this genre the 'moral meme' – it does not represent anything specifically Italian, but rather engages with moral ideas recognised and praised well beyond the community and its local issues.

This genre is favoured by adults and the elderly; usually, but not necessarily, by those who are religious; and, in particular, by women. Most of these people do not themselves choose to appear on Facebook. Therefore the shared meme stands not only for an intimate thought, but also for a sort of visual presence – usually romantic, with bright colours and an optimistic tone – with which these people like to be associated. This aesthetic corresponds to an overwhelming everyday presence of visual materials with moral implications that can be seen inside their homes.

This practice could also be related to the fact that most religious people do not like posting religious materials online. They consider that religion is an intimate matter that should not be displayed to such a diverse public. A similar concern to keep the most intimate aspects of life for more private circles is also seen in the way most parents are reticent about posting photos of their children on Facebook. Young priests are the only people in the region who post religious material on a regular basis, such as photographs of the Virgin Mary, cult objects, small prayers or invitations to religious events in the local parish. In contrast, lay people prefer to post images that refer indirectly to holy ideas and events. Some moral memes may contain verses from the Bible, quotes from Catholic saints or an invitation to meditate.

The importance of Catholicism does not rest simply in its practice, but in a way of life that reflects the larger cosmology. It would be easy to say that because of Catholicism things happen in a certain way. However, the fact that most non-observing Catholics and atheists follow similar norms to those of Catholics suggests that such an explanation is far too simplistic. For example, many atheists respect similar moral principles to those of the Catholics, except that they have removed God from the centre of their focus. Many non-Catholics end up being as conservative as Catholics because they have to replace the permanent sense of protection by God with other mechanisms, such as their own definition of morality or moderation.

(a)

(b)

Fig. 3.2 Photos from inside a house which resonate with the moral memes (photos by the author)

This suggests that what keeps people in order is morality. Even if generated by different sources, morality in Grano is expressed in similar ways, which creates the sense of a very conformist society. The reason why Catholicism is only a marginal reference in this book is that it guides

(a)

(b)

Fig. 3.3 'Humorous' memes. The first meme (a) reads: 'What did you do today at school? ... Dad, you can read everything on Facebook.' The second meme (b) reads: 'That moment when ... [you realize that] even the ugliest person you know is *fidanzata/o* and you are not.'

(a)

Ognuno è un genio.

Ma se si giudica un pesce
dalla sua abilità di arrampicarsi sugli alberi,
lui passerà tutta la sua vita a credersi stupido.

— Albert Einstein

(b)

Fig. 3.4 'Clever' memes. The first meme (a) reads: 'Everybody is a genius. But if a fish judges itself on his ability to climb trees, he would spend his entire life thinking he is stupid.' Albert Einstein.[6] The second meme (b) reads: 'A great deal of progress rests on the will to progress.' (Lucio Anneo Seneca).[7]

the everyday life of most people in Grano without necessarily being made explicit. Rather, Catholicism is seen as lying in the orderliness of a living room, in taking good care of your family and in the frequent visits to your 80-year-old grandmother. Catholicism is about respecting such everyday duties. Agnosticism, in turn, seeks for a morality that is less rooted in everydayness and conventions. So we should understand the extreme popularity of memes in this light: they represent a very simple way of making morality visible while representing explicit guides to people's values whether in relation to the idea of family, community, religion or humankind.

Among the memes that do not have an explicit moral message, the most popular types are the 'humorous memes' and the 'clever memes'. The former usually refer to some current event and the latter to an intelligent thought or ingenious expression which is often more important than the picture which accompanies it.

The purpose of the clever meme is to pass on knowledge and human experience. Most of these memes contain quotes from famous authors or scientists, and usually people do not feel like adding any personal comments when sharing them online. They sense their own words would be poor and insignificant when compared to the messages the memes transmit; most people seem to say: 'Look, here is a nice or a true thing; I'm letting you know what I like and what I think is true, moving or beautiful, but these ideas do not belong to me, they come from a much greater mind!' Clever memes also have moral implications and people value them as representing undeniable achievements of the human spirit.

The huge popularity of memes suggests that this is the prime way in which many people relate to bigger issues, be they moral, intellectual or social. Sharing memes on a certain topic creates opportunities to compare and relate to other peoples with similar tastes and ideas, which represents a subtle route to social differentiation. For many, internet memes represent a precious stock of ideas that point to the higher structure of society, without contradicting too much one's actual setting. Previously ideas would be discussed inside the family, in front of the television and in other smaller social circles. Now, by way of memes, people have started timidly to penetrate into the public sphere in what is proving to be a popular way, with their own alternative ideas to those promoted by the mainstream media. Memes help people express complex ideas and critiques of higher levels of society, often without actually articulating these ideas themselves.

Memes tend inevitably to be about morality, but pretty much everything else that is posted on Facebook in Grano also tends to have a moral component. We suggest that in Grano morality is the main force that assures social conformity. Most people practice morality on an everyday basis. For example, the local dialect that everybody knows is almost never used in online postings, but as an exclamation or a short commentary usually meant to deride a particular situation or to express affection. The official Italian language is seen as the proper way to speak in public, so it becomes a moral duty for everybody to talk in Italian on social media. Postings on Facebook represent a way to present yourself to the public permanently, so the local view is that you should do it in the most appropriate way.

The majesty of nature

It is not only the beauty of life that is celebrated on the internet. Beauty is also seen in specific material forms, such as the Italian landscape and cityscape and, especially, in the local scenery.

The second image in Fig. 3.5 represents a caption about coastal Puglia. It was shared from an article in a local magazine which praised the fact that Puglia was included in the 'Best value travel destinations of the world for 2013' by the *National Geographic* and *Lonely Planet.*[8] People in the region agree that the local landscape is really beautiful and they should be proud of it. As in the case of moral memes, this represents a sort of universal truth that cannot be challenged. As a consequence, the local landscape is intensively photographed by people from Grano, day…

…and night.

This is by far the most popular type of personal photography people upload to Facebook. Especially during the summer, people photograph the landscape endlessly in everyday as well as more dramatic settings: at sunset, when the sea is too calm or when the sea is too agitated, such as during a storm. This genre is equally popular across both genders and all, occupational and social backgrounds. It reflects the beauty and majesty of nature in the wild and carries no intention, unlike tourist guides and travel agencies, of attracting outsiders to these areas. Rather, this genre of photography has become a landmark of the popular grass-roots movement to praise the local area as being unique, pristine and untouched, values that contribute to a regional sense of environmental responsibility. These ideas are used heavily in the fierce resistance by several environmental movements and activists to what they see as ugly and damaging modern developments, such as the exploitation of the

(a)

(b)

Fig. 3.5 Photos shared from the internet showing the city of
Venice, Italy (a), accompanied online by the status message: 'Our
Venice...Goodnight', and (b) the coastline in Salento

(a)

(b)

Fig. 3.6 Photos taken by people in Grano and uploaded to Facebook

Salentine coastline for tourism or the construction of the new express road to the southernmost point of the peninsula.

Angela discovered in the summer of 2014 the pleasure of daily morning walks to the seaside. This routine is considered extremely healthy and is practiced especially by women in their fifties and older. For example Angela, who likes taking photos with her old mobile phone,

Fig. 3.7 Photo taken by a young adult in Grano and uploaded to Facebook

or Elena, who regularly cycles to and from her house in another village in Grano, feel that it is in the middle of a natural wilderness where they are free and happy. Angela is a school teacher in her early fifties and all three of her children are studying at university in Milan or Turin. Elena is a retired public servant and her four children all live with their own families. The two women have always been extremely active in the morning: they would wake up early, prepare everything their families needed for the day, rush to take their children to school and then go on to work. Now, however, as Angela's work programme is more relaxed and Elena has only one nephew to look after, they have a sense of there not being much to do in the morning any more. In this context, walking through the vast fields and empty roads around Grano gives them a strong sensation of liberty and charges them with energy. Angela shares this feeling with her loved ones by means of photography and endless tales of her walks, and Elena wants to keep as fit as she always was in her earlier, active life. During the warm season Angela uploads the photos she has taken during her long walks to Facebook every couple of days and accompanies them with short comments.

In the photos shown in Fig. 3.8, Angela praises the beauty of nature and the local area, but also responds herself, in relation to this beauty, through her daily encounters with it. However, this hobby has not come about simply because Angela has more time on her hands than others, nor is she alone in enjoying it. Emilio, for example, an accountant

(a)

(b)

Fig. 3.8 Photos shared by Angela on Facebook after morning walks. Each of them was accompanied by a status message, respectively: 'It is a symphony of colours at the back of my house today... 🌸🌿🌸 🌿🌹/ I portray it like this and wish you plenty of ♡' and 'There are roses that blossom [in the middle of winter], have a nice Sunday!' (b).

who works in Lecce, uploaded 400 photos to Facebook between August 2012 and December 2015, out of which 183 are photos of the local landscape.

Sometimes landscape photos also contain a discreet human presence, for example people who are not intended or not choosing to be there.

Fig. 3.9   Photos of nature with a discreet human presence

When the photo shows a young person, the stillness of the land-scape could be used to balance out other more dynamic elements of the picture, such as a motorcycle. Sometimes young people employ this technique to express rather anecdotally that they were part of a land-scape and they had a great time.

In all these examples, contemplating the landscape means that the person borrows something from its beauty and majesty by being able to internalise and appreciate it.

In the context of this constant preoccupation with and admiration of nature, one outstanding topic on Facebook is the preservation of the local terrain. The few environmental associations in the region and many individuals run extremely visible campaigns against major intervention plans in southern Salento. These include the Trans Adriatic Pipeline (TAP) project developed by the European Union to bring natural gas from the Caspian region and the plan of national and regional authorities to extend the motorway (*Super Strada 275*) to the headland town of Capo di Leuca. The social movements that oppose these projects are known as 'no TAP' and 'no ss275' campaigns respectively, and centre on major environmental points, such as the likely reduction in the air quality, the seizure of agricultural land and the cutting down of a few thousand olive trees. For campaigners, social media is a prime way to advertise protests and gather support in the area, and this is quite successful as people in the region are extremely sensitive about their territory.

(a)

(b)

Fig. 3.10 Popular genre among young people while contemplating the landscape

Personal photos

Uploading photos of children on Facebook is a problematic issue in Grano. Most parents are extremely reserved in uploading photos of their children online as they are concerned that people might use these images in ways they cannot control. This is opposite of the parental outlook in the field sites in England and China, where Facebook is dominated by baby pictures. This could be related to a tradition about the 'evil eye', as many anthropologists might suspect, but nobody in Grano even hinted at this. Rather, we suggest that this is related to the much stronger tradition of Catholicism and the hierarchical structure of society which imposed, on most people in Grano, a restraint and strict limits regarding the visibility and public display of their families. In respect of this preference, we will not reproduce any images of children here.

Sometimes uploading photos of children together with adult members of the family is acceptable because, in this case, the photos are not simply about children, but about particular relationships that exists in their family. In Grano whole families gather together mainly for family reunions, such as for birthday parties, wedding ceremonies or Christmas dinner. These occasions have a compulsory nature that grants families the right then to share group photos. Photographs of a few children captured in such moments and seen among so many adults are regarded as acceptable for sharing online.

However, there are parents who post constantly about their children, even if they do not upload too many photos of them. Typically mothers post much more often than fathers about their children, from a nice line their 4-year-old just came out with to a short status outlining an enjoyable day at the beach or an evening out with the whole family. The most popular type of posting for mothers is to announce their children's achievements, especially out of school: diplomas obtained at a national contest of Taekwondo, personal performances in local music contests or participations in any of the numerous workshops for children organised in the region. These are appreciated on Facebook because people get to signal not only their children's talent or achievement, but also the care and diligence they have put in as parents in raising their children. Children are seen as the most important reason to exist, so their success is automatically reflected as a personal success for the parents.

One father of three who posts regularly about his children puts a lot of energy and economic resources into giving his children a 'proper' education. His postings express this care as they are dominated by references to his children, especially what he enjoys most about their behaviour. He wants his online friends to know how he appreciates his children's education. Every now and then he shares music videos and short pieces of sports footage, but almost never a photo of himself or his wife. So, unless you knew him personally, you would not learn much about him from his profile page. Indeed, in Grano this scenario is not the exception but the rule: people tend to use Facebook to emphasise the one particular aspect of their lives which they are most fond of and which they consider to be suitable for online presentation.

Single and group photos

Teenagers are the group that post the most photos of themselves and their friends. The 'selfie' genre is dominated by women and small groups of friends. Young men upload selfies only when they feel particularly confident about how they look, or when they are posing with a close friend. Selfies can be glamorous or not, edited or not. Young female teenagers can spend hours preparing themselves for an edited selfie. They change outfits and try out different make-up styles before shooting several photos, then they edit them using applications such as piZap and iPiccy[9] and, finally, many consult friends before uploading a selfie to Facebook. The most popular selfies can have more than 140 'likes' and are responded to, in double figures, by comments such as 'Beautiful!', 'You look smart!', 'I love you' or a stream of emoticons.

The fact that most of the time when they take selfies teenagers want to look good and presentable is not necessarily an expression of any sense of personal vanity. Rather, as we will see in Chapter 5, the personal image is related to bigger social concerns and to relationships. The self-deriding type of selfie is almost completely absent among teenagers in Grano, who prefer to capture everyday settings and postures. Group pictures are not usually edited as the idea is to point out the place where these people were together, their relationship and perhaps the activity.

Young adults post far fewer photos of themselves than teenagers. Many prefer group photos that are taken on special occasions, such as when going out, meeting old friends or attending a ceremony. Normally young adults do not edit their photos as this would be considered too self-indulgent.

Young adults tend to use selfies in more sophisticated ways. It is considered inappropriate for adults to have close-ups of their own faces in photos or to spend too much time caring about their online image. Rather, they are expected simply to be presentable at all times. Care taken over personal appearance is a response to a sense of constant observation within the community, and it is seen as bestowing moral qualities on people. Therefore if you do want to express something

Fig. 3.11 Photos of teenagers

in a photo you had better do it in the first shot and in a slightly self-mocking way so that you can demonstrate you are not too serious about your online image. Young adults often prepare their selfies so that they contain an entertaining element, such as a nice gesture, a more sophisticated angle or some unusual background. Usually only a few shots are taken and then just one, or a short sequence of photos, will be displayed. Men post selfies much more rarely than women.

(c)

(d)

Fig. 3.11 (*continued*)

Instead, it is usually friends who insist on taking a close-up photo of them.

In contrast to many of the pictures shown in Figs. 3.12 and 3.13, which are created by means of mobile technology and with the intention of being shared on social media, the following photos are

(a)

(b)

Fig. 3.12   Group selfies of young adults

(c)

Fig. 3.12 *(continued)*

seen as more conventional images that are then later integrated with social media. What these pictures reflect is a deeper sense of the passing of time.

Some adults post photos where they do not look into the camera and sometimes express ideas in more abstract terms. One consequence of this abstraction is that the exact meaning of the photo is understood only by a close circle of friends and family. My ethnographic material supports sociologist Pierre Bourdieu's point that the more highly

(a)

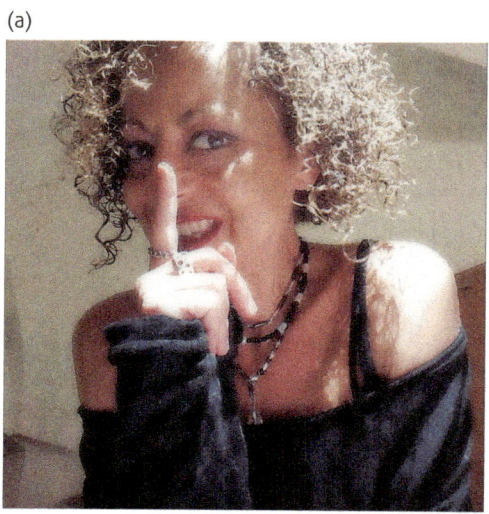

Fig. 3.13 Examples of selfies and photos of young adults

(b)

(c)

Fig. 3.13 (*continued*)

educated people are, the more they enjoy abstract genres, such as art and photography.[10] What is particular in Grano is that most people can appreciate, even if they do not adopt, tastes that are normally associated only with particular social groups. The reason for this is that people may see different social groups groups as representing certain ideals, which is a crucial part of the argument of this book.

Fig. 3.14 Family photo at the graduation ceremony of the youngest daughter (a) and everyday photo at the sea near Grano (b)

Cute pets and delicious food

Among the most popular everyday items photographed and uploaded to Facebook are pets and delicious food. Pets are usually cats and dogs, and more rarely donkeys from the nearby farms, and the photos tend to be of them in cute poses. Food pictures are of delicious looking dishes or

(a)

(b)

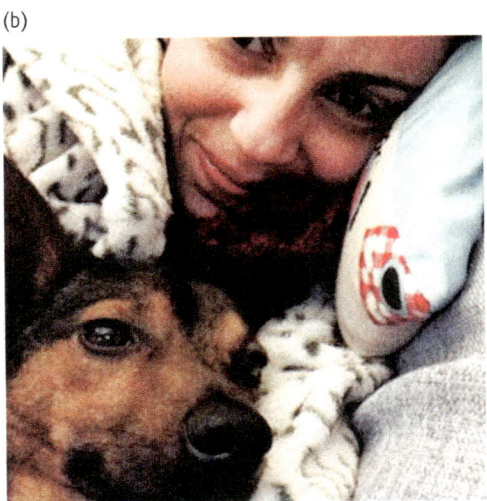

Fig. 3.15   Photos of own pets uploaded to Facebook

those that demonstrate a special skill, pictures of food being prepared, arranged or consumed in style. Both pets and food are associated with leisure, but in different ways. While many people are seen to be able to produce good-looking and high-quality food,[11] pets are usually associated with higher social status and with some sort of indulgence. In this context photography of food is a quite common genre across all social categories, while photos of pets are uploaded especially by young people and those from higher social classes.

(a)

(b)

(c)

Fig. 3.16 Everyday photos of food. The first and the last photos were accompanied by the following status messages respectively: 'And now at work' (a) and 'Amici! Ciao!' (c)

The strong tradition of home cooking is combined with attention to healthy cooking, traditional dishes and ingredients, and good photography in the photographs uploaded to the internet. The result owes much to the important influences of the 'slow food' movement in terms of what is regarded as representing refined taste, ecological concern and self-indulgence as constant reminders of belonging to the middle-class.[12] However, when food is cooked in a more popular way, such as food prepared for public festivals, it might not look so stylish.

Creativity

We have seen that artists, entrepreneurs and artisans are among the most intensive users of Facebook in Grano because they see this service as an unmissable opportunity to advertise their work and keep contact with friends and customers. Grano is dominated by the material and visual items they produce online and offline, from domestic objects to the avalanche of event posters and advertisements for local businesses and cultural events. All these need permanent online visibility. In the meantime people take this opportunity to introduce personal elements into their online postings to show that their work is an integral part of the community.

About half of the hundreds of social and cultural events organised in Grano every year are promoted by individuals who have developed a passion and skill in graphic design. Some of these people have also specialised in producing films or organising events, so for them Facebook has become critical in increasing the visibility of their work. Small crafts produced by individual amateurs are proudly displayed on Facebook. These include paintings, collages, small poems or brief thoughts. Perhaps the most popular type of work is the laborious installations that depict the scene of the Nativity (*presepe*) and are handcrafted in virtually every house in Grano before Christmas, in a true tradition of domestic artisanship.

Another particular form of creativity is the crafting of the self, mainly through singing, dancing, acting and practicing sport. This again is massively advertised by professionals, such as local musicians in various bands in Lecce, the opera house in Bari, *pizzica* (traditional folk song and dance) groups or players in the local football and volleyball teams. Amateurs also post their work in local dance schools, the two amateur theatre assemblies or the numerous private classes

(a)

(b)

Fig. 3.17 Photos of artisan work uploaded to Facebook

in singing and playing instruments. In contrast, people rarely post the remodelling of their bodies on Facebook. Going to the gym, beauty salon or hairdresser is not seen as a person's own work, and therefore not to their own merit. We will see in Chapter 5 that these activities are considered implicit and embodied in the actual person, which can be admired on Facebook in pictures of everyday activities in Grano or at parties, and not as special events.

Looking for something special

Apolitical postings include various genres, for example memes, sharing news items and written statuses, that they all point to people's need to show something special online. News items from regional and mainstream newspapers or articles on technology, science and culture, taken from glossy magazines, are shared to indicate the issues with which individuals identify themselves. In particular, many people in Grano are preoccupied by health issues, so articles on science and medicine are quite popular.

Adult women particularly enjoy sharing memes with 'Good morning' or with birthday wishes during the year. Many feel that such a gesture denotes increased care for the one to whom these wishes are addressed.

A very important distinction should be made between text and non-text-based postings: written status messages that are not accompanied by visual material are usually seen as a sign of erudition. However, visual materials shared on Facebook, such as photographs, short videos, thumbnails of web pages and internet memes, are more popular and are not associated with the self.

(a)

Fig. 3.18 Sharing of interesting moments. Kindle status message: 'My new reading companion. Welcome 😊' (a), sharing the works of the Japanese crochet artist Toshiko Horiuchi-MacAdam (b)[13] and photo of a local concert from a particularly unusual angle (c).

(b)

(c)

Ph. Carmelo Baglivo

Fig. 3.18 (*continued*)

(a)

(b)

Fig. 3.19 Sharing of special moments: 'Happy Birthday' meme (a) and photo taken by an adult woman of her grandmother (b)

It is extremely rare for a very personal state of mind or feeling to be announced openly on Facebook. So many posts cannot be deciphered in this way, except by a very limited audience such as close friends who know the key intimate details. For example, the bunch of flowers (Fig. 3.20) has a very precise meaning. For several months during 2014 the woman who uploaded this photo on Facebook was being intensely courted by a man of her own age. He used to offer her fresh

Fig. 3.20 Photo of a bunch of roses uploaded to Facebook

flowers, usually roses, at the beginning of each week so that they would brighten the rest of her busy week. The woman was uncertain whether it would be a good idea to have a romantic relationship with the man, but she accepted the flowers as if from a close friend. Every few days she or her mother cut the stems of the flowers and put them in fresh water. This photograph was taken at the end of the week, when the flowers were not so tall. Whatever her romantic feelings might have been, the woman wanted to take the photo because she thought the flowers were really beautiful, and because she wanted to tell her admirer that she took good care of the flowers all through the week. This is just an example of how something that could simply be appreciated for its beauty will also often point to deeper meanings that are only intelligible to a very small audience. This illustrates how people see Facebook as a tool to gradate public visibility.

In this context, the spectacular is to be found not in personal relations, but in the wider world, the local landscape or some of the local events. A situation where the spectacular can be clearly associated with the person occurs when photographs have been taken at tourist destinations, usually outside Italy. Generally women post such photos much more than men do, and there are cases when teenagers and young adults share a few dozen photos from their holidays. Usually these photos are admired by most people in the 'friend' list, but only close friends and family 'like' or comment on them. The reason is that holiday photos are considered rather personal.

Political postings

Politics occupies a special place on Facebook, as it is by far the most dis-
puted topic in Grano. Young and adult men post about politics much more
than women or teenagers. The three main genres of posting are political
memes, news items from the mainstream or regional media, and the person's own political comments. The first two categories are accompanied
by brief comments or indications such as 'incredible, do read and realise what these people are doing...' or 'speechless...'. Political memes
usually express either current political situations or generic ideological
themes. News articles are shared by people with a higher cultural capital who are extremely well informed, read a few journals a day and regularly watch political debates on television. Some of these people tend
to post relatively more philosophical comments and elaborate status
messages.

The posting of political memes and shared material on Facebook
has allowed people the opportunity and forum publicly to share political criticisms and ideas that previously they would have only shared
with their families and close friends. The consequence of this is not
that more people from the region are involved in politics because of
the internet and social media, but that more people are encouraged to
participate in a public sphere that was previously restricted to just a
few – mostly local politicians and intellectuals. This suggests that
people use social media to share ideas that often challenge the higher
structures of society.

Photos posted from political scenes are usually quite spectacular
and dramatic, such as rallies, fights in parliament, war and violence in
the world or unlikely actions of major Italian politicians. For example,
in the autumn of 2013 an innocent posting of 'Good morning', accompanied by a photograph in which Nicky Vendola, the president of the
main left-wing party in Italy and governor of the region of Puglia at
the time, shook hands with Silvio Berlusconi, caused a severe out-
break of rage and heated discussions over a period of three days. These
took place on the Facebook Wall where the photo was initially posted
despite repeated attempts by the owner of that Wall to calm down the
situation.

Sharing political photographs and videos is much more popular
among people with a medium level of education, and it is often done to
express frustration and anxiety. In recent years the dominant political
subject shifted from critiques of Berlusconi to those of the rather unstable Italian political scene. The relatively new political force *Movimento*

(a)

(b)

Fig. 3.21 Political memes: a critique of the Milan Expo 2015 (a) and a meme inspired by the developing exodus across Mediterranean Sea towards Southern Europe (b)[14]

5 Stelle focused on producing online material.[15] As this political movement has built its success on the internet environment and free online content, they produce a constant flood of short videos showing initiatives by political leaders, criticisms of the government, rallies and an internal election scheme in which candidates could present themselves on YouTube, which are all very visible on Facebook.

Political postings can also be witty and humorous (see Fig. 3.22). Paolo is a 34-year-old man who works on a temporary basis in a central bar. He is a revolutionary spirit and very interested in politics. He actively comments on other people's postings but, for himself, he just shares interesting social and political news. From his Facebook page, you would not know whether he was married or had children. However, when you talk to him, he is extremely communicative and can tell you stories for hours. He just does not see any reason to put any of these stories online. He thinks that private issues should be discussed with friends and only what is 'really' public should be put on Facebook. Out of his preoccupation with politics, Paolo created a particular online character who is now well known in Grano as being smart, attentive and always up to date. It is within this online space that he can enjoy working and engaging with ideas in a way that his paid job as a bartender does not allow him to do.

Fig. 3.22   Edited photo of a handmade *presepe* that reads: 'Prosperous' Christmas and 'Fascinating' New Year! [Signed] Mario Monti [Italian prime minister at the time] (© Biagino Bleve)

The way most people use Facebook is not to protest or change the world, despite many having strong feelings about it, but to laugh about a well-known situation that nobody seems to be able to change. It is true that this marks a shift from the practice of reading the news as a more private and passive pursuit to a certain empowering of citizens, as many authors have remarked.[16] However, in Grano political postings do not usually denote an increase in information and political activism, but rather a broader acknowledgement of the way individuals understand and practice politics. This also suggests a new sort of political violence in which the subject under scrutiny is not a distant and autocratic power, but sometimes their own peers and people from the community. It is this sense of *realpolitik* having descended on Grano via Facebook that makes people involved in politics extremely sensitive about the online material – as can be seen when the mayor exclaimed after receiving numerous birthday wishes online: 'I had no expectations that Facebook could bring me any good surprises anymore...'.

Discussion

The stories and illustrations in this chapter show why Facebook can be understood as neither a reflection nor an extension of a person's true self. Rather, people in Grano use Facebook to reflect their different needs for social visibility. These needs could be related to a personal talent, looks, sensibility, the importance of family life, social solidarity or involvement in politics. The 'audience' could be the local community, friends from Grano, the group of intellectuals in their Facebook account or the ex-colleagues from their university who now live in other parts of the world.

Facebook represents an environment where all these groups and networks can be brought together and where the average user has to find ways to respond to this diversity. The result is that most postings tend to relate in different ways to the general and the universal, by emphasising one specific feature that is at the core of their social group, such as a passion for music, football or politics. The true self is reserved for the family, God, friends and is not seen as representing something that should be of interest to the larger world. Facebook reflects just what the individual, as the result of local social forces, perceives as being 'showable', 'desirable' and not too intimate.

Most people do not see the point in trying to be too specific on Facebook. They have their offline relationships and personal media where they can be specific and thorough. This is expressed in the quite popular practice on Facebook of posting generic comments that are intentionally ambiguous so that only closest friends or family members will actually know what they refer to because they have the right keys to decipher the comments. For example, when Enzo writes a witty status on Facebook criticising an Italian celebrity who has just appeared on television wearing extremely high heels, only his close friends know that he is particularly passionate about such shoes and always spends a fortune buying high heels for his girlfriends.

This shows the limits to public display, but also that Facebook is an inclusive and comfortable realm that corresponds to how people like social life to be in Grano. Many people do not use this service to connect to the wider world or to create private relationships with those who share similar tastes. So people in the region tend to agree that they enjoy Facebook, but do not take it too seriously. In a local context in which everybody knows everybody else and most people do not really need to communicate online locally, Facebook helps to establish a sphere where individuals feel they can show what kind of person they want to be. Most of the time this means upholding the particular position they already have in their society.

In short, this chapter has shown the limits of seeing social media as technologies simply used for communication. In Grano they are also not used for self-representation since most of what matters about a person is not posted. Instead the people of Grano use social media in a much more limited and specific way. People use this new visual field to complement the other things they do and the other places they express themselves by finding something that previously did not have such an easy outlet. Sometimes people use social media slightly to overstep, in an acceptable way, the local norms by expressing, for example, a feeling of pride in their local landscape or a particular genre of political opinion or sophistication through slightly clever angles and informal posing. In each case social media can be used to add a small element to what is already known about a person, in the same way that a people might have a small hobby, such as baking cakes and memorising poetry. However, most of the online audience does not know everything about the person who posts. Social media adds something worthwhile about them that is quite, but not very, personal, hence the general view in Grano that posts should be moral and 'good'.

4
Social media and social relationships: setting layers of intimacy

In some ways the previous two chapters pose a problem because they do not really reflect the way anthropologists understand the world. Much of Chapter 2 is concerned with how most people in Grano use public-facing social media in order to replicate the conformity already seen in their society, and how this conformity varies with age and social status. However, in anthropology this manner of using social media should be secondary to our prime interest, which is the study of relationships themselves as played out in social media. In Grano, as in most places, there are firmly established norms and conventions for relationships, such as those between *fidanzati* (engaged couples), married couples and siblings. At the same time, many people for all sorts of reasons that could be economic, social or emotional live lives that might not conform to these norms. So anthropology is concerned with explaining not only the categories and the norms of relationships, but also the very varied ways in which people actually conduct these relationships.

Chapter 3 suggested that in most cases, all things being equal, people in Grano do not really need Facebook. In other words, if we had just studied this platform we would not have understood too much about their society: Facebook does not represent people from Grano, it just shows us glimpses of the people and their relationships. There is a sense that Facebook does not add much to community life as people already have many ways of expressing the same things offline. Indeed, public-facing social media are very particular and partial. As such they only become important when they are seen to resolve a particular issue, fit a new niche, provide a good means of expressing some particular relationship or when things start to break down and become difficult, such as when highly educated individuals cannot find employment or when spouses separate. People know what they have lost and Facebook helps them bring these things back into their lives.

As public-facing social media do not provide a complete picture of the private relationships people in Grano have, we should move our focus on to the more private media. Some analysts study media to see if they 'reflect' or 'represent' patterns of relationships. We shall see that this approach does not work very well. Instead we need to see social media as vehicles people use to navigate relationships and, to some extent, to create new forms and variations of these. Women have a leading role in maintaining communication and structuring relationships. At more intimate levels of communication, it is women who use and drive the use of social media most intensively. We will start with the normative relationship that is represented by the nuclear family, and then focus on the mother-children relationship. We will also explain why spouses rarely express aspects of their marriage on Facebook or in any other public online environment, while parents and especially mothers tend to post quite a lot about their children.

However, there are many aspects of these relationships that remain completely separate from, and largely unaffected by, social media, including some of the most important ones. If we only studied what is posted on the social media platforms themselves we would fail to recognise this. We have to pay as much attention to the types of relationship in which social media are not used as to the ones in which they do play a part. Therefore we will also look to the non-typical, more complicated relationships. As it happens, because of the continuous modernisation of Grano society, these sorts of relationships have come to be very common. We will explore two case studies: a family split between Italy and Switzerland because of male migration to work and a single mother who tries to establish a romantic relationship that could lead to marriage. In both situations it is private communication and the more private social media that contribute to attaining both the normative and the ideal for these relationships.

The normative relationship

There is a huge literature on family relations in the south of Italy and, in particular, on the role of women in the household economy.[1] This points in different ways to the distinctive unity of the nuclear family and its role in maintaining social relations with extended family and the rest of the community. My ethnographic material suggests that in Grano the nuclear family could be further divided into the core, represented by the mother and her children, around which the figure of the father gravitates. This model is not only expressed by distinct roles, practices and work within the family, but it is also physically visible: mothers sometimes sleep with their children until they turn teenagers while the fathers may occupy the children's room decorated with sweet teddy bears and filled with toys. Indeed, mothers are always surrounded by their children, in a plethora of social circumstances, while many fathers might attach to this core temporarily and in very specific situations.

We have seen that spouses can reflect this separation on Facebook by posting according to their individual tastes, rather than showing what they have in common. But this is very different from how spouses relate to each other in more private spheres. It is on WhatsApp and the phone that they relate to each other continuously, intensively and practically, but at times also very romantically.

'I don't really need Facebook. All I need is WhatsApp.' This is what Silvia always told me, from my first interview with her. Silvia is a typical middle-class woman in her early forties. She is married to Giovanni and they have two boys aged 13 and 8. Silvia does not work outside the home and Giovanni co-owns a café in Grano with one of his brothers. They are extremely busy most of the week. He works every other day in the bar from 6:30 in the morning until late evening. Silvia supports her husband's work in essential moments: she brings him a hot lunch when he is on duty and serves occasionally at the bar in the busy periods or when they are short staffed. She then has swimming lessons four times a week, goes to the gym three times a week and drives her children to four different after-school activities. The bar is open Saturday and Sunday as well, which leaves them with little free time outside their annual holiday.

While Silvia is extremely reserved on Facebook and rarely posts anything, she is very happy to have her smartphone because she feels it brings so many people much closer. She has decided to use an iPhone she received as a gift from Giovanni, and to give her much-loved old smartphone to her two sons to play games on. Meanwhile she keeps yet another iPhone, received more recently from Giovanni, packed in its original box, unsure about what use to make of it. She speaks to two of her sisters and her brother every day for a few minutes, and sometimes talks to her older sister continuously for hours. Silvia usually calls her siblings from home, after she has finished some specific job and while waiting for the next task – for example, in the second part of the morning, after putting vegetables on to boil and before going to collect her

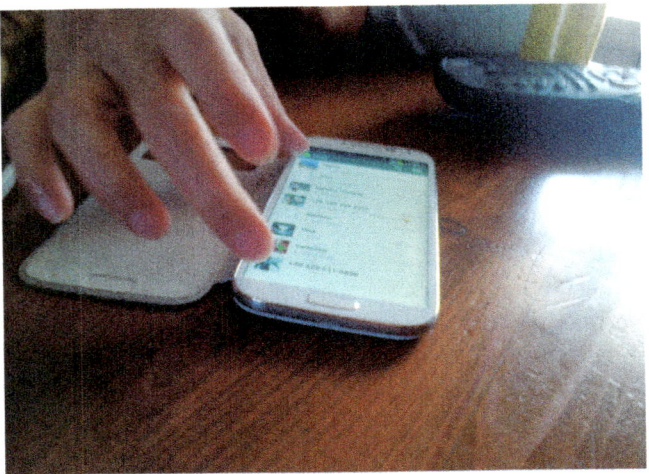

Fig. 4.1 Silvia explaining how she uses WhatsApp

children from school. They talk about everyday matters but, lately, she had been focusing on regulate updates on WhatsApp from her brother who had taken his family to Dubai for six days. Silvia showed me pictures taken by her brother of the tourist attractions in Dubai, such as the Raj Hotel, the artificial lakes and the luxuriant shopping malls. She remembered how excited she had felt when she had first seen all these places in the photos and could not believe her brother was actually there. As he kept sending his siblings messages on WhatsApp explaining how they were feeling, what were they going to do next, Silvia had a surreal sense that she was there too, as she sat at the kitchen table or drove her children to their swimming lesson.

Giovanni does not send Silvia many pictures, but he is quite active in texting short messages during work. Even when he's at the bar, although he cannot afford to stop for more than a moment, he sometimes finds a few seconds to send Silvia a short message. He usually places his smartphone near the cash machine where he can keep a sharp eye on the ongoing WhatsApp conversation. Silvia is most happy when she receives unexpected messages from Giovanni and often rushes to reply, hoping he will read her message on the spot. But most of the time Giovanni will not reply to his wife's message until half an hour or an hour later. Being able to exchange a short sequence of messages in just a few seconds gives them both a profound sense of intimacy that was unachievable through standard text messages. Their large-screen smartphones can be situated conveniently behind the bar and on the kitchen table while both spouses move busily around them; a short glance from the corner of his eye in Giovanni's case and a discreet *beep* in Silvia's is enough to cause them to engage with one another without leaving their work. In Giovanni's case, his role as a busy bar owner vies for attention with his smartphone: he spends three or four full days a week at work, hardly seeing his family.[2] Silvia keeps him updated about what is going on with their kids during the day, so their conversation is less about coordinating roles than about sharing in constant updates. To Silvia's more practical updates, Giovanni responds with witty comments and suggestions. It is a continuous dialogue which builds the unity of the family.

But this is hidden from other people, including the wider family. Silvia is the hub for siblings and friends. She takes decisions as to what kind of information should stay within her family and what should be relayed to Giovanni. In contrast, Giovanni is in constant contact with just two other people via the smartphone. Both are good, old friends from Grano. He usually talks to them in the late afternoon. Their conversations are more opportunistic; for example, they arrange to meet each other in the evening, to talk about work or to share entertaining videos related to some current political event. So it is Silvia who sustains family relations and creates a sense of domesticity. By constantly chatting with his wife, Giovanni is assured that his family is doing fine, and he can work hard like his father and his grandfather did, if in different circumstances.

Giovanni is part of the new *professionisti* which has emerged over the last two decades from the lower middle classes in Grano: without higher education or emigrating to work, they have managed to build a relatively comfortable life by means of constant hard work. They contrast with the previous class of *professionisti* who were much wealthier but who, in just one generation, have moved away from commercial and real-estate activities, now seeing these domains as being less prestigious than they were. In Chapter 6 we will see that, for the old *professionisti*, this attitude relates to the rising appeal of higher education, which will lead to either good careers, usually in the north of Italy, or other prestigious jobs for those who decide to return to Grano, such as jobs in education or local administration. What is important for the present discussion is that people from lower social and economic backgrounds were the ones upholding traditional family values. This contrasted with people from higher classes and the highly educated who may have elitist tastes and more liberal attitudes. Taking a wider perspective, it can be seen that the normative values were imposed by the lower and middle classes and then appropriated and slightly restyled by each strata of society. We will see in the remainder of the book that this was the result of a particular combination of a strong tradition of social differentiation and the ideals of egalitarianism and modernity.

Silvia and Giovanni demonstrate a traditional marital relationship in a modern setting as they construct a dense web of constant communication. As in the case of many married and romantic couples, communication is an essential part of their relationship and, as such, local values mean that it cannot be put on display on public-facing social media. If in the previous two chapters we have seen that public-facing social media help the individual relate to the ideas and values they are expected to uphold, this chapter points to the fact that most personal relationships are expressed exclusively through the more private social media and by means of dyadic communication. WhatsApp has become central to personal relationships because it provides people with a virtually unlimited yet private visibility that cannot be expressed on public-facing social media which is subject to strong, delimiting social norms.

What is privacy?

In my household survey, 48 per cent of respondents declared they had never changed their Facebook profiles to private. Most of them did not know there was such a possibility, although some had tried on different occasions to find out how to restrict access to their Facebook profile to fewer people. We have seen that this is related to how people understand their society: people in Grano are simply not used to thinking in terms of private spaces about things that are as clearly public-facing as Facebook, YouTube or Twitter. Indeed, the online environment is considered 'free' (*libero*) and as designed to facilitate interactions. Therefore people see no reason why it should be private. The household survey also showed that only 20 per cent of respondents thought that owners of social media use their personal information in ways that could harm them, and far fewer were actually concerned by this. An interesting exception was represented by those with higher educational capital, who tended to see Facebook less as a free environment and more as an asset that should be protected.

For most people, property, such as a house or a piece of land, belongs to the private arena and therefore cannot possibly be the subject of a post on Facebook. The default place to put any content that is intended for slightly larger audiences than a person's own family or closest friends, but which for different reasons is considered not for public consumption, is on WhatsApp.

Isabella is 26 years old and has been *fidanzata* for eight years to a man from a nearby town. As we have seen in the Introduction, marriage is seen as requiring a solid ground and the couple must have between them, typically, at least one stable job and a house. In recent years economic circumstances led to severe difficulties in reaching either of these two conditions and even thinking of getting married became quite problematic. So Isabella has had the shortest period of engagement of all her close circle of friends, each of whom has been engaged for 10 or even 12 years.[3]

Isabella is happy that she works full-time as a shop assistant in a clothing shop. She is also proud she has time to study for her undergraduate degree and will probably graduate in a year's time. She started to study law at the University of Salento six years ago and, after a series of misunderstandings with the management of the school, she transferred to Bergamo. All through this time, her *fidanzato*, Salvatore, supported her in her determination to complete her studies even against the will of her family, who were urging Isabella to get a full-time job. The couple's biggest problem is that they have not been able to save money for the marriage. Salvatore works on a temporary basis as a builder, and Isabella's recent employment as shop assistant is the first stable job either of them has ever had. They estimate that the wedding ceremony alone would cost at least €10,000. Their families cannot raise even a small part of this sum, so the plan is that once Isabella has graduated the two can start saving money for the wedding. This means they can if all goes well get married in perhaps another couple of years.

Until then the two live and work in different towns, each living with their parents. As the two towns are 10 kilometres apart, they do not manage to see each other very often during the week. The two compensate for this by spending most weekends together and sometimes sleeping over at each other's home. This arrangement also allows them to spend more time with their friends: Isabella's closest friends are six female former fellow students from her secondary school in Grano, all of whom happen to be engaged to friends of Salvatore. Isabella actually met Salvatore because he is the cousin of her best friend at secondary school who introduced them to one another. Since all her best friends were already engaged, Isabella thought she should also take this important step. This strengthened her friendship with her female classmates even more. Isabella always enjoyed the fact that they had the same tastes and very similar passions: from what to drink and what to wear to whom to take as role models. Belonging to this group where she could share her most intimate thoughts and feelings always made Isabella feel safe and comfortable.

With the advent of WhatsApp, the sense of intimacy increased in an unprecedented way: *le ragazze* (the girls), as Isabella calls them, now share one WhatsApp group. They could start the day with a simple *buona giornata* ('good morning'), a question or an entertaining video clip. 'A video can really change my day!' laughs Isabella. They send messages all through the morning, and those who do not work contribute the most. However, because her work is less demanding in the morning, Isabella prefers to switch off her smartphone and read some copied coursework for her degree. Around lunch time the WhatsApp group is most active as most of its members have more time on their hands, and there are so many messages to catch up with. The afternoons are reserved mostly for making plans for the evenings, which sometimes include meeting their partners. When preparing to go out or for a family reunion, women often ask for approval or advice on their outfits, make-up and hairstyles – and they do this exclusively on WhatsApp. They often exchange selfies to confirm they adopted advice given or to solicit further suggestions. The group is then active again before the women go to sleep, and sometimes a few of them can use it until well after midnight.

I ragazzi (the boys) also have their own WhatsApp group. Whereas women use their group whenever they feel down, or are extremely happy, to give each other ongoing support, and always to check when someone is less active for no good reason, 'the boys' tend to be much more reserved. The most common topics for their WhatsApp conversations are football, jokes and work. Four of the men support Juventus Torino (which is by far the most popular football team in Grano), two support Internazionale Milano and one supports AC Milan. Therefore they always have difficulty in agreeing on issues related to football, which is reflected in continuous reciprocal mocking on this topic. Around the times of Juventus's football matches their WhatsApp group reaches its peak activity because that is when the seven friends support or guide each other most frequently. In contrast to the women's group, the men discuss less personal matters: they often exchange entertaining videos, deride Italian politicians and politics and, after a poor performance of the national football team in the 2014 World Cup finals, they derided Italian football. In Grano men in general rarely use private social media to discuss private issues with other men. Rather, men mostly use this media with women, including when flirting or trying to build a romantic relationship.

Then there is a third mixed group on WhatsApp, which is the least used by all the seven couples. Besides its utility function for setting up meetings, discussing issues of common interest or sometimes to let the others know what some of the group are doing at a particular time, there is relatively little sharing or impromptu messaging going on here. It seems as if this group was created simply to balance out the existence of the gendered groups which were seen as essential.

What is important is that both Isabella and Salvatore know that in many ways their *fidanzamento* depends a lot on the unity of their respective friends of the same gender – especially for the women. It is this unity that currently is substantively supported by WhatsApp. Isabella sees many women of her age becoming less attached to their peers as they start to work or move closer to their marital partners, and she recently started to sense that she needed to foster stronger relationships. WhatsApp has come to do just that: to reinforce the kind of stability and external reassurance she needed most. Isabella feels that she is young, good-looking and bright, but she is not very sure if these qualities will be sufficient to pave the way to a good marriage. The girls' WhatsApp group provides her with a continuous confirmation, external but not very public, that she is doing the right things in preparing for her marriage. It represents another level of intimacy that Isabella needs in order to preserve the commitments she feels to her *fidanzamento*.

This suggests that social media are used to express and extend particular patterns of sociality within concurrent layers of intimacy. But we should not think that, in contrast to Isabella, Salvatore tends to neglect his status of *fidanzato* by watching and talking endlessly about football. Rather, in his case, it is not WhatsApp or mediated sociality that clarifies his values. In Grano men tend to rely much less on their peers when it comes to establishing a family. As we have seen, for them this mainly implies being able to buy or build a house, possibly with the help of the family. Regular chats with his peers on any social media or phone could not possibly contribute to this in any way. We have seen that unmarried men define themselves in relation to the public, rather than to the more private or domestic, spheres. So the entire society, including his *fidanzata*, is expecting Salvatore to contribute to something very concrete and tangible; only when the house is ready will Salvatore be entitled to relax, take part in small talk and play games on his own home console. Even if, for both partners, the anxiety of not yet being married is similar, it is nevertheless focused on very different things: on the body for Isabella and outside the body for Salvatore; in the interactions with her peers for Isabella and in the interaction with his parents for Salvatore; in a delicate balance between virtue and sex-appeal for Isabella and in a more pragmatic and an apparently detached attitude for Salvatore. However, these two distinctly different outlooks actually strengthen the couple.

Unfit until married

Many foreigners might be puzzled when they see the apparent misfit between many young Italian couples: when walking or having an *aperitivo* during summer afternoons, women might be wearing elegant dresses or two pieces, glittery high heels and expensive accessories, while the men often wear shorts or inexpensive denim jeans, with sandals or light shoes and a Lacoste T-shirt with a turned-up collar. Women have elegant bags, while men carry nothing because their hip bags are associated with work. In many cases the only accessory they have in common seems to be the pair of sunglasses that everybody wears: usually black and elegant, adding a sense of individual mystery – a combination of prestige, refinement and discretion.

Similar discrepancies between relative sophistication for women and negligence for men can be seen in older couples. On the other hand, if many young couples' clothes seem completely mismatched, the discrepancies in clothing are relatively less obvious for married couples. This suggests that only through marriage can a certain similarity in appearance be achieved, and this is partly because many married women are responsible for buying clothes and caring for the external appearance of their entire family. This can certainly vary with age and social status, but we can say that, overall, the clothing mismatch of young unmarried couples expresses their particular relationship of not yet being married – they express a collective manifestation of individuality. Individuality *per se* is seen as wrong and cannot exist without the support of other individuals of the same gender who present themselves similarly. For example, *fidanzate* can wear adventurous dresses and stronger makeup if more of their peers are doing the same. This represents a sort of general rehearsal for the wedding, after which spouses start to pay more attention to dressing and behaving in ways which match each other. In this context, the abundance of personal photography exchanged on WhatsApp between *fidanzati* can be seen as a constant effort to maintain the ideal of marriage and to prepare themselves to fit into the conventional roles of a married couple.

This discussion shows not only the cultural traits which challenge different prejudices related to public appearance, but also to the use of new technology and smartphones. For example, it is commonplace that elderly people and some younger adults in Grano accuse the younger generations of not having 'real' relationships because of social media. They could take the image of a large noisy group of young people hanging around in a *piazza* or in a bar while some of them text or talk on their smartphones as denoting a lack of socialisation and sensibility. But the story of Isabella and Salvatore, as well as of their friends, suggests that this judgement is simply not correct: well-dressed women and jovial, more casual men can be using their smartphones not because they are more distant one from another, but because they really want to be much closer. The problem is how close society will actually let them be.

This section shows that, in a context in which there are very specific norms on public display and behaviour, social media have come to help people to express particular patterns of sociality, without convening the expectations of the community they live in. When people sense that some particular relationship should not be too public, they find ways to express it in new, adjustable, private spaces. Social media help create alternative layers of personal presentation – between the less-relaxed public domain and the very personal, intimate one. These layers can be scaled both ways: upwards towards the public sphere, for example, when people reach a certain level of confidence or social status, and downwards, towards more intimate relations, when they want to adjust or clarify the various misunderstandings and ambiguities that the public display has implied. It is throughout this continuous process of scaling that social relationships are constructed.

Love through messages

Elena lives with her youngest son, who is 18, in a small village a few kilometres south of Grano. She is a quiet, discreet person and not too fond of going out. She enjoys the comfort of her stylish home; the small back garden, with its abundance of flowers, and the company of her washed-out, cross-breed dog. Elena spends most of the time in her spacious kitchen, which is decorated with an elegant, dark-brown wainscot, light, gauzy curtains, and colourful plastic flowers – so unlike the usual austere, stone-dominated interiors of Grano.

Elena's husband and their two older sons have been working in Switzerland for more than four years now. Initially the entire family left for Switzerland some 24 years ago. Her husband, Agostino, was told of a job by one of his brothers who was already working there in construction. Elena followed him shortly afterwards with their two small boys. She had her third son in Switzerland. All through their stay there she did not work, but volunteered from time to time for different social projects. Her two older sons graduated from vocational schools and the entire family considered their Swiss diplomas to be the greatest achievement. Nevertheless 14 years ago, when Elena's husband was promised a job by one of his cousins in Grano, the family decided to return to their home town. Here, they did not have to pay rent, the cost of living was much lower and they were close to the rest of their family. The house inherited by Agostino was half-refurbished, but Elena was not very happy. She commented that the decision to move back to Italy had been her husband's – 'as always' in her life. She had never felt she belonged in the small town where she was born. She often felt a stranger in Switzerland as well, but there she had managed to build a special intimacy with her sons that was difficult to continue in Italy. A too-close relationship with grown-up children was at odds with local norms of sociality.

After 10 years in Italy, during which Agostino lost two jobs due to the difficult economic times, he decided to emigrate back to Switzerland. Again one of his brothers found him a job there and, shortly afterwards, his two older sons decided to join their father. Elena remembers holding back the tears in her deep blue eyes when, exactly 10 years after they had returned to Italy, she accompanied her sons to their train back to Switzerland.[4]

Now Elena is 64 years old and her youngest son is about to finish his high school studies. Even if she feels extremely alone and constantly dreams of returning to Switzerland some day, Elena knows this would be very difficult: her family never settled properly in Switzerland and, as her husband is reaching retirement age, it would be expected that he would return to his home town as many Italian men do.[5] However, it is likely that her two eldest sons will not return to Italy, where their Swiss diplomas are not recognised, and that they will also encourage their younger brother to come and work in Switzerland. What has kept Elena afloat all these years has been her immense love for her sons, and the countless evidences of love they have given back to her.

Elena joined Facebook three years ago because her eldest son insisted and set up a profile for her on the platform. He sent clear and detailed written instructions on how to start up the computer and to log on to the service. She then started to really enjoy it and to be online quite a lot. She is now friends on Facebook with her three sons and 26 of their friends. It was these friends who requested her Facebook friendship. Elena is well known for being an open-minded and hospitable mother: each summer when her family returns home for vacation she repeatedly invites her sons' *fidanzate* and their numerous friends to her luxuriant garden, prepares fresh food and bakes tasty marmalade cakes for them. Some of these reunions turn into small ad hoc parties. Elena feels she is truly happy when she has all these young people spending time light-heartedly around her.

When her family is back in Switzerland, she does not know how to bear the huge physical distance from her loved ones. She found comfort in being her sons' confidante – the person they always came to for advice when they needed it. She remembers when her eldest son separated from his *fidanzata* after eight years of engagement. He called her on her mobile phone from Switzerland, at huge cost, and Elena remembers in great detail how they talked and cried for an hour and a half. He had been separated from his *fidanzata* for several days, but he had waited desperately hoping that she would change her mind before telling his mother about it. Elena had stopped the car on the side of the minor road she was driving on and listened carefully to all the details of the story, feeling completely useless being so far from her son. She remembers entering her home and crying at the thought of what her son was going through and that she was not there with him. She said she had only cried like that once before – when the same son had bought his first motorcycle. Without telling her of this acquisition, he uploaded with great pride a few photos of his bike on Facebook. Elena just looked at the photos and cried. It had been a 1,000cc bike and she knew it was too powerful. She kept thinking of the accident he had had as a teenager with his scooter, which resulted in hospitalisation for a month. She had pleaded day and night with the doctors and nurses until she persuaded them to allow her to stay there with him.

Elena finds that Facebook can be cruel and prefers to talk to her sons on the mobile phone because then she can really tell how they are. Elena has one smartphone and a Lycamobile subscription with 600 free minutes to Switzerland. Her two eldest sons both have a few hundred free minutes. She could use up all her free minutes in less than a week, but she knows she should distribute the free calls judiciously over the month. With Agostino she talks for just a few minutes every few days and then one of their sons will continue the conversation.

Elena also hates talking on Skype with her family because she thinks this medium is just too intimate:[6] actually seeing them – in Switzerland – is simply unbearable. She prefers the mobile phone where her sons seem so much closer to her, where she can notice every intonation of their voices, while thinking of them with love. In contrast, Skype does not allow her imagination to roam free. Seeing her children online and not being able to hug and care for them is intolerable. Her eyes are distracted by the objective reality of their average looking rented flat in Switzerland and, for some reason, she is less able to focus on what her sons are saying to her.

Her youngest son lives with her in Italy and Elena uses a second smartphone to talk to him. They communicate mainly via WhatsApp, which her son considers to be a less intrusive way of keeping in contact. As this is the only mobile phone with an internet subscription, Elena also uses it to exchange WhatsApp messages with her family in Switzerland. However, she finds that these messages, and especially the photos. make her rather sad: she feels the photos do not reflect the reality of what is actually going on in Switzerland. As she lived there for almost 12 years, she just knows that the reality 'out there' can be really tough, especially without a woman in the house to take care of her family. So when she receives photos from Switzerland she immediately knows if they misrepresent reality. As a mother, she feels responsible for knowing the 'reality' and not just random fragments of it.

Finally, Elena also has a third mobile phone, a standard feature one she uses to talk to her friends and relatives in Italy. She mostly receives calls and rarely makes any calls. But she keeps this phone as a sort of reminder of her earlier life in Italy. On this phone she still has the same number she had when she first acquired a mobile phone, and the main emergency numbers are saved here, such as her doctor, accountant and the different professional workers who help her in running the house. She considers all these people not close enough to give them the new mobile phone numbers. This phone seems to represent the outer world which Elena does not want to mix with the personal one, represented by her family.

Since her husband left Italy for the second time, Elena has felt even less like going out of the house. She limits her outings as much as possible, including her trips to the shops. As her youngest son is now a young adult, her opportunities to socialise even as a parent outside the house have become even fewer. Elena argues that in Grano people gossip a lot, even when there is nothing to gossip about. She says that even if they see her going into a shop, they might comment: 'Who knows where she is going?' And she is right, they probably would – especially as she is seen as being different from many women in her village. Having lived for many years 'outside' the village, people feel that she has developed 'strange' tastes, which are reflected, for example, in the way she has decorated her house. Elena has installed a few small statues and pots of plants in front of the house and the back garden is full of plants – not cemented or tiled like most people's gardens are in Grano. Furthermore, Elena knows that a housewife who does not live with her family is seen as a contradiction in terms, and that she should therefore be even more careful than usual to keep her respectability intact.

As a result, Elena is condemned to stay in the house as much as possible. While her occasional outings are rather formal, dull and always in a rush, she considers her actual connections to be via the internet and the smartphone: in the absence of her family it is these media devices that maintain the sense of home.[7] Elena spends at least four hours a day on Facebook, where she mainly observes her contacts. In particular she likes the romantic memes containing ideas that reflect her own thoughts. Some of her preferred memes resemble pretty much the two poems she showed me: they were written by her two older sons and dedicated to her some 15 years ago on Mother's Day. They are handwritten with blue ink in nicely ordered verses on small pieces of paper, thinned by time, and in one case under a big bunch of flowers drawn by her son. She keeps these gifts in her purse together with her ID card and an icon of the Virgin Mary. Every now and then she takes the poems out and reads them, almost crying. Similarly many of the internet memes she shares online stand for particular memories they bring to her.

There is a need in Elena for the romantic, as it represents a missing aspect in her life. Elena told me how her husband had pressurised her into marrying him. They had been very young, and after several years of *fidanzamento* he had felt that she was about to leave him. She has tried, but has not been able to love him. After they had their first two boys, Elena and Agostino were informally separated for a few difficult years. They were still living in the same house, but Agostino occupied the ground floor, which had a separate entrance, and rarely visited his family. He used to give Elena very little money, and it was informally suggested by the *carabinieri* (police) that he had even taken the family car into the countryside and dismantled it rather than giving it to his wife.[8] Elena had been forced to sell several pieces of her gold jewellery to pay the electricity bill, and had constantly needed to invent stories to justify to the children the strange absence of their father. She remembers that it was most difficult to stand bravely in front of them and invent excuses for him when, for example, they would see Agostino pass by their window without even waving 'Hello'. She had tried to cry only when the children were sleeping. We can see how the close relationship between

Elena and her three sons was an attempt to compensate for the broken and tense relationship with her husband.

From the beginning of her marriage, Elena decided to keep the unity of the family. But, by constructing such a special intimacy with her children, Elena had actually limited her husband's access to them. This was not to do with revenge, but rather from a sense that, in the context of an unstable marriage, she needed to focus even more on consolidating a secure core between herself and her children. During this process she was constantly torn between her personal feelings and the expectations of society. Many people in her small village applauded her efforts to 'take [the family] forward': three decades ago a single mother separated from her husband for reasons such as a conflictual relationship was hardly acceptable. The forbidding of divorce by the Catholic Church was a strong force, but Elena's decision to keep the family together was more about her determination to be a good mother. Even nowadays many single mothers face huge difficulties in being accepted, even by their more liberal female friends, to join activities where families or the idea of family are involved. People are worried about transmitting to their children a model of a separated family and, as such, single mothers are often regarded as a potential threat to the unity of couples.

Therefore Elena's choice to stay at home, despite being an extremely active and joyful person, can be seen as representing an attempt to preserve her integrity, but it is also because she feels at odds with the community. By locking herself inside her house for days at a time, she is declaring publicly that the modest social life of the town is indeed not as important as her relationship with her sons. Instead, daily phone calls, Skype and WhatsApp messages with her sons are really important for Elena. Her comfort lies with where her children are, and now they are mostly online.

The process of trying to keep the unity of the family during long periods of male migrant labour overseas was typical for generations of families in the southernmost region of Puglia, and indeed in most of the south of Italy. This story highlights the ways in which new technologies contribute to changing patterns of family ties and enduring nostalgia for the homeland. As we have seen, social media do not really help Elena and her family ease their tumultuous 'cross-border lives', which include an idealisation of the united family and a nostalgia for the homeland, because they render more visible this separation by hundreds of kilometres.[9] So Elena has chosen to set the level of visibility of this physical separation so that it does not add any more anxiety and disquiet than is necessary.

Let us now take a look at a case where a single mother is using private media in an attempt to establish a family. In the context of a demanding everyday life and strict social restrictions on meeting single men, she relies exclusively on private communication to access what she would otherwise struggle to reach.

The single mother

Rita is a 42-year-old single mother. She graduated with a Bachelor of Arts in literature from Rome, but she never managed to find work in this field. She returned to Grano six years ago, when she realised that the relationship with the father of her newborn child had ended. Ever since she has tried to find a romantic partner, but she has not been able to find a man who was prepared to take responsibility for a stepchild. Rita was never *fidanzata* and she knows that by leaving Grano to study she rejected not only a customary but also an easy way of life.

After living for a few years in her mother's house, Rita decided she should take her life into her own hands: she converted her father's studio into a nice, unpretentious apartment, decorated it with personal drawings, and moved in with her daughter, Anna. Rita considers herself a liberal woman and tries to raise her child in the same way. However, especially when her daughter started school, Rita found that there were many compromises she had to make if she wanted her daughter to be properly integrated in her class: she stopped dressing herself in bright colours, started to iron her shirts and sent her daughter to vaguely useful extra-curricular activities like the rest of her class did. However, she never arrives early to collect her daughter from school like everyone else in order to engage in small talk with other parents.

Rita knows that people comment on her daughter lacking discipline and routine; that they eat at irregular hours and sometimes not at home; and that she was the first to withdraw her daughter from gym classes and then from the costly Taekwondo lessons.[10] As an unemployed single mother with little financial help from her husband, she finds it impossible to follow the standards most people in Grano have for raising their children. However, the community does not necessarily see that the father is absent or not interested in caring for his child, but rather that the mother-child bond is not as strong as it should be. Rita's more liberal attitude contradicts many mothers' practices of caring for their children. Rita feels almost obliged to establish a family with recognisable routines and everyday concerns. This unit would then be recognised as stable by most people in her community. She might dislike the lifestyle, but she also recognises that trying to attain this ideal is the surest way for her daughter to be accepted as 'normal'. So, even if she is not a particularly religious person, Rita can hardly wait for her daughter to start catechism classes. She knows that this highly normative practice will restore some 'normality' to her daughter and to herself.

In contrast with many mothers, Rita almost never posts her daughter's accomplishments on Facebook. For her, mothering is rather intimate and delicate, and should in no way be displayed in public. She hangs the poems her daughter writes and her paintings in a few special places at home rather than posting them on Facebook. In this way, she thinks that her friends and family who visit her at home can observe these works and engage with them more profoundly. Sometimes this will include her daughter explaining, commenting or drawing attention to some detail. For Rita this is the normal way for her child to open herself to the world. Instead, what Rita does upload to Facebook are entertaining photos of her daughter playing with friends, falling asleep in a hammock or going to the sea with her grandmother. These are expressions of how Rita sees childhood, as a period in which children should develop their own personalities. Rita does not need her daughter to prove that she is a good mother, so she uploads to Facebook only those photos that give her daughter a voice of her own.

However, what is really private for Rita takes place on her mobile phone. Bruno is a man from a close village who has courted her for almost two years. They have known each other since they were kids and most probably he has been in love with her since then. He spends quite a lot of time with Anna and dreams of marrying Rita someday. Rita's family is pressuring her to marry Bruno as he is seen as a great choice. But she feels trapped by these pressures which do not let her think peacefully.

Here is an exchange of messages between Rita and Bruno from a time when she was angry with him because he had taken Anna to the cinema when he was supposed to be looking after her at home:

Rita: I forgave you
Bruno [*not understanding why she said so*]: OK, I still didn't, but tomorrow morning, yes
Rita [*angry*]: What should you forgive me for?
Bruno: Shut up and sleep!
Rita: I take orders from nobody! You sleep!
. . .

Bruno: Come on, if you sleep and then you finish your housework I'll take you to the cinema

. . .

Rita: The *Wolf of Wall Street* [the film was playing in the cinema at the time]

. . .

Bruno: Now go to sleep!
Rita: Stop it! You are playing with your [promise to go to the] cinema!

. . .

Rita: When you have done your housework, we'll see. Now, enough and sleep!
Bruno: OK, fine, but please don't tell this to A [Anna]. Come on, if you sleep I will even buy you popcorn! Come on! God! Sleep!
Rita: I want cinema! I want cinema! I want cinema!

This conversation happened between 00:24 and 00:42 on the 24 October 2013. Rita remembers it was a cold night and the chilly northern wind was blowing her shutters when she put Anna to sleep. She had heard several *beeps* on her Nokia phone and had known it was Bruno texting again. She had not wanted to reply until her fury had simmered down and she had finished tucking Anna in. In the interview, both Rita and Bruno explained to me how the story had evolved. She and Bruno had just stopped messaging each other less than one hour before, while Anna had still been playing in her room. They were arguing because Bruno had broken what she had thought was a mutual agreement not to take Anna to see the children's movie that was running at the cinema. In the above dialogue Rita is trying to play the entire situation down, and is suggesting that the two of them go out themselves to see a movie. They both know they probably would not do that, but as they were messaging they were actually creating a warm intimate atmosphere.

Bruno knew that after the first angry exchange of messages he should give Rita some space, but also that he should finish the conversation on a positive note that would allow him to continue it the next day. So he opened his window for a while and made himself a large *panino* (sandwich) filled with some two-day old prosciutto he found in his fairly bare fridge. He turned down the volume on his big flat screen TV in the sitting room that was running a lively political talk show and entered his small bedroom; he switched on the light and plunged into his simple double bed holding his iPhone in front of his eyes. He waited for a few minutes before sending off the first message in the conversation above to Rita.

Both Rita and Bruno knew they should be careful while exchanging messages not to show too much. Bruno knew that Rita knew he loved her, so he just wanted to express care and support to her and her daughter, while leaving enough space for them as a family. In turn, Rita really needed support and affection and was not very sure where her relationship with Bruno would lead to. Instead, both were sure of their strong friendship. In this context, the continuous exchange of text messages throughout the evening reflected their existing relationship, which was characterised by uneasy hesitations over whether to transform it into something other than friendship. Through smooth, non-intrusive and delicately worded private messages the two were working out their relationship before deciding to display it publicly. And they did that for about eight months.

The intimate exchange of text messages late at night is typical in many love relationships in Grano and probably elsewhere in the world. What is really interesting in Grano is that not even the smallest hint of these early relationships permeates into the public domain. So, until they have a normative relationship, couples are reluctant to show it online. It is this contrast with, on the one hand, the deep and wholeheartedly intimate conversations via private chats on Facebook, WhatsApp and phone calls and, on the other hand, the jovial, detached and witty public appearance on Facebook that creates in many couples a continuous sense of romantic bliss and deep intimacy and tenderness.

However, we have seen that private conversations can structure different layers of intimacy mapped out over several platforms. This may be a response to a personal need to find a platform that is best suited to reflect a particular relationship, such as in the case of Elena, or it can be used to set up group visibility, such as in the case of Isabella. Sometimes different social media can be used to reflect actual commitment to a relationship. For example, Alessandra started to first use Twitter when plunging into an intense love affair with a man in Rome. She set up a Twitter account at the national fair where she met him. She had never used Twitter before, and had closed down her Facebook account a few years earlier, when she separated from her husband. The new couple started to use Twitter intensively to melt the physical distance into a never-ending dialogue. After a few months they turned to Skype and started to talk almost daily for a few hours. However, Alessandra often felt 'useless' and 'angry' because she could not 'really be' with her lover. Even though they could see one another on Skype, they could not share the same intimacy they had enjoyed when they had been together in Rome. Sometimes they were bored after five minutes on Skype, not knowing what to say next, so each started to do domestic chores in order to try and fill the periods of silence and embarrassment. Even if they were now finding out many more things about themselves, they sometimes felt that the sharp visibility of Skype is inappropriate for their relationship: they could see each other's houses, which felt strange as they rarely spent any time together in either of them. Nonetheless they both felt Skype was better than Twitter because it added more elements to their relationship. Still, after a few months, the couple's use of Skype dropped off as they started to travel the 600 kilometres that separated them more often, and they decided to move on to Facebook. Alessandra created a new Facebook profile, with a discreet presence, and started to send friend requests to her closest friends.

In this case, the three different social media platforms represented tools the couple had used to reflect the progressively greater commitment they made to their relationship. In the end, by re-joining Facebook, Alessandra signalled, if initially only to her close friends who had known about it, that she had finally succeeded in starting a new relationship.

All the stories in this chapter suggest that social media do not increase the complexity of social relations, despite what we might think at first glance, but rather provide new spaces where people can express the complexity of their social relationships. Previous communication media could not do this mainly because they were in fact either public, for example web pages, forums and newsletters, or private, for example phone calls, text messages, emails and internet chat rooms. Social media changed this completely because they extended the domain of *possibilities*: that is, people can now scale each of their relationships within the same environment and choose between an increasing number of possibilities regarding how they present themselves at any given time.

Setting layers of intimacy

So far, we have seen that Facebook is not necessarily used to reflect, reproduce or strengthen relationships. With the exception of celebrating a handful of events that are seen as being both private and public, such as *fidanzamenti*, weddings, anniversaries or graduations, when different personal aspects can be displayed online, people tend to exclude most of the intimate elements of their lives from their online postings. Actual relationships are already known or, as in the case of Rita and Bruno, yet to be built, and there is no need to suggest them online. Facebook can be used to confirm a relationship to close friends only, such as in the case of Alessandra. This suggests that the use of Facebook is creative and expressive in Grano, but within the limits allowed for public visibility and the constraints of social expectations. So people really need private and dyadic media – to express personal relationships and those that cannot yet be publicly displayed.

At the same time, if the norm is the happily married family, as in the case of Silvia and Giovanni, people do not really need Facebook to demonstrate their relationship. Giovanni works every other day in a very busy place and Silvia inhabits spaces that are extremely visible: the house, her husband's bar, shops and playgrounds, while being in permanent contact with schools and other places of education for her children. In their case, showing their relationship on Facebook would be repetitive and burdensome. Instead, using WhatsApp to live it intensively when they are not together is their main priority. Their relationship is for themselves and for their family, only its general visibility is for the community.

In contrast, the two women who followed after in this chapter are at odds with their society, but for very different reasons. Rita has faced strong difficulties while trying, for six years, to integrate herself and her family into Grano life, mainly because she does not wish to follow many of its routines and norms. Refusing to conform to what mothers of her age do would have been acceptable if she had either a very low or a very high social position. As Rita is at neither of these extremes, she is condemned by society into trying to be 'normal'. But she can hardly conform with this now – 'normal' was what she was when she left Grano more than 20 years ago.

In contrast, Elena is a typical mother. Despite her familial problems, she has always been seen in her community as a brave woman and mother. The fact that, since her husband left to work in Switzerland, she refuses to leave her house too often is part of her effort to preserve this reputation. Many people in the village know that Elena talks every day with her family in Switzerland, while in fact she talks mostly with her sons and follows them closely on Facebook.

Now the ideal of establishing a family is perhaps expressed most strongly by the youngest couple in this chapter. Isabella and Salvatore are struggling to reach the status of married couple. While most of their efforts are driven by this ideal, they do not have the slightest prospect of a house that would objectify and protect it. Instead, they have WhatsApp groups. In this context the 'girls' group' acts in a similar way to how the house acts for Elena. Isabella and her close friends use the intimacy of their WhatsApp group to support each other in their complicated journey towards married life. As *fidanzamento* is seen as a temporary position which leads to the 'real' social standing of being married, most people have difficulties in making this relationship visible in the same public and neat way that building a house, raising children or dressing appropriately objectify a marriage. The solution is to display it to a smaller and closed audience that can recognise it is an essential part of the project to build a real marriage.

This suggests that for people who are not yet married, the ideal of the family pushes communication towards more intense intimate interactions, using a variety of personal media which try to replicate the relations existing in fundamental institutions such as marriage and parent-children relationships. In contrast to the public displays which express a common agreement on what the public sphere should be, the more private media contain all the tensions of real personal relationships. They can also be much more chaotic and less regulated because many individuals struggle to agree on the proper ways in which their relationships should be acknowledged in public.

Looking to display the right social position

Attempts made to display the right social position suggest a parallel between social media and marriage itself. A real relationship is only legitimate when it has sufficient substance, so you do not marry until you have that substance, be it love, a house or family approval. Similarly you do not go on Facebook until you can prove what you put online, and, vice versa: you close down your Facebook account once, for example, you have had a child from a casual relationship. You feel that the new status of 'single mother returned to give birth in her home town' simply does not fit anymore with the image you constructed just a few weeks before on Facebook. This suggests that Facebook is the place that gives public legitimacy to public values.

We have seen this by following two main components. The first is what social media do, but also do not do, in relation to normative relationships. We have started with the normative relationships represented by married and *fidanzati* couples. We have seen that Facebook as a public platform does not at all reflect the ways these relationships are experienced, but private media can do this. Intimate relationships have a rather restricted social visibility because, in Grano, it is the status of a relationship that should be displayed and not the relationship itself.

The second component is how we can learn more about what social media can do in relation to non-normative relationships. We have explored the non-typical, more complicated relationships represented by the families of single mothers and those separated because of work migration. These situations are considered atypical not because they are not very frequent, but because they are contradicting what is generally seen as the normative relationship. The ethnographic material shows that in these situations social media become relatively more important for individuals because they use them to attain the normative, that is the more typical, relationship.

These two perspectives support the suggestion that Facebook represents the wider accepted social realm that it is meant to reflect, if only partially, and the appropriate social position, while private social media give people the possibility to construct different layers of intimacy. If public-facing social media are used to show conformity to ideas that circulate in society, the more private social media are used to fight the small, everyday struggles of personal relationships. It is this more anxious and well-guarded intimacy of relationships that allows for the calm, worry-free and more assenting public sphere to exist.

In the next chapter, we discuss why the local notions of beauty and the burden of complying with a whole range of aesthetic values cause people continually to craft their social appearance in accordance with social ideals, and how they use public social media to reflect this process. Then, in Chapter 6, we focus on the impact social media have on education and work, which are seen as the strongest sources of ideals in relation to the higher political economy of the state. We conclude that people use social media to map out the dual nature of their relationships – the public and the personal, the visible and the less visible – in a continuous attempt to fit themselves into a series of ideals proposed by their society.

5
The imposition of beauty

> **Socrates:** So then: should we say that the appropriate is that which when present makes things *seem* beautiful or makes things *be* beautiful, or neither?
> **Hippias:** I think it's what makes things seem beautiful. It is like when somebody puts on well-fitting clothes or shoes, even if he's ridiculous, he is seem to be more beautiful [...]
> **Socrates:** If, then, beauty is the cause of good, goodness would be generated by the beautiful. So it seems that we take seriously wisdom and everything that is beautiful because that which they produce and generate, the goodness, deserves to be pursued. Then maybe based on what we discover, the beautiful looks like the father [*sic*] of goodness.
>
> (Plato, *Hippias Major*, pp. 294a, 297b)

Everybody in Grano would agree that Luana is a beautiful woman. She runs, together with her younger sister and their mother, a fine leather shop in one of the main commercial streets in Grano. The shop was established by her father almost 40 years ago and ever since then it has represented the main source of income for the entire family, bringing in more money even than her mother's good salary as a teacher of Italian. After completing secondary school, Luana never considered looking for another job or leaving Grano.

In her early forties, Luana considers herself quite attractive and does as much as possible for other people to notice this. She is quite tall, which for people here is a standard for beauty, as the local saying goes: *Altezza metà bellezza* ('Height is half of beauty'). She remembers that it was during the first few years after completing her education that she started to believe that she had a lot of potential for *essere* ('being') really beautiful. So she worked on her physical aspect in different ways: she first joined local gym classes, then changed her hairstyle periodically and improved her make-up techniques. Finally, she underwent several small aesthetic surgeries.[1]

Luana was *fidanzata* with Gabriele for several years. He was equally tall, dark-eyed, with curly dark hair and a large forehead. He had practiced bodybuilding as a hobby since his twenties, so when the couple used to walk together on Sunday afternoons many people agreed their appearance was *uno spettacolo* (stunning). As a common friend put it: 'they were perfect'.

But two years ago, after a short period of living together, Luana broke their engagement and moved back to her mother's. She felt she needed to start a new life. She felt she had become 'more mature' and autonomous. She stopped dyeing her dark black hair and started to spend more time looking after herself. Now she focuses more on trying out slightly new hairstyles and make-up until she finds a particular style that more closely fits her idea of beauty. Luana follows a strict diet recommended by a nutritionist in Lecce, and her mother now also enjoys eating the raw greens, seeds and dry salads that Luana discovered on a recent trip to India. In 2014 Luana joined a pole-dancing class in Lecce. She is particularly excited about this new sport because it is developing muscles she did not know she had and strengthening her body even more.

In her work on the rise of the fitness culture in the Western world, sociologist Roberta Sassatelli relates the central place of the gym and fitness in Italian and European society to a particular awareness of one's own body.[2] She explains that, by engaging constantly in gymnastic activities, individuals are currently attempting to administer in a confident and autonomous way the resources of their bodies. This represents a popular embodiment of the more elitist classical ideals of European culture – a pure and perfect body – in a modern context. Indeed, Luana has put this project at the centre of her life: she can spend €400–500 a month on maintaining an attractive appearance, yet she works for almost five days a week in an average shop, like many other working people in Grano.[3] For most of the year she only spends nights out with friends at the weekends . Three evenings a week she goes to the gym for two hours and has a late dinner with her mother. Luana then goes to her room to watch television and fall asleep.

Her busy everyday schedule does not allow Luana to spend too much time beautifying herself at home: 'if you are taking constant care of yourself, you do not need too much time to take care of yourself at home,' she says. She just uses a few anti-wrinkle creams in the morning and before going to bed, combs her straight hair with a few firm gestures and never does her fingernails as her plastic nails last for at least two weeks. Luana also does not like jewellery, and hardly uses any accessories other than her elegant Armani sunglasses; her beauty consists now in maintaining a perfect and strong body.

Her sister, Eva, has a quite different idea of beauty. She does everything that Luana does but on a much smaller scale: gym, regular visits to hairdressers and beauticians, and healthy diet. It is her married life and non-observant Catholicism that restrains Eva from expressing her beauty as blatantly as her sister. She has been married for nearly nine years and has two children, aged nine and six. Back in high school she had been considered to have the potential to be 'a beauty' someday: she had won a few beauty contests and many of her friends had encouraged her to follow a modelling career. However, she had wanted to marry the man she loved and have a 'normal' life. Her husband managed to obtain a good position in local administration and they started to enjoy a comfortable married life.

Eva knows it is considered inappropriate to look 'perfect' when rushing your kids to school in the morning, or entering the greengrocers on the corner or the butchers. Instead, it is when she is going out with her family that she grooms herself more attentively and sometimes wears elegant clothes or uses more make-up. In many situations women do not leave home before spending a certain period of time beautifying themselves and selecting their clothes, making sure their outfits are neat and that their family is equally well dressed. Dressing reflects the social and economic status they believe that they still have despite the recent economic difficulties, and social media have to reflect this. For most married women in Grano, the idea of personal beauty does not really make sense outside the family.

In general, married women in Grano could be described as having a less conspicuous, but constant and enduring, kind of beauty. By not stressing too much their physical beauty, they instead express their status as wife and mother. In contrast to her married sister, Luana never dresses in the same clothes on two consecutive days; she arranges her hair in two or three different ways during the week and sometimes adds some eye-catching accessories such as a wide leather belt with a large metal buckle or a brand new pair of sunglasses. A married woman would not normally do any of this. She would probably be relaxed if in the morning she put on the same clothes as she wore the previous day as long as they were clean and she looked decent.

She would also rarely change her hairstyle in two consecutive visits to the hairdresser and, in general, would try not to attract attention to her appearance in any particular way. Spending one-third of the average salary on maintaining an attractive appearance, as Luana does, is inconceivable for middle-class married women. They rather compensate for this cost and focus on appearance, which would be considered a luxury, by putting in extra work on maintaining a clean and neat appearance instead.

Now, with Facebook, women have another space where all these efforts can be made visible. For example, Luana does not upload photos of herself to Facebook very often and her profile is private. This means that she lets people know and admire her offline rather than online. Actually she has little time to spend (*andare*) online, except during the summer when she likes uploading photos of time spent with friends. She uses the service mostly to make appointments with people she likes to spend time with. She does not like to see *cose pesante* ('heavy things') posted on Facebook, such as posts on the more philosophical thoughts or those that engage in political debates. She considers all these a waste of time.

Luana keeps just a few photos of herself public on Facebook. These were done by a friend who is a professional photographer. The photos are in black and white, and they show Luana in romantic dialogue with the spectacular scenery of the Adriatic coast: she is very well dressed and looks beautiful, but does not try to be 'too' attractive and never looks into the camera. In several of these photos her profile is photographed against a century-old watchtower that guards the rocky coast. However, Luana only engages with the majesty and uncontested beauty of nature in these photos that she has made public. In contrast, many of the pictures on her private Facebook profile show her photographed at close range, sunbathing in a bikini on a boat, or while drinking a fresh juice with friends.

This suggests that Luana embodies a project of beauty itself: publicly it can be admired from a distance, in less detail and sometimes as seen in harmony with the greatness of nature, while it is within a close circle of friends that Luana reveals her true self. This is consistent with Luana's offline attitude. Her customers admire her beauty and professionalism discretely when stepping into the shop while, during weekends, summer holidays and with close friends, Luana reveals deeper aspects of her personality. This outlook is similar to that regarding religious faith: we have seen that it is 'normal' to strive to be a good Catholic without necessarily showing this on Facebook.

It is this dual quality of her appearance that distinguishes Luana from other people in the community. Her preoccupation with looking attractive and fit is more like a craft, like painting, for example. The rule is you might let other people see the product of your work, but you present it as a craft. This project is in no way narcissistic because it is normative. As we will see later in the chapter, it is the social duty of *bravi* (good) citizens to craft their physical appearance in a way that can be appreciated socially.[4] This suggests that the use of social media should be seen in the larger context of the history and norms of the region. Reading the following sections, we will see how these norms have made people work on themselves constantly and enjoy complimentary online public appreciations.

Where do all these ideas come from?

Let us take a few steps back and put everything in the context of Italian society as people from Grano see it. In the Introduction we saw that the *società contadina* (rural society) that characterised most parts of Salento up to 1950s underwent dramatic changes in just a couple of decades, mainly driven by the massive industrialisation in the north of Italy and central Europe. This imposed on Grano very precise ideals and cultural references generated by the increasingly prosperous north of the country. For example, older people remember how huge trailers carrying washing machines and plastic domestic goods flowed through the streets of Grano in the early 1960s, basically selling new and modern ways to care for the home. At the same time the entertainment industry had grown spectacularly and had come to be dominated by the glamorous world of Rome, especially in the cinema, which expressed both refined and popular tastes.[5]

The roots of the cultural obsession and norms for *bellezza* can be traced way back in time, for example, to the Middle Ages, when in the fine arts it was seen as a divine attribute. This was associated gradually with femininity and had an important role in matrimonial exchange.[6] Hundreds of years later, in the late 1970s, many Italians started to see the model for *bellezza* as emerging in the city of Milan. Any middle-aged women in Grano remembers that if their mother had beauty standards set by famous actresses, such as Serena Grandi, Laura Antonelli or Gloria Guida, who were all associated with Rome, in the 1980s and early 1990s they themselves grew up with a completely different kind of beauty, more glamorous than that appreciated by the previous generation.[7]

In the 1980s and 1990s the fashion industry flourished in the north of Italy, and models such as Cindy Crawford and Yasmin Le Bon who worked mainly in Milan, marked a profound professionalisation and internationalisation of beauty.[8] The new kind of beauty was more tangible and tailored than the *bellezza classica* ('classic beauty') of the previous decades, which for most people had been limited to distant admiration. However, as before, it was aimed mostly at women.

These new qualities of *bellezza* were the result of a spectacular increase in diversification of goods and services related to beauty. Media and mass consumption proposed a popular engagement with the idea of beauty, style and glamour: virtually everyone could afford to beautify themselves. The sudden rise of *modelle* (models) in the 1970s corresponded to the spectacular take-off of the *moda Italiana* (Italian fashion) and *il stilo Italiano* (the Italian style). Famous fashion houses such as Versace were trading with great success in New York and elsewhere.[9] Even if innumerable small workshops from various regions in Italy participated with materials, knowledge and work, for most people the fashion industry was synonymous with Milan. Even today, Milan remains, for southern Salento, a model not only of economic success but also of desirability.

This rapid development of fashion and style can be seen as a secular response to the Catholic aim for a beautiful Christian life and being a good person. It came on a wave of optimism, affluence and mass-consumption, and corresponded with a major shift in public attention from Rome and the Vatican, representing the pillars of a united Italian state, to Milan as the locus of economic success. As Italian commentators noted, the economic and public success of Silvio Berlusconi is related, among other things, to the fact that he successfully surfed this wave of popular enthusiasm.[10] In particular, the media giant owned by Berlusconi made innovations in the entertainment industry by placing an essential focus on stereotyping and promoting a particular kind of feminine beauty. The most popular television shows such as *Striscia la Notizia*[11] (Strip the News) and *Non è la RAI*[12] (It is not RAI) pushed the *veline* (television showgirls) not only as a mass consumption product at the heart of the Italian celebrity culture, but also as a lifestyle model for generations of female teenagers.[13] Even if this was vehemently criticised in Italian society as misogynistic and degrading, many women in Grano in their mid-thirties remember how they grew up dreaming of becoming such media celebrities. This could also relate to the aim of popular television to drive bourgeois tastes and subjects into popular audiences.[14]

However, the Italian fashion industry started to lose ground less than two decades after its inception. Especially after the economic crisis of 2008, the business market and policy makers started to rally around the famous *qualità Italiana* (Italian quality) as a distinguishing mark of national style. Domains that used to be outstanding, such as the arts, design and craft, were invoked as supreme proof of Italian excellence. In this context, different versions of 'beauty' seemed to carry a new burden: the responsibility to represent those things that both Italian media and its audience agreed still existed in abundance: the beauty of the Italian land- and seascape, cities, art and history, or the quality and aesthetics of the different regional traditions and cuisines. All along, the physical beauty of the people accompanied in different ways the praise given to genuine Italian quality. For example, major motor and football shows were presented by young attractive models or celebrities, who in contrast to *veline* were seen as less superficial, more expert and wearing more decent clothes. In a successful show on RAI2 (a major channel on the national television network), young female hostesses presented powerful new cars by driving them in spectacular Italian holiday resorts, such as snow-covered chalet resorts in the Alps or exclusive sea resorts. The various kinds of beauty that Italians agreed on were packaged into an attractive format for a popular audience.

There is a powerful critique of the current decline in the 'authentic' values of beauty in the successful Italian film, *La Grande Bellezza* ('The Great Beauty'). In Grano this film, which juxtaposes the decaying of the majestic beauty of Rome with the meanness of Rome's hypocritical, high-class inhabitants striving for ephemeral values, including false beauty, appealed to most people, and especially to the highly educated and those who had lived in Rome for a period. When the film was screened on national television in the winter of 2014, just after it had won an Oscar for the best foreign language picture, everybody in town watched it compulsively. The streets were emptier than usual and some bars screened it on their big screens, where only music and football are normally played. In the days that followed, the film was discussed intensively in families, between friends and in the local media in a similar way that the San Remo Festival is usually discussed every year. Many views can be summarised in the indignation expressed by one women in her forties: 'We [Italians] have so much beauty, and Rome is *bellissima* (extremely beautiful), but what are we doing with it!?' She continued that human beauty should be about truthfulness and honesty, even if the person looks old or unfashionable, that it is as if nature is teaching us a lesson that we should not ignore. In her view, only natural beauty can now match the majesty of the many impressive constructions that humankind used to erect.

Later in the year, the theme of the 2014 San Remo festival was 'beauty'. The impressive set design was inspired by the film *La Grande Bellezza*,[15] 'just apparently abandoned, in which harmony, elegance, and memories of distant splendour still exist'.[16] RAI News commented bitterly that it was: 'a metaphor for the country'. The television celebrity and co-presenter of the festival Fabio Fazio explained: 'Great beauty for us Italians is a necessity, it gives importance to what we are.'[17] In a monologue given at the festival by the popular actress Luciana Littizzetto, she addressed many issues relating to beauty and diversity, including a plea for a return to 'normality', and she derided those women who are obsessed with beauty, dedicating themselves to 'stirring, shaving and suction'.[18] Her words were welcomed with frenetic applause and unanimous approval in the media, which appreciated her attempt to restore feminine beauty as represented by the natural and the genuine.

Nonetheless, if important segments of current Italian society are trying to find a way back to celebrating natural beauty, for many people in Grano external beauty is something that can be achieved through regular effort and care, and stylish accessories. Thus people with incomes well under the average will save up to buy expensive branded bags, jeans, sport shoes and sunglasses, and will go regularly to the gym and their hairdresser. One young adult woman who had just separated from her husband told me that she had a few wardrobes full of branded bags. Her husband used to give them to her as a gift after each major domestic fight. She told me sadly: 'I would have preferred him to love me instead. I did not need those bags. I never really liked them.'[19]

Physical beauty live

So how do people express these ideas on Facebook? Let us take the cases of a teenager, Elisabetta, and a young adult woman, Simona. These women enjoy posting selfies on Facebook, but for quite different reasons. Elisabetta normally uploads a photo of herself every two weeks or so, usually without any additional comment. Most of the times she adopts a serious face and focuses on one feature of her appearance at a time: her dark brown hair, big eyes or a fine accessory. Each photo might receive between 20 and 40 'likes', with the most popular ones receiving more than 100. Most comments praise her beauty, the quality of the photos and, in the case of distant friends, how much they miss her. They are dominated by a series of ingenious emoticons including sets of purple hearts and all kinds of smiley faces.

As with most teenagers in Grano, Elisabetta takes the selfies with her smartphone usually inside her house after preparing herself assiduously. She might wash her hair and comb it for a long time, polish her nails and try out a few pieces of clothing. She always takes a few shots, selects the photos carefully and then edits them online. Many of the photos are close-ups and cropped so that the margins are touched by her shiny hair. People who see these photos agree that Elisabetta looks very attractive, sometimes because of her direct and sincere look, other times because of the nice details of the photo: a single delicate earring or a barely perceptible smile.

However, many of her friends recognise that Elisabetta is actually quite different offline. She is much younger and less serious than she portrays herself on Facebook, and seems to always look relaxed and casual. Elisabetta wants to be seen as an average person who is able to adopt a good-looking and glamorous style when she needs to. This attitude is crucial in her desire to find a *fidanzato* (fiancé). Elisabetta senses it is her duty to look smart and attractive in what seems to be a more permanent environment, just as, she feels, you would not put everyday photos into a photo album. Many of the comments on her Facebook photos recognise her intention to connect personal beauty with purity and virtue. Elisabetta sees beauty as an essential step towards her future life and also as a civic responsibility. She crafts herself on Facebook not in relation to some individual ideal, but in relation to a social one.

In contrast, Simona does not need any public validation of her beauty. She uploads a much more limited range of photographs on Facebook where she might create an aura of mystery for people who do not know her so well. Many people in Grano remember that she was considered a beauty in her teens, but she never profited from this in any particular way. Now, in the context of sporadic employment and strong commitment to her relationship, Simona takes the visibility of Facebook as a sort of game. It is a game because she feels there is no commitment to the online audience: she can be extremely discreet about herself, while she can also show what makes her different. Simona sees her beauty as a sort of tool that connects her to the social life of the town, without saying anything deep about herself: she simply lets people who know her better associate her appearance in every photo with some deeper aspect of her personality. For example, a melancholic air while in her partner's house in *campagna* (a rural area) in summer expresses her profound dissatisfaction with the way people in

Grano spend their summers,[20] or a photo where she stands against an old white façade while smiling directly at the camera signifies a particularly good moment in her relationship and a mood for urban life. Close friends can then see through the beautiful photo to the purity of her soul.

Simona feels that posting interesting photos online is her way to be popular without doing anything spectacular. Not being married yet, she has found this space where she can be creative and pursue her ideals. Her reserved and discreet attitude on the streets of the town, while walking her dog on the same route every day sits alongside her fierce discipline of regularly controlling her privacy settings and the way she appears on Facebook. This represents her particular way of being moral. Simona feels free to enjoy the mystery and the independence of being a young woman, while always thinking of ways to overcome the numerous social norms that surround her.

Still, both Elisabetta and Simona agree that when people like the photographs they upload to Facebook they feel happy. They pay particular attention to the comments their photos receive, as this is how they feel they can really tell if people just like a beautiful photo or whether they appreciate these women in particular as the subjects of the photos. In many comments they receive there are several recurring semantic references to beauty: *bella* ('beautiful'), *quanto sei bella *-** ('how beautiful you are'), *bella sei* ('you are really beautiful'), *bedda!!* ('beautiful' in the local dialect), *bella foto, bella te!* ('beautiful photo, beautiful you'), as well as interjections and emoticons that express the same kind of unreserved admiration, such as *-* and 😍 and variations of these.

All four women presented so far in this chapter have different aims in life, but the ways in which they present themselves offline and online suggest they all see beauty as a civic responsibility and as being in line with the ideas and norms of the society in which they live. Simona, as a highly educated and unmarried woman, sees photography on Facebook as a technique of completing her offline appearance in a creative way: for example, she does not have enough money to style her hair as often as she would like. So, washing her hair, taking intriguing, self-made photos and uploading them to Facebook is a particular way to show her physical beauty and her ability to craft it. This is in contrast with Luana, who lets professionals craft her beauty. In a way, this is the same as the difference between classical photography, when professional photographers used to shape events and capture people according to different collective ideals, and the current situation, where most people own a personal camera and are able to photograph themselves in a manner of their own choosing.

So this points to the Italian concept of style being wide-ranging and not just aesthetic. It is very much related to the idea of craft and artisanal production. Crafting refers to a final product that is aesthetically pleasant and useful. This could be a ceramic piece, a car or a building, but also an agreeable rhetoric style, an exceptional scientific thought or an elegant pose when wearing a fine outfit. These are all equally admired and appreciated, but in each case the technologies, the hard work and the tricks that have led to the final product are not shown. Similarly people never display on Facebook any of the myriad cosmetic products, attempts and techniques they tried, nor do they talk about these online. Instead, we have seen that these aspects are reserved for discussion with a friend in front of the mirror or on WhatsApp. For most people, it is through constant display that personal beauty can be recognised as a craft.

This suggests that, in the same way that many people in Grano put huge amounts of time and effort into their offline appearance, they are now also extremely careful in curating their Facebook page. They do this by selecting and editing the photos they upload, and showing their support for online friends with comments and 'likes'. Their online persona is a public assertion of who they are and of how they want to appear in public. Facebook is thus a core representation of one element that characterises the person. It could point to the social position or the capacity to craft themselves. But how do young women relate the capacity to craft beauty to the higher ideals of society?

Style and mass consumption

The relatively rapid commodification of personal beauty in Italy that happened in the extraordinary years of the 1980s and 1990s has continued in different ways up to the present day, where it notably conquers the youngest sectors of the population. Mass-produced goods reduce the once insurmountable distance between high fashion and popular tastes, and make 'beauty' increasingly accessible. In Grano a pair of D&G sunglasses that used to cost more than €240 in 2012 cost just €160 in 2014. Branded sunglasses for eight-year-olds were the latest trend, and many hairdressers and beauticians confirmed that in recent years between 60 and 80 per cent of their young clients have requested styles and treatments either as seen in media or as proposed by the big fashion houses. One shop owner commented on the convergence of tastes to include those of the young population: *Non sono anziani più. Ci sono solo giovani* ('There are no old people anymore. There are only young people').

In her work on clothing in Madrid, anthropologist Marjorie Murray shows how the inhabitants of this city spend their entire lives trying to embody the ideal of Madrid.[21] This involves paying particular attention to clothing and accessories, but sometimes also to not working too hard and spending a lot of time in collective leisure activities. Murray explains that people embody these practices with a very specific idea of the individual's responsibility to wider society, and in particular how this relates to Madrid having had the responsibility, historically, for representing Spanish values.

The same kind of social obligation to dress well and be neat is found in Grano. The sheer number of expensive shops for such a small town reflects the permanent preoccupation with looking good. Even in their daily chores, people enjoy using new branded shopping bags for carrying food to a close relative or carrying an old side-lamp to the repair workshop. My research suggests that in Grano this concern for public display does not stem from a sense of superiority, but rather from a particular combination of the traditions of egalitarianism in *civiltà contadina* (peasant culture), the ideals represented by aristocratic tastes and the normative behaviour imposed by Catholicism. For example, while new fashions and styles proposed by the big houses in Milan

Fig. 5.1 Annual fashion catalogues discussed by a local hairdresser (photo by the author)

embody fine taste and exclusiveness, most people in Grano adopt these only when many others from the same social and economic background do the same. They know that each individual should not stand out too much, so the easiest way to resolve this is if everybody is stylish.

In this equation, local stylists and clothing retailers are seen, especially by the young population, as essential connections to high style and taste, so it is these professionals who hold the monopoly on beauty. For example, each prestigious retail shop in Grano has at least one brand that is entirely made in Italy, which is seen as the standard for quality. While just a minority of the local population can afford to buy these brands, it is the duty of shop owners to refer to such fine products. By doing this, they transfer the responsibility for buying cheaper and lower quality to their customers, while they preserve the position of being good business people who appreciate quality and support Italian industry. So we can see how these local beauty professionals adapt the ideals proposed by glamorous Milan and beautiful Rome to local specificities and sensibilities. Young girls adopt the newest hairstyles and tattoos of Belén Rodríguez,[22] which denote the current ideal of beauty; young boys buy denims and wear Lacoste T-shirts, as the major football players do; housewives and cooks adopt recipes they see on television; and most young people have clear preferences regarding branded garments and accessories. This has become all the more striking in the years of economic crisis when wages have been quite low while these items remain very expensive.[23]

Fig. 5.2   Selfie taken during hairstyling and uploaded to Instagram

It is therefore the task of a small army of beauty professionals to sort out all these ideals and craft beauty so that the normative behaviour can be respected. As their clients do, they know that beauty and style should be aligned with people's social positions, otherwise the results will be socially sanctioned. Young people can mock you and older people can give you a critical glance for what they consider to be inappropriate. This is reflected in small, everyday gestures, such as when using make-up. In Grano a golden rule is never to wear bright make-up on both the lower and upper parts of the face. On most occasions, lips and eyes should not have pronounced make-up at the same time. Women who contradict this rule are seen as unusual, eccentric and may be suspected of being frivolous. However, strong make-up is accepted in exceptional settings, such as for marriage ceremonies or in the performing arts.[24]

So for most people the true skill lies in the ability to craft themselves. People do not judge other people simply by their exterior aspect, and beauty is in no way limited to the surface of the body. Rather, in the case of adults, it is expressed in relation to issues such as individual work, skills and behaviour, which vary significantly according to social position. Most middle-class women who work exclusively in their own homes are seen as beautiful if they are well-dressed and modest, while those from higher classes can acceptably be overdressed and wear expensive jewels in ordinary day to day life. The individual work women carry out on themselves and their families on an everyday basis, before rushing into the streets of Grano or before taking a photo of themselves and uploading it to Facebook, can only be visible if rigorous standards of beauty and public appearance are respected. All these rules set limits and norms to feminine beauty on which women constantly draw in Grano. Let us seen now how these norms are reflected in social media.

The everyday beauty of married women

If people were asked to point to a typical feminine beauty in Grano, they would probably choose a married women (*donna sposata*). We have seen that married women see their own beauty in strict relation to their duty to have a beautiful family. Women who work exclusively in their own homes (around 40 per cent of women in Grano) place a relatively higher emphasis on the way that they and their families look. A key element of this is the responsibility most mothers feel to make their children look neat and clean when they go out. Married women are also in charge of buying

(a)

(b)

(c)

Fig. 5.3 Photos uploaded to Facebook by married women showing family photos blurred in the background (a), flowers received as a gift (b) and an open personal notebook (c)

most of the cosmetics for the entire house, taking their children to the hairdresser, and doing most of the Christmas shopping. There is a strong sense that people other than their family should see their work and the care they give as wives. For example, the ironing of clothes can only be appreciated if the family members often change their T-shirts: children every two days and the husband every day. This is a basic and common way to demonstrate you are a good woman. It also suggests that married women do not localise beauty in the physical aspect of their person, but rather they disperse it in a myriad other things that surround them, from domestic objects to family accomplishments, and rarely in their own personal hairstyles. It is the duty of these other things to point to the inner beauty of the woman.

Giuliana could be described as a typical housewife. She never leaves the house before she is perfectly dressed and wearing faultless make-up. She likes dressing simply, in dark tones, and usually wears a delicate necklace. Her black hair is impeccably straightened, cut to just above her shoulders and always shining. Her nails are cut straight, of medium length and polished in fashionable nuances of cream, while her clothes always look like new and fit perfectly. Giuliana's husband, who has a good job as a car dealer, is always very presentable and their two boys are clean with neatly combed hair.

However, all these preparations take a lot of time. In Grano domestic tasks have carefully allocated slots throughout the day, during periods of time when people are not socially visible, and this represents a challenge. These times can be mornings for housewives; afternoons, during business trips or when commuting to work for employed people; evenings and nights for teenagers, and so on. Alterations in the daily routine normally have to be sanctioned by the family and, if they become regular, they will be also observed by the rest of the community. The biggest fear for many is that their partners may be having an extra-marital affair and the challenge, if you alter your daily routine, is to prove you are not.

In this context, the constant preoccupation with justifying time becomes a main duty. Women who work exclusively within their household have to invest their time in something that can be recognised as valuable: a clean house, a neat physical aspect for themselves and their families and well-behaved children who do well in school. This is part of a context in which their daily interactions with many categories of people is quite limited: they are not supposed to talk to men on the streets or in bars as this could be seen as a sign of being unfaithful, or to other married women for too long during the mornings because this could be seen as gossiping or laziness. Thus Giuliana spends almost an hour a day grooming herself, Silvia in the previous chapter takes swimming lessons four times a week after taking her children to school, and many married women go to the gym in the evening once their husbands have taken over some of the domestic responsibilities.

The young and older housewives usually have a stable network of peers who support their lifestyles. For example, Giuliana is best friends with three other housewives who live in the same part of the city. They visit each other almost daily; during the summer afternoons they might spend several hours at each of their houses in turn, sitting in the small courtyards in front of the house drinking fresh juice, eating homemade cookies and watching their children playing. In these regular visits Giuliana feels most happy: she is surrounded by people who share a similar lifestyle, friends she can trust and who can really understand the contented relaxation that comes after a full day of work and solitude, and she does not have to be particularly well groomed.[25]

This suggests that ordinary beauty is an archetype and a standard at the same time. It is an archetype because it points to the higher ideals in the community regarding style and morality, and it is a standard because everybody can adopt and recognise it. A married woman who looks 'too good' in an average situation might attract serious questions about her morality. Instead, the standard of taking care of themselves minutely, dressing neatly and, more recently, shaping their bodies assures them of an expected and not very ostentatious kind of beauty. At the same time, women know that people judge and gossip a lot, so by maintaining a good-looking and neat appearance as a norm they can be attractive in a perfectly acceptable way.

What of all this actually goes on social media?

So far we have seen that beauty is not seen as a narcissistic selfish indulgence, but rather as a difficult social burden and obligation. A common expression was to compare Facebook with a *vetrina* ('shop window'), which we have seen can, in Grano, be quite elaborate, or to *mettersi in mostra* ('display oneself'). My research shows that married women are extremely careful when selecting what they will post as they sense a moral duty to represent not only themselves, but also their whole family.[26]

Giuliana has rarely posted a photo of herself on Facebook during the last three years. And this is not the exception, it is the rule. Most married women in Grano hardly ever post photos of themselves online. In most photos uploaded to Facebook they are photographed with their kids or in groups. As Giuliana seems to say: 'I decided many years ago that I am married to Claudio and this is exactly what I am doing now. The fact that Facebook was invented meanwhile should not change this situation.' Her restrained use of Facebook reflects her commitment to her marriage and her defence of this social position: a young housewife posing on Facebook while her husband works and her children are at school would be seen as inappropriate.

Instead, Giuliana enjoys posting on Facebook some of her inner thoughts and the main accomplishments of her daily work. Thoughts and feelings are usually expressed through memes and rarely through a status message. Those thoughts she appreciates most she writes down in the 'Notes' section on Facebook. A photo of a neat school book points to order, predictability and thorough guidance in education; a poem written for Mother's Day reflects her relationship with her sons; and a photo of her friends playing with the kids at her home points to notions of friendship and care. In the relatively few pictures taken at home, Giuliana is careful to ensure that the parts of the house that appear as background to the picture are tidy and in good order. She might move the flower bowl and the white crochet doily on the kitchen table back to their place, or straighten up the new soft carpet in the sitting room before taking the shot. The house is her responsibility and the failure of the house to look right on such public media as Facebook would be seen somewhat as a personal failure. Family photos are rare, but they are posted for key moments, such as birthday parties around a big cake covered in thick cream and red roses, at the Christmas table or during the holidays. It is important that all the four members of the family are present, to denote unity and commitment.

This suggests that Giuliana's Facebook page reflects her interior beauty. Married women tend to craft their Facebook pages in relation to their deeper aspects: housework, family and personal thoughts are not displayed as mere 'products', but as existential values. Married women are relatively restrained on Facebook and more expansive on private-facing social media than other people because they most strongly wish to reflect these values, and not to expand or popularise them. Close friends and family usually support and protect any opening up to a larger public through 'likes' and comments, which create a sense of familiarity on a public medium such as Facebook. This is a useful addition to an anthropological attempt to understand what these values are and how they work.

What about men's beauty?

If married women are only moderately active on Facebook, married men are even less active; some do not use this medium at all. Many feel they do not have anything to show online. Those who perform routine work do not see any reason why they would post about things they actually discuss in conventional ways: with work colleagues, superiors, clients, friends, over a coffee or with acquaintances on the street. Many think there is simply no way to reproduce this diversity on Facebook. How can they compress this variety and mix of sensations into just a few shots or rushed lines? And why would they take the shots in the first place? In the next chapter, we will see how these constraints are related to the traditions of visibility for men's work and their socialisation.

It is even more unusual for young men to emphasise their physical aspect online. There are exceptions, such as a few teenagers and gay men, but usually even these exceptions will accompany a focus on their physical appearance with other issues, such as humour and self-derision. Men's physical beauty is sometimes appreciated and discussed online, but it is usually their female friends who might bring it up and comment on it online. Men prefer to display informality, as they do offline. For example, the old sign of distinction in men was to shave their faces regularly or to grow elegant moustaches, but this can now be replaced with smart unshaven looks. This movement of men towards informality and apparent negligence is the opposite of the feminine move towards added care and elegance, and Facebook is making this clearer.

My research suggests that in Grano *bellezza* (physical beauty) represents an immense burden to the whole society, but especially to women. We have seen that married women attempt to manage this burden mainly by distributing it over a multitude of subjects and practices, which is evident in the way women organise their online space. In contrast, unmarried women can afford to have much greater visibility online.

Many people think that it is social media that has made people more concerned with the normativity of looking good or being witty because they are more visible. But so far we have seen that the opposite is true in Grano: actually, the main drive for this comes from tradition, television and other sources, and the main spaces people do this are in the home and when out in public places. So people need social media in order to show that they are not personally vain. At the same time, by choosing attentively what to display on public-facing social media, people are enabled to legitimise their particular attitudes and concerns. In short, they use social media to show that beauty itself is a social and not an individual issue.

Inner beauty – eloquent speech

Mr Donatello is the mayor of the largest commune near Grano and I came to know him quite well. He is relatively tall, athletic, in his early fifties, partially grey haired and always smiling and benevolent. He usually wears elegant dark suits and unbuttoned light shirts. Mr Donatello is married with three sons and is considered a good-looking man, extremely affable and is always pleasant company to have around. Furthermore he is renowned even among his many political opponents for being a wonderful speaker. Actually many argue that this was the reason he was elected, albeit with a fragile majority, for the third time in a row. He was contested from all parts of the political spectrum, but everybody agreed he was by far the best public speaker of all the candidates. With his calm, tenor voice and natural charm, he could keep any audience absorbed for several hours. As some people argued, when he talks you have the feeling that things will be resolved or at least that they are not as bad as some say. Mr Donatello is particularly popular among younger and older women who find him calming and agreeable.

The obsession with public speaking in the Italian elite dates back not only to the establishment of the public intellectual as the central figure in the life of continental Europe during the Enlightenment, but also to its roots in the ancient art of rhetoric. The Roman philosopher Cicero is credited with having created a language and rhetorical style that became most influential in the establishment of modern Italian law and politics, as well as in Western European public culture.[27] In Grano we can see glimpses of such skills in the tradition of *comizi* (political assemblies); in the hypnotising discourses of politicians; in the interminable introductions to public events and intellectuals' insistence on their work. Public speaking is intrinsically linked to social position and prestige. In this setting, even if the content of public discourses is not particularly convincing, good rhetorical skills can keep an audience really captivated and attract their goodwill.[28]

Mr Donatello and most local intellectuals, journalists and authors do not restrict their intellectual skills to the offline world. On the contrary, they feel obliged to continue charming their audiences online as well. Their oratorical skills are so associated with their persona, they simply cannot be something different in another public sphere. In the same way as entrepreneurs have to advertise their businesses if they want to stand out from the competition, intellectuals have to publicise their ideas. Like most public figures in the region, Mr Donatello has chosen to have a Facebook profile that has very few if any references to his personal life. Most of his posts are about the local administration, decrees and public events in the region. But, despite his popularity on Facebook, he receives only a few 'likes', hardly any comments and almost nobody shares his posts, no matter how interesting they are. People are reluctant to engage with public figures online as this would indicate political support which might clash with innumerable other online contacts. For example, 'liking' or commenting on the post of a right-wing author would automatically turn you into a right-wing admirer even if, offline, things were not that straightforward. In other words, it is exactly the public visibility of Facebook that prevents many people from socialising online with public figures.

As a result most people consider Mr Donatello's online interventions as either inappropriate or plain boring. His Facebook presence is simply a reiteration of public ideas in a space where people expect at least some level of personal detail and engagement with issues that go beyond the local community. The fact that intellectuals in Grano tend to fill their Facebook pages with long comments on political and social events, personal articles or interventions in a way that is supposed to reflect their offline activities makes their online presence rather insignificant when compared to their oral performances. This is perhaps because they do not use other media, such as YouTube, to make up for their lack of ability to express themselves orally on Facebook.

Public figures are particularly concerned with the promptness of their comments and responses online. For example, a timely and witty answer to a hot issue denotes knowledge, interest and a constant preoccupation with the life of the community, nation or humanity at large. Thus they turn Facebook, which as we have seen is mostly local, into a veritable 'Twitter for Grano', where they broadcast but almost nobody responds or comments. Permanent vigilance is part of their job. The art of posting a powerful line, a sly remark or a flamboyantly critical paragraph is an essential part of what defines a public intellectual. These also represent ways to express their inner beauty. But unless they alternate these qualities with personal details, most of their online followers are not really interested in their online presence.

Absolute beauty – landscape

In Chapter 3 we saw that perhaps the most popular genre of photography among adult people on Facebook is that which shows off their local landscape.[29]

Fig. 5.4 Photo of the Adriatic coast taken north of Grano and uploaded to Facebook together with the comment: *Perché spostarsi?* (Why move to another place?)

The photo in Fig. 5.4 was uploaded by Michele, an IT worker in his late thirties, in July 2014. It was one of his most popular photos on Facebook with 20 'likes' and eight comments. One friend commented by uploading a very similar photo, shown on the right-hand side of Fig. 5.5. It is not only that the pictures are very similar: the coast, the calmness of the sea and the time of the day that they were taken, but they also seem to be in an timeless dialogue between nature and viewers. This sensation is created by the lack of any human presence so that the beauty of nature can be admired silently and respectfully, exactly as when the photos were taken. It is in the face of this beauty that the comment that accompanies Michele's photo makes sense. As another friend commented: 'Indeed no reasons to move away! . . . maybe just reasons to fall in love!!!'

In the context of the present discussion, these photos express an absolute kind of beauty. The beauty of the local landscape is something that does not need to seek public affirmation, as most people in Grano see it as a fact and a given. This is also reflected in some popular expressions both in the media and in Grano such as *nostro territorio* (our territory, or our landscape) and *nostro cibo* (our food). They imply an aesthetic excellence, but also a nostalgic sense that the genuine qualities that constitute it are about to be lost or forgotten. The possessive pronoun *nostro* comes from the Latin *nostrum* (ours) and perhaps owes its notoriety to the way in which the Roman Empire used to call the Mediterranean Sea *mare nostrum* (our sea). Along with the obvious possessive implications,

Fig. 5.5 Artisan work representing the beauty of the local territory, including two traditional peasant constructions (photo by the author)

the Romans saw in the idea of *mare nostrum* and the ruling of the Mediterranean shores a vital source of peace and reconciliation for their Empire.[30]

A similar sense of pride and belonging is felt towards an entire array of traditional pieces of architecture, such as *pajare* (stone shelters in agricultural fields), *masserie* (manorial houses) and *pozzi* (underground water basins). In contrast to nature, which supposes greatness and intactness, a built structure is admired when it involves diligent work and embodies some sort of local ideal. For example, *pajare* and *pozzi* embody the genius of peasantry to master the rough environment and *masserie* symbolise aristocratic high taste. Online comments such as: 'How beautiful [about an old house]! Who would build something like this today?' or 'How much work our mothers used to do every day [in the collective agrarian consortium] and also raise so many kids of their own...' could be nostalgic views on tradition, but they also point to the qualities of work that will be discussed in the next chapter. For now, it is important to note that images of nature and the built environment, uploaded to Facebook, represent a permanent kind of auto-discovery of the *bellezza del nostro territorio* (beauty of our territory), in contrast with many 'ugly' modern interventions. For example, some environmental associations focus on removing decaying modern structures from the landscape.

This suggests that the majesty of nature cannot be paralleled by human beings, only imitated through their continuous work on primary sources, such as stones and their own selves. This observation supports our argument that human beauty is considered beauty when it is recognised as a craft. But it also explains how many other elements contribute to this appreciation. For example, houses, food and children represent perfect opportunities to demonstrate your crafting skills – although they are not optional, but rather follow conventional rules. People are expected to be able to create beautiful things that everybody can praise, whether they are builders, chefs, *artigiani* or women. Facebook is thus used as an opportunity to display personal skills, as well as to demonstrate that crafting is a never-ending process that improves itself with time. While the perennial beauty of the local landscape is seen as representing a universal truth that cannot be contested, the beauty of a person is not a given, so the individual must continuously strive to achieve it. It is public-facing social media which make this effort evident in different ways for different categories of people.

The ideal of beauty

This chapter suggests that Facebook is regarded by most people in Grano as a window that opens up a view both towards the exterior appearance or landscape, and the interior of the human mind or domestic family. For both, people follow clear guidelines as to the type and level of beauty and style they are expected to reach. But we have seen that Facebook is regarded by most of the adult population as a burden, that is, one more place you have to think about as a public expression of yourself: what to wear, what to make appropriate and how to behave. Many people use Facebook in order to fulfil a social obligation that otherwise has little personal benefit. This is maybe most evident when we see that, in comparison to women, most men do not really bother uploading much to Facebook. However, whereas in all other research sites in the 'Why We Post' project beautification by young women is done for the benefit of or to attract individual men, this is not the case in Grano. Here women display and develop their beauty mainly in response to a social norm and not necessarily for men.

This suggests that we have to completely re-think beauty in different parts of our society. We have seen that in Grano beauty could represent a social burden that is imposed especially on individual women and relates to the wider values and projects of representing Italy itself as a stylish and beautiful place. While many young unmarried women feel obliged to spend much time and effort making sure they look beautiful in public and on Facebook, most married women are expected to keep to the norms of appropriate beauty by having a strong body and elegant clothes, but also by showing evidence of keeping a clean and tidy house, a neatly clothed family and well-behaved children. We have suggested that this obligation is always in relation to higher ideals, which can come from the local community, tradition or from Italian society generally. Most people sense a civic duty to display conformity with these ideals and social media help them do this more efficiently – by uploading photos on Facebook they show how they actually relate to these ideals. Clothing and style can represent a personal comment on beauty, in the same way that gossip and small talk provide everyday comments on society and politics. The duty to dress well and to be neat, to keep the house clean and tidy or to be eloquent and witty at all times represent objectifications of the local culture.

However, ideals do not come solely from higher levels of society through fashion, television and media, but also from particular individuals in each society. For example, Luana and Mr Donatello are two extraordinary figures who embody particular ideals. Luana has built a name for herself as being good-looking, so now she has a responsibility to the town to take on the private craft of being the most beautiful that she can be, in the same way that a good painter has a public duty to be a recognised painter or a saintly person to become a saint. The ideals of human beauty combine physical characteristics, such as strength and height, with virtues. Luana and her ex-*fidanzato* took their physical characteristics and worked on them in order to achieve an ideal of beauty that was particularly powerful in their society. But this sustained effort would have been worthless in the absence of a permanent representation of other local values. Thus Luana is also considered beautiful because she is a discreet person who lives with her mother, works with her sister in their family business, talks affably with her clients and always dresses herself impeccably, and is neat and clean. Then during her *fidanzamento*, despite her numerous admirers, she was strictly faithful to Gabriele.

In turn, Gabriele is in no way more special than any other young adult of his age, with the exception of his spectacular musculature and somewhat smart clothing. However, as in Luana's case, these relative exaggerations were meant not necessarily to show individuality, but rather to embody particular aesthetic qualities associated with glamour, celebrity and the media. Had Luana and Gabriele not continued to represent popular social ideals, each of them would have been considered to be simply extravagant or frivolous.

We suggest that the nature of an ideal does not require that people really actualise it: for example, if a clean house, neat clothing and well-behaved children are usually markers for women's diligent work and care, most women do not really want to be so perfect and so neat. Instead, what many people in Grano do want is to be associated with such high ideals. They can do this by emphasising their physical aspect, personality, personal values or through their profession. Thus each individual can become a model in the local public sphere, thereby transcending, for example, the models proposed by television and mass media. They do this by showing a capacity to integrate ideals that come from Italian society with local ideals generated by the traditions of family life, peasant sensibility and Catholicism.

Now we have seen that these traditions have imposed the need for particular attention to a set of publicly visible requirements which, among other things, resulted in people with similar social and cultural backgrounds feeling an enormous social pressure to be similar to each other. For example, the only way women can be impeccably dressed and groomed is if all other women in Grano are dressed and groomed in that style – and fashion is particularly good at reconciling the tendencies towards social equalisation with the desire for individual differentiation and change.[31] People try to 'be different together' and this is why they allow a whole array of local and national experts, such as designers, fashionistas and hairdressers, to instruct them in which styles and accessories to adopt. These experts act in a very dynamic consumer market working to give social acceptance to individual desires, which also means not transgressing the norms corresponding to the different levels of the local social hierarchy. It is only those individuals who for different reasons contest this hierarchy who go against the norms for visibility.

This suggests that people in Grano have different indirect ways to express conformity to their respective social positions. For example, married women find out they do not want to upload photos of themselves to Facebook, intellectuals start to bore people with their ideas expressed online, teenagers and different rebellious individuals extend online the limits of their freedom and everybody agrees on the magnificence of their countryside. The presence of high-cost elegant items in a low-income region whose economy is rooted in an artisanal tradition should be seen in the context of people's preoccupation with personal appearance (as expressed by beauticians, hairdressers and retail shops) and public places of socialisation (such as the *piazzas*, cultural events, cafés and restaurants). Facebook could be any of these places at a time: it is a place where you both display and craft yourself.

It is this aspect of Facebook that helps people to breach various limitations in public visibility and to participate in what they recognise as the public sphere. Similar to watching television, most people in Grano do not really want or dream of becoming celebrities, actors, presenters, models or fashion workers. Rather they simply enjoy knowing, watching and engaging with these things. While the massive importance of television in Grano is related to people's desire to learn as much as possible about the society they live in, Facebook allows people actually to engage with these issues in a variety of ways and within one single environment. In their book about the webcam, anthropologists Daniel Miller and Jolynna Sinanan argue that new technologies help people to carry out ideas that existed in their societies, but were more difficult to achieve with previous technologies.[32] People recognise that historically the ideals to which they aspire develop, and in some ways increase, so that each new technology helps them fulfil some earlier aspiration and leads to the development of the next set of goals for the future. Thus new technologies are simply a small but dynamic and visible part of our humanity as a cumulative and on-going project.[33] Following this line of thought, we suggest that the ideals expressed by social media are seen by most people in Grano not as some sort of outcome in themselves, but as guides to an on-going social process that gives people their socially sanctioned aims in life.

Crafting beauty

This chapter shows that the view that Facebook is what drives people to expression of their own good looks is wrong. We can see that in Grano there is a much deeper historical agenda that drives people to an almost feared responsibility to create good looks, whether in their physical appearance or in their life in general. Facebook is used in Grano to reduce this social visibility to a set of elements that reflects peoples' positions in society. Different kinds of beauty are expressed on Facebook in order actually to balance out more normative values with higher ideals in society.

We see that most people do not look for individual differentiation but rather for collective differentiation, that is, finding groups that will collectively adopt new lifestyles and choices. Social media allow people to display multiple versions of individualism, but only when these are within an expression of social conformity. Many people in Grano want to demonstrate that they can look stylish or display proper behaviour, rather than expressions of individual creativity in matters that conform with local conventions. So people use Facebook to do the opposite of what many critiques would expect: they do not highlight social differences, but rather point to social structure and groups. In most Facebook postings it is the social position or role that is being confirmed, whether in subtle ways or in reference to largely shared ideals.

This complements the findings in Chapter 2, which explores social media as a communication between people and argues that public-facing social media represent and express the offline only partially. In contrast, this chapter shows that the maintenance of a public value and normative ideal obliges people to filter out and show essential personal details on Facebook that complement or explain their offline visibility. The fact that some people use Facebook to challenge this visibility, as some teenagers and 'urbanites' do, for example, should be seen as reinforcing this process because their behaviour is consistent with their respective roles in society. In this context, Facebook represents a detailed collection of what this society has agreed should be admired and considers really worthwhile. It is a collection of partial representations of people that, in its totality, constitutes a pretty fair reflection of their larger society.

6
The wider world: ideals of work and ideals of education

So far we have seen that people distinguish very clearly between different forms of social media in relation to what kind of public or group visibility each one brings. But we have also seen that public-facing social media is only used to display a partial representation of people and their relationships. For example, much of what concerns the local community, such as unemployment, poverty or contested gender relationships is not explicitly articulated in public. Unlike some of the other sites of the 'Why We Post' project, especially Trinidad, Brazil and Chile, sensitive issues are always discussed on social media provided they are associated with distant institutions or individuals, typically the corrupt Italian state, the unstable situation in Europe, the unfair world beyond or a notorious tyrant. These are largely accepted issues which belong to the public sphere. At first sight this is puzzling. People do express on an everyday basis, by the way they speak, dress, cook or raise their children, that they belong to Grano and not to other places, or to a certain social category. However, most people do not show these things explicitly in public, being intrinsic parts of themselves and therefore not easily separated or singled out.

This chapter discusses how, by engaging with general and largely accepted issues, people can actually express very clear ideas about what is going on in their own community. We focus on how people articulate on social media their ideas about work and education, two topics identified as critical in Grano and Italian society generally. A third topic, politics, is an inherent part of the discussion. We focus again on Facebook, as these concerns are almost absent from Twitter or Instagram. We suggest that although discourses on work and education are expressed critically on public-facing social media, the way people display their own work and education is much more subtle because these are seen as existential issues that correspond to very precise ideal models.

What kind of work is shown on Facebook?

The first observation is that most people in Grano rarely post anything on Facebook regarding their own work. State employees and bankers might say that the nature of their work means it would be inappropriate to talk publicly about it; lawyers and doctors might refer to professional discretion and a lack of time as impediments to their engaging with this subject on Facebook; and manual workers would not see any reason why they would post about their work or why anybody would be interested in it.[1] On the other hand, Facebook is massively used during work time, especially by those who work in an office or in retail, who often use social media to 'escape' the work environment.

However, there are three professional categories that stand out from the rest in reflecting their work on public-facing social media: local entrepreneurs; people with liberal professions, including artists, artisans and intellectuals and women who work exclusively in their own household. We suggest that this is related to traditions of visibility regarding the products of their work. All these categories have in common a relative autonomy and the belief that their work is an essential part of themselves, so displaying it means that they are showing the values for which they stand.

Local businesses, or why social media turn entrepreneurs into teenagers

Maybe the keenest to exploit social media are local entrepreneurs. They are the most consistent and visible users of social media in their age group. A successful business owner can pay well over €100 a month on their mobile phone subscriptions, have two or three smartphones, send hundreds of text messages a month, talk for a few hours on the phone every day and use the mobile internet heavily. They know they should be always available and prompt on the phone, and be able to reply to text messages well after midnight. Those who have started a new business in a very congested market – such as a fashion outlet, an optician's, a café or a bar – are most active online and invest regularly in their online presence. This is seen as mandatory to create those networks that the established businesses already have.

Perhaps this is why on Facebook many well-established entrepreneurs in Grano do not make a clear distinction between their professional and personal life. It is standard practice for a middle-aged entrepreneur to have a Facebook profile for their business rather than an individual profile or a Facebook business page. In many cases such a profile is also used for more private matters. For example, the owner of a fish shop uploads photos of impressive ships and nautical sports downloaded from the internet, together with promotions for fresh fish and photos of his 12-year-old daughter on the same profile, called Pescheria La Balena (The Whale Fish Shop). This creates a somewhat surreal effect where business is mixed with personal detail, daydreams and private stories. In particular, running a private fish shop means that most days there are a couple of hours when there are no clients. Marcello, the owner of La Balena, does most of the heavy work in the early morning before opening the shop: he unloads the fresh fish delivered by his cousins who are fishermen in Grano Porto, prepares it and displays it in the glass cooler, together with the fish that is left over from the previous day and the frozen fish. In his always cold and damp shop he keeps his large-screen laptop on the edge of the small box where the cash register is, always logged on to his Facebook profile. In most of the idle periods Marcello browses the internet and waits for somebody to chat with on Facebook. Whenever a client enters his shop he rises promptly from his tall rotating chair and takes up a position between the large double-sink and the cooler, greeting and sometimes continuing a previous conversation or anecdote. Marcello works in a professional manner, talking in detail with each client and trying to make them stay longer in his shop and buy as much fish as possible.

Marcello has created a Facebook account specifically for his business and finds it normal to spend time on the internet at work rather than at home, where he prefers to spend time with his family. His work involves a limited set of business partners and clients, and therefore he does not really need social media or mobile phone to stay in contact with them or to advertise his business. For Marcello, Facebook is just a compromise between his need to explore the world and to express that he runs a business. Before being a fishmonger, Marcello worked at sea for 15 years for different Italian and Greek ship-owners. He used to be mainly a sailor, but also occasionally managed the boats. So, he has always been used to working by himself, to the permanent sensation of liberty and of to the limitlessness of the sea. When he decided to retreat to the cold white tiled walls of his fish shop, he found he desperately needed the internet. Marcello's Facebook page is dominated by blue: the deep blue of bright skies and the darker nuances of endless seawater. These are contrasted with the elegant silhouettes of white ships and sail boats, swimming dolphins and large fish. For Marcello, Facebook does not only counter the monotony of his work and fuel his need for vitality and freedom; it is also an active part of his life. It is the repetitiveness of sea photos, the banality of short comments and conversations, and the occasional creeping in of his daughter that make Facebook a crucial part of his existence.

Bigger entrepreneurs use social media in a very similar way. Alessandro owns one of the three most important bars in the modern square. His business is extremely demanding: he not only sells coffee and drinks, but also pastries, panini and mini-pizzas, and has further specialised in producing crêpes and ice cream. He never closes the bar before 22:00 and during the summer he can stay open well after midnight. He is always rushing between the multitude of suppliers, clients, various state institutions and his own family. For example, some of his clients often ask him to prepare their coffees himself using his personal recipe that mixes 60 per cent of Arabica beans with a secret mix of other different types of coffee, at the same time as having to look after his bar, make regular orders for his wife's fabric shop and prepare the weekly musical events that he, together with eight other businesses in the square, sponsors during the summer.

This frenzy of activity is reflected in his expansive use of technology. In summer he pays around €2,000 a month on electricity because of high-consuming equipment: three cooler cabinets, one freezer, an ice-cream machine, a high-performance air-conditioning system, two slot machines and a flat-screen television that plays a music channel most of the day. For himself, Alessandro has two smartphones and a basic feature phone; he runs a personal Facebook profile with more than 1,300 connections and a Facebook page for his bar with some 900 followers. His own profile is much more used than his business page: Alessandro is quite a popular character and feels he does not really need a business page. Also asking people to 'like' it could be quite embarrassing, he feels.

Like many other small entrepreneurs in Grano, Alessandro long ago stopped making a very clear distinction between friends and clients; between friends on Facebook and contacts on his mobile phone; or between friends on Facebook and *veri* (real) friends. His universe is just too abounding to try and do this. So he often sees all the various media he uses as one big single entity. For example, many of his private comments go on Facebook and he picks up news from Facebook in private conversations. Alessandro does not try to adapt his online presence to one single social status of entrepreneur, member of community, husband or parent. He is rather the sum of these parts and most people in Grano know him simply as Alessandro and his place as Café Alberi.

Now Marcello and Alessandro use private media for their personal relationships in different ways. While Marcello, who has more time on his hands, calls his wife and some of his brothers daily, Alessandro prefers to text on WhatsApp as he finds this quicker and more efficient. As such, in a way, their behaviour is closest to that of teenagers: they are driven by their numerous contacts and by their own curiosity to use Facebook intensively, while they do not have a clear daily routine in terms of when they use it. For example, Alessandro alternates periods of intensive Facebook postings with periods of inactivity and uploads to Instagram just a few of his best photos from Facebook. Like teenagers, entrepreneurs use Facebook to tell people much more about themselves than most people do in Grano. The reason is that commercial activities can be seen as opportunistic and mercantile, especially in this period of economic downturn, so small entrepreneurs need some level of personal detail to humanise their Facebook presence.

Liberal work needs online presence

In Chapter 2 we have seen that the use of public-facing social media increases with a person's level of education and cultural capital. While education is rather an individual matter, cultural capital is constantly evaluated publicly and is not necessarily related to education. What is essential in maintaining an important cultural capital is the degree to which one's 'cultural' products can be rendered public. This is probably most evident for artisans and artists.

Valentina has worked in her parents' *bottega* (ceramic workshop) since she was in secondary school. She is 39 now and has two teenage sons. She has always worked hard, initially as an apprentice of her father, an established pottery maker near Grano, then as a regular employee in his family business, along with her mother and her younger sister, and now, more recently, also as a designer. Valentina literally works every day of the week: she starts her work day after ten in the morning and could work up to nine or ten at night. When the workshop has to deliver major orders, especially during the summer, she sometimes does not leave work until after midnight for a few days in a row.

Valentina joined Facebook much later than most of her friends. She had so many things to do every day that she really seemed not have time for Facebook. However, when her responsibilities grew in her father's business, one day in the winter of 2013, Valentina realised that she really should be on Facebook: 'my clients kept asking me for my Facebook account [to stay in contact] and I had to create one.' Initially she used a pseudonym as her profile name and an abstract painting as her profile picture. She started by posting short phrases in which she talked about herself in quite an enigmatic way and sharing more artistic images, such as graffiti works and vaguely surrealistic photos. It was only her very close friends who knew the real identity of this profile and were able to understand the rather coded language she used on Facebook. Gradually she started to reveal her true person: initially by indicating in the second name of her profile the colour of her hair – *nera* (black); then, by adding a series of edited close-up photos of herself showing her hair, one eye with intense make up in black and red, and a semi-profile taken from the back.

This gradual revealing of her true person took more than half a year. The problem Valentina faced was that by continuing this game she could not really fulfil the reason for her Facebook presence in the first place: to keep contact with her customers and, implicitly, represent her workshop. She knew she could neither be like her father, who had used Facebook for years and developed a very specific online presence in which he alternated amusing everyday observations about himself, such as 'This morning I looked in the mirror and could not recognise that face', with photos of products from the workshop. Nor could she be like her mother, who had a Facebook account she rarely used.

It was only in September 2014 that Valentina changed her Facebook profile picture to one where you could clearly recognise her. This was particularly successful and all her close friends 'liked' the photo immediately, which also meant they approved of Valentina's decision to behave as 'normal'. Still, Valentina wanted to be different so, for the rest of the year, she continued to upload half a dozen photos of herself that were edited in strong colours: in one she mocked an old advertisement for Coca-Cola and in another she was portrayed as lost between stars. But she also started to post some details of her work and to upload photos, at the request of many parents, from the several *laboratori* (workshops) she organised for children.

Eventually, Valentina ended up behaving online like most other young artisans in Grano: her Facebook profile was more about her profession than about herself. Other examples include Luigi, who posts exclusively about his stone carving and is considered to have a quite monotonous profile, and Maria, another ceramic artist who also posts short personal stories, created by a series of ingenious photomontages, and attracts constant appreciation. What all these people have in common is a distinct use of Facebook exclusively to serve their work. For artisans, it is of secondary importance to post personal details online, making them appear more professional than entrepreneurs. This is because artisanship is associated with moral qualities, so artisans do not need personal elements to demonstrate who they are. The term *artigianato* is most often applied to good quality manual work, as opposed to industrial or standard work, and describes the best *gelato* (ice-cream) as well as the finest interior housework. So it encompasses a large variety of appreciations. Valentina's timid start with Facebook, followed by the elusive presentation of the self and ultimately the strong focus on her work, is an example of how this awareness is emerging online.

The same tendency to use Facebook mostly to reflect their work can be found in people with other liberal professions such as artists, authors or public intellectuals. They might not be very numerous, but they are active and very visible in the public sphere, and people respect them as opinion leaders. Each of them tends to have several hundred online followers. Their online visibility is related to the traditional visibility of the products of their work. We have seen in the previous chapter that their rapid reaction to public issues on Facebook is seen as denoting expertise, involvement and a preoccupation with the life of the community. Many individuals with liberal professions see these attributes as being central to their work because they see their work as forming an important part of their social responsibility.

Subtle reflection of work on Facebook

In the previous chapter, we have seen how married women see domestic work as an essential part of their beauty. In particular, those who work exclusively within the household feel a supplementary need to display their daily effort, but not in a manner that is too obvious. They are like artisans, with the exception that they do not display the work, but rather the *products* of their work.

For example, Maria Angela has never worked outside the home. She is sure she 'would never work [as an employee] if she could'. She wakes up just before 7.00 and, while her two sons use the bathroom, she quickly spreads a few *biscotti* with marmalade or butter and prepares coffee in her coffee machine for two. Then she rushes to help the children finish getting dressed, sits them at the kitchen table, sometimes gives them a cup of milk directly from the fridge and checks their school bags.

Her husband Antonio works at the Chamber of Agriculture in Lecce, so he drives the children to school. Therefore by 8:25 Maria Angela is already free! She quickly rinses the dishes, cleans up the kitchen table and takes a general look to see if everything is in its place. If it is a Monday, she plugs in the vacuum cleaner and starts to hoover the entire house. She does not vacuum more than two days a week, but on Mondays the house usually looks really messy after the weekend. Maria Angela also fills up a washing machine ready to turn it on later at night when the electricity is cheaper and opens all the windows to air the house. Maria Angela is happiest while putting the house in order and preparing a tasty lunch for her family: 'I look forward to them leaving [the house] so that I can start doing my own things... but then I cannot wait to see them back!' After ten she goes to buy something for lunch from the nearby shops: food and bread from the corner shop and vegetables from the greengrocer. Then she returns home, turns on the television and starts to prepare lunch.

Sometimes she is moved to tears by news of the waves of North African immigrants landing on Italian shores, or so many desperate families having nothing to put on their table, and her mind runs to her children again; she looks at her watch and estimates when she should go and collect them from school, rushing to finish her work. Even if lunch in Grano can be relatively simple, it takes at least an hour to prepare it for a big family, as in most cases it is cooked fresh and leftovers are only ever kept for dinner. However, on Thursdays, Maria Angela usually orders a whole roasted chicken or fresh sausages from the butcher because she spends the entire morning at the flea market; and on Sundays Antonio likes to prepare their lunch himself.

However, all this daily effort is virtually invisible on Facebook. It is in the afternoon, when the boys are doing homework, watching television or playing in their room that Maria Angela has some time for herself and checks her Facebook page. She scrolls down the NewsFeed, shares what she finds nice or impresses her, a meme or a news item, and sometimes comments on her friends' postings. Every few days Maria Angela checks the page of her parish and reads attentively the recent postings or comments. When she finds a small prayer, she recites it quietly. However, she rarely feels the need to upload a photo of her own. Stopping while preparing lunch to take a photo and upload it to Facebook would be nonsensical.[2] Instead she prefers to post photos of her two sons. In the photos, they usually stand still and look straight into the camera, a little upwards. Maria Angela does not like to photograph them when playing or not paying attention to the camera. She usually uploads the photos when sitting together with her children in the afternoon: now her older son is almost 12 and he often helps with posting the pictures on Facebook.

Indeed, most personal photographs on Maria Angela's Facebook profile may look formal, staged and somewhat sombre. She does not see photography as a work-in-progress, but as a finished product that has a very precise meaning: her sons are visiting grandpa or she is on holiday with Antonio. Her domestic work is not explicit but implicit in her Facebook photographs: it is because of this work that her sons are well-behaved, well-dressed, have their hair combed and her family always looks happy. Family members smiling at the camera are a product of this diligent work and care, and nothing can be left open to interpretation: for example, she would never post photos of the two boys fighting even if they do look 'sweet'. This suggests that domestic work is not seen as complete unless the products of this work are recognised and appraised by the community.

This contrasts with artisans and public figures, whose work is seen rather more as a process and a technique, and has been invested with public visibility, authority and recognition from different political and economic forces coming from higher classes and the state. Artisan, intellectual and to some extent entrepreneurial work should be displayed on Facebook repeatedly, in detail, and always stressing any new achievements. It is this permanent endorsing of work and relating it to higher models in society that can demonstrate your work as being valuable. Instead, women's domestic work is much less noticeable on Facebook as they do not need permanent validation of their labour: they need time for the products of their work to grow up, have accomplishments and turn into what they were meant to turn into. This particular craft is not public, but more an intimate and often personal mystery.

The sense of contentment and fulfilment felt by housewives that is evident in Grano, and the absence of any plans to work outside the domestic sphere, clearly distance this case from current debates in feminist theory and economic anthropology on, for example, the formal recognition of housework carried out by women[3] or the gender division of labour in the household economy.[4] In Grano the role of the housewife as domestic worker is regarded as critical to the moral and economic output of the family as a whole. As we see in the Introduction, many married women act as true managers of the household and see their sustained effort to take care of their families as a responsibility that does not need constant public scrutiny. Therefore women, especially those who work exclusively within their household, see Facebook as an opportunity to display the achievements of their work, and not the work itself.

Facebook helps them to demonstrate their particular role in the community, which was previously acknowledged only by a much smaller circle of family and friends and limited to sporadic social occasions. They can use Facebook as an unprecedented opportunity for social visibility.

So far we have seen that the work displayed on Facebook corresponds to a social ideal and expresses skills and constant practice. Let us now look at how this is related to education, the other critical aspect for people in Grano.

The ideal of education and inequality

When asked about the use of social media and new technologies, a school teacher commented promptly: 'What could we teach students? They should teach us instead!' There was a sense among teachers that they were outdated with regard to new technology, and many were strongly reticent about adopting it. For example, many teachers argued that the electronic registers which had recently been introduced had made their work more difficult. Some of the younger teachers took over the task of filling them in for their older colleagues on a regular basis. This created further issues as the online system could be accessed only from central locations in the staff room or from home. The condensed timetable with only a single break of 20 minutes, combined with school finishing just before lunch time, make it difficult to access the online register during class. The problem also is that the online register, being a new technology, conflicts with their daily routine. It means that teachers have to stay on after school or work extra hours at home.

The vice-president of digital learning and inspector for the Lombardia region declared recently: 'Can you imagine a class of 30 students all connected to the internet while the teacher explains Leopardi? In two seconds all will be on Facebook.'[5] She continued to say that the new technologies could be useful if they helped to create a new way to provide an education. In other words, new technologies could be useful if they were part of a revolution in the education system. However, most teachers are not convinced that such a revolution is needed. They have seen very few of the recent promises made by government ministers regarding the implementation of new technology actually being kept: multimedia blackboards (by Fioreoni and Gelmini in 2006 and 2008); a national plan for digitisation (by Profumo in 2013); and most recently €15 million to fund wi-fi coverage (by Carrozza in 2013). So teachers in Grano were really reluctant about the government's recent initiative to implement electronic manuals and tablets: it was not only unclear when and how this would happen or when training would be delivered, but also there were rumours that school personnel would have to support the costs of tablets, with some headmasters making arrangements partially to subsidise these or to arrange bank loans.

This situation shows that the sense of disjunction between education and social media discussed in Chapter 2 is not simply a consequence of antagonistic views on such technology between teachers, and sometimes parents, on the one hand, and students on the other. Rather, in Grano public education seems to be planned without the inclusion of new technology and media. This might be also related to the fact that most initiatives for digitisation were thought about exclusively in terms of urban areas.[6] As a result, while most parents support the use of new mobile technology and social media by their children from a relatively young age (10–12 years old), they also have a sense that these may impede their children's school education.[7] This is related to the belief that a 'good' education is seen as a combination of school and home education and so, as school is seen as being essentially outside technology, many parents try to balance this out with more intensive use of personal technology by their children.

Separate educational paths

However, let us first see how education is structured. The most prestigious secondary education is represented by the *liceo* (theoretical high school). This is seen as ideal among middle and higher classes in Grano as it gives their children the highest chances of entering a university.[8] Things become complicated when parents have to choose between the two main educational paths: *liceo classico* (humanist) or *liceo scientifico* (scientific). *Liceo classico* bears the weight of being the oldest secondary school in Italy and, until 1969, it was the only school that granted access to university.[9] Much of its prestige comes from being specialised in subjects extremely respected in Italian society: history, philosophy, Latin and ancient Greek, which prepare students for distinguished careers in the humanities and jurisprudence. In contrast, *liceo scientifico* focuses on sciences, languages and, since the 1990s, also computer science and information technology.[10] Thus it has built a reputation for preparing students for scientific universities in particular and, implicitly, for good but not necessarily prestigious jobs, such as engineering and IT. It is the *liceo classico* that is considered by many to really 'open the mind and vision' and prepare students for understanding the world.

Further down the ladder are the technical and vocational schools which educate most of the qualified working class in Italy. As the director of the vocational school in Grano put it, 'here is where the students that remain come [after the other secondary schools have filled their places]', including students with behavioural problems and with low educational performance. Nevertheless, with more than 800 students, the vocational school is the biggest secondary school in Grano and the less advantaged people from the whole region see it as the only place where their children can learn a *mestiere* (profession) that hopefully will some day turn into a *lavoro* (job). Thus this school accommodates students from very different social and economic backgrounds and with very different prospects for the future.

The vocational school was also where a policy for regulating mobile phone use within the perimeter of the school was most difficult to reinforce.[11] The main reason was that many students and parents advocated their right to be in touch with each other at any time. One teacher exasperatedly told me the story of a mother who called her son during class to ask him how he wanted his pasta because she remembered that somebody in the family did not eat what she had planned that morning to prepare for lunch. For teachers these are unnecessary intrusions, while for some students and parents this sense of being in permanent contact can be highly important. Most parents who send their children to vocational school know that, in fact, after completing their studies, their children will largely rely on their families and not on the schools to find jobs in the region. So, despite teachers' advice, students do heavily rely on social media for study and many parents encourage this, even if it means breaching major school rules: for example, by exchanging homework via WhatsApp or finding solutions on the internet to virtually any problem.

A similar restriction placed on teachers, concerning their right to be in constant contact with their family, was resented by the younger teachers at the *liceo scientifico*, when the head teacher tried to ban the use of mobile phones by teachers during classes, despite knowing that this ban was in line with a government order set in place in 1998.[12] Some agreed that such a rule makes sense for the students as the receptors of the education, while the teachers felt that they had learned enough by adulthood and had gained an entitlement to use their mobile phones at any time. Like the students in the vocational school, teachers were now claiming the right to be in contact with their families in urgent

(a)

(b)

Fig. 6.1 Box where students are required to leave their mobile phones at the beginning of class (a); files prepared by staff on students using mobile phone cameras during school time (b)

situations. Therefore the conflict seems to be less about opposing sides, and more about everyone wanting to be on the same side, that is to be allowed to use mobile technology at all times, regardless of their social roles as teacher or student. This reflects a deeper clash between divergent views on the role of public education: many teachers are trying to maximise the effectiveness of their teaching and wanting the students' undivided attention during class, while students and their parents see that formal education is simply a part of a whole situation where education at school and at home, as well as traditional forms of solidarity, are all equally important.

In this context, most parents think the multitude of practices and interactions outside the formal education system are essential for their children's future. In particular, they see social media as enhancing their children's chances in life: they improve results at school, give children networking skills and access to information the schools cannot offer and enforce peer networks which might prove essential someday. Social media also link young people up to a sort of 'modernity' to which many aspire. All these ideas are probably expressions of the fact that Grano is a relatively small place and the family is of dominant importance. However, more than half of the Italian population live in places with fewer than 20,000 inhabitants.[13] We have seen that in Grano 'good' parents put a great deal of effort into raising their children and, in the case of the middle classes, this includes complementing school education by practicing sport, mainly football for boys, and Taekwondo and volleyball for everybody, as well as in some cases private tutoring in English, the sciences and different arts such as singing, dancing and drama. Parents see these activities as being just as mandatory as eating bread or watching television news. They are an intrinsic part of education, as a prime commodity that a good family has to offer their children.

The huge gap between home and school education is also reflected by a recent report that showed that 65 per cent of Italian families with at least one child have a computer at home, while on average there are just six computers for every 100 students in Italian schools.[14] In my own household survey, 70 per cent of households had at least one notebook or PC which was used as a family device, rather than as a personal one. These figures show that much of the children's IT education is happening at home rather than at school, and imply that parents from higher social and economic backgrounds can better transmit computing skills to their children. Many people contrast the importance of home education with the efficiency of public education, which online is often presented as the product of a corrupt and inefficient system.

These two memes had been posted on Facebook by two young women: the first had been shared by a mother from a popular satirical Facebook page.[15] It received 32 'likes' and 18 comments, which was double the average response for her postings. The second meme had

(a)

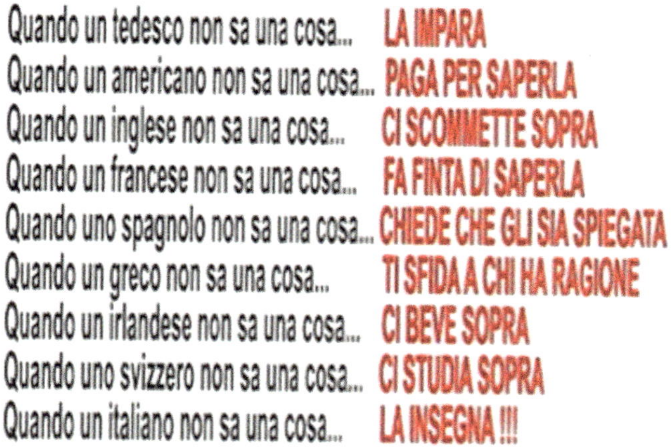

Quando un tedesco non sa una cosa... **LA IMPARA**
Quando un americano non sa una cosa... **PAGA PER SAPERLA**
Quando un inglese non sa una cosa... **CI SCOMMETTE SOPRA**
Quando un francese non sa una cosa... **FA FINTA DI SAPERLA**
Quando uno spagnolo non sa una cosa... **CHIEDE CHE GLI SIA SPIEGATA**
Quando un greco non sa una cosa... **TI SFIDA A CHI HA RAGIONE**
Quando un irlandese non sa una cosa... **CI BEVE SOPRA**
Quando uno svizzero non sa una cosa... **CI STUDIA SOPRA**
Quando un italiano non sa una cosa... **LA INSEGNA !!!**

(b)

Ma perchè ce l'avete tutti con me? Sono solo una delle tante porche che ha fatto carriera in Italia.

(Cit. Peppa Pig)

Fig. 6.2 Memes shared by people in Grano.
The first meme (a) reads: 'When a German doesn't know something…they learn it/ When an American doesn't know something…they pay to learn it/ When an Englishman doesn't know
something…they bet on it/ When a Frenchman doesn't know something…they pretend to know it/ When a Spaniard doesn't know
something…they ask someone to explain it/ When a Greek doesn't
know something…they challenge you on who is right/ When an Irish
man doesn't know something…he drinks on it/ When a Swiss doesn't
know something…he studies it/ When an Italian doesn't know something…he teaches it !!!' The second meme (b) reads: 'But what do you
all have against me? I am just one of the many pigs who made a career
in Italy.'

been shared by a teenager student under the brief comment: 'This time even Peppa is right.'[16] The post received 12 'likes' and was commented on four times. We should note that Peppa Pig has a particular position in Grano: it is hated by many adults, among whom it has the reputation of being irritating and filthy, while it is quite popular among children. Some mothers refer to her as: 'that annoying naughty piglet' because its character clashes with a few fundamental values: a certain order and cleanliness, a certain way to follow and obey your parents, including being less autonomous. Peppa Pig and her brother George are always challenging their parents and escaping their control, which is unacceptable for many parents in Grano.

Now, as we see in Chapter 3, people use social media to reflect in a subtle way on the higher political economy of the state. They can openly criticise political and economic structures or can use a meme to point out different issues they find intolerable in their society. If in politics this is most visible and can be exploited in moments of maximum intensity, such as during electoral campaigns or political crises, public education is perceived as a far more rigid system that many people feel it is useless to engage with. For example, young people in Grano who are qualified as school teachers hesitate to apply for teaching positions because they see the process to obtain a permanent position as being too complex and not very transparent. This means that, on the one hand, people feel trapped by social rules about, for example, which high school they should go to or what profession they should learn. On the other hand, many see the safest escape from this trap of choosing the correct training route is to rely on their existing personal networks and become more connected, including by means of digital and internet technology.

At the same time, a collective value means individuals do not criticise members of the community in public. For example, people never discuss or challenge their children's teachers on Facebook, even if they feel extremely upset by the way they are teaching. Instead people displace all these issues by focusing on matters a considerable distance away from Grano: they might be angry about the high rate of unemployment in Italy, the failure of central government to create employment, injustices in recent work legislation, corruption or preferential practices to obtain employment.[17] It is acceptable to criticise the Italian state and its actions and, sometimes, distant issues are seen as much safer than very specific local ones. What people criticise are not concrete cases, but rather ideals that the Italian state fails to meet.

Social inequality online

Young people from impoverished backgrounds do not in any way allow their relatively difficult economic and social conditions to be displayed online. Their difficult conditions are already reflected in their being enrolled in the least prestigious schools. In contrast to their better-off peers, they have to make extra effort to use the genres and language required in online social spheres. For example, they do not use the local dialect in postings, even if for many this is their current way of speaking to their peers, or when setting a photo of themselves they are careful to eliminate those details that might show they are different, such as a run-down house or poor items of clothing. Many see their presence on Facebook and in different online groups as mandatory if they want to reduce the gap with others of their age. So they use social media in ways that aim at levelling off social differences.

Giorgia is a 16-year-old student who lives with her parents and her five brothers in a modest council house in the centre of Grano. Nobody in her family has a stable job and they depend on weekly help from the church. She is friends on Facebook with both her parents and the three eldest brothers who work on a temporary basis in different parts of Italy, mostly as waiters at seaside resorts. They are most active on Facebook: they post numerous photos with co-workers in different affluent places and try to keep a constant connection with their friends from Grano. Giorgia loves seeing all these beautiful pictures and her brothers

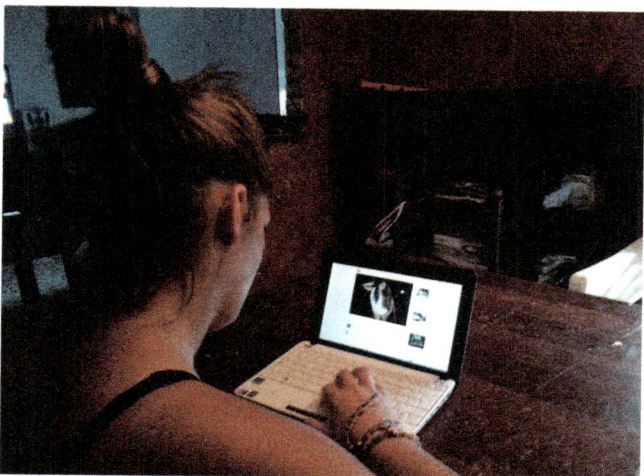

Fig. 6.3 Giorgia sitting at her notebook in *salone* (photo by author)

smiling and being happy. Facebook is the main way she communicates with them as she does not have a smartphone so cannot use WhatsApp. She uses Facebook on the family notebook acquired by her father some two years before for just €80.

Indeed, her father encouraged everybody in the family to join Facebook and friend each other. Then he found the cheapest internet subscription via USB (of €19 a month) and arranged that a friend would pay for it when he does not have enough money. The father argued that this was the only way 'to move on' and preserve the unity of the family. In Grano there are virtually no jobs for his sons, so migrating to work was the only solution available. Still, he thinks they are too young to 'disappear' and be limited to only sporadic telephone contact. And on Facebook you can 'really tell' how they are doing. The mother looks several times a week at the photo of her eldest son and his new fiancée posted on Facebook and she said to me with a big smile of happy anticipation: 'She looks like *una ragazza brava* (a good girl)!'

From the very start of using Facebook, none of Giorgia's family members have ever said anything to suggest online that they are poor; they know that their close friends already know this and there is no reason for bringing it up online in any way. Giorgia uses her older brothers' online stories to cover up any social differences with her peers: 'liking' or commenting on a photo taken by her brothers in an affluent restaurant from an exclusive sea resort on the Adriatic coast represents a way of borrowing something from that wealth. These pictures prove not only that her brothers work and earn a living, but also that she has access to places that only better-off people can usually visit. Like many young people from lower social and economic backgrounds, Giorgia's family use Facebook to reach out to a world that otherwise is not very accessible. Without permanent employment, without higher education and while having to worry about much more than others of their age, Facebook remains one of the few means by which low-income young people can demonstrate they actually are not very different from others. Ironically, a service that does not bring economic advantage to its users is their main weapon in their constant endeavour to escape poverty.

This potential is taken for granted by most teenagers from lower social and economic backgrounds, and makes their parents particularly happy because they see in Facebook a place where their children can relate to current issues in the same way as their better-off peers. This is in startling contrast with what happens in schools and other institutions, which are seen as simply reproducing many of the inequalities already present in society. These parents have no money to send their children to football or dance classes, nor can they help them to do homework, but online these differences seem less important. Many parents recognise that the online environment has brought a sense of fairness to Grano, even if they are not too sure how this can actually lead to employment.

On the other hand, for most parents, social class seems to create daunting barriers even in the online environment. Normally adult people from the lowest classes do not relate very much online with people from higher classes and vice versa. The former use Facebook in much more restrained circles and in more restricted ways than the latter, so their online presence never really takes off. The story of the father of Giorgia should be seen in this perspective: seeing that the possibilities to connect online with his peers were limited, he turned to his family, which is active and interesting online. Here he found content that could appeal to his own peers and thus succeeded in enriching and expanding his presence online.

The relative success of the highly educated

The highly educated young adults who return to Grano represent a distinguished category of Facebook users. Typically, after graduating most of them remained for a few years 'in the north' trying to find jobs suited to their qualifications. Many ended up working for years in different under-qualified part-time positions, such as waiters, shop assistants or day-carers. Those who return to Grano have usually decided to do so when something has gone wrong: either they have broken up with their partners in the big cities or they have to take care of their ailing parents. Sometimes, their partners have dragged them home after deciding that they cannot cope any more with the costs of living, especially after having a baby. They then rediscover the quality and ease of life in their home town, and enjoy spending time with their families and renewing old friendships. However, at the same time, many started desperately to miss the cosmopolitan life they had in Rome, Bologna, Milan, Ireland or England. All these places are seen as centres of civilisation, style and good taste, or as lively, full of opportunities and events. Many left-wing people also miss the moments of student solidarity and 'true' political activism in these places.

Matteo holds a Bachelor of Arts and has never had a stable job. At 36, he is quite an active member of the local organisation of the biggest left-wing party. For some two years Matteo has been regularly writing short commentaries on various social issues, ranging from poverty to discrimination on Facebook. He shares news accompanied by smart remarks that now attract a good number of 'likes' or comments. Since he was watching the television news anyway, reading several newspapers a day and keeping in contact with his former graduate colleagues from Rome, he decided that he should overcome his shyness and post his own thoughts when something important happens, and indeed 'there is always something going on in Italy!'. So because of this practice Matteo has earned a reputation for being an intelligent and witty character with a particular focus on sensitive social issues, and many people enjoy talking to him on the streets and offering him a coffee. He now feels much less oppressed by the smallness of the place, or the sense of solitude and monotony in the daily rhythms of life than he did when he first returned to live in Grano. More importantly the everyday gestures of admiration imply appreciation of his particular social status, which is essential if he wishes to become some sort of public figure someday.

Bianca is another unemployed person: she is 42 years old and holds a Masters degree in Sociology. She had never thought she would need more than her basic Nokia phone to communicate and had joined Facebook only recently, mainly because she needed to be part of a Facebook group created by the small agricultural association to which she belongs. Soon she was asked to manage this group, and started to read more on micro-farming, organic agriculture and traditional agriculture in Grano. Bianca is now well known in her community for taking brave and penetrating positions online, such as when militating against the use of agricultural land for other industries. She has also written several articles in the local press and has established a reputation for being a strong social and environmental activist with a clear mind, someone with whom people and institutions can discuss issues.

In a way Facebook rescued Matteo and Bianca from the perpetual *status quo* in which they were living in Grano: they could not find work to meet their aspirations, they had no capital to start their own businesses and they also had difficulties in terms of setting up families of their own. In the current economic climate, living in Grano is the most viable option for them. Over the last couple of years many highly educated unemployed people have started to use Facebook more intensively. They have not been able to find work because they are so highly educated and society pushes individuals to aim for jobs that are suited to their training and social ambition. Equally, their education and work experience made them reluctant to enter the local system of relationships and recommendations that could assure them safe jobs in the public sector. They found the system disgraceful and appalling, and to give in to it would feel like a real failure. So Facebook helps them to express all these issues at the same time and, although there is no economic benefit, they do gain a very clear social benefit: they are able to try and recuperate the social positions they think they are entitled to without needing to use their parents' networks.

This is probably more obvious in the case of those who come from a commercial tradition within the family: for many, higher education meant that they did not want to continue the family business and moved out into more theoretical fields, such as literature or philosophy. So they lost both the opportunity and the propensity to become business owners. We see in Chapter 4 that this place was then taken up by people from lower classes who had invested in assiduous work and had taken economic risks instead of following the route of gaining a higher education. And just as entrepreneurs are most active online to support their business, many highly educated people also use Facebook to demonstrate their special skills and knowledge.

Highly educated women face an additional problem. As they have missed the boat of *fidanzamento* and marriage – and as many had romantic relationships during their university studies – they find it extremely difficult to find a romantic partner now they are back in Grano. So, in a way, they are victims twice over of their higher education – it first led them to leave the town during the years that were essential for the project of building up a family, and then it proved to be inadequate for the labour market. Talking to them I had a sense that many felt that all the years they had spent up north they had been living in a dream, and now back in Grano they struggled to reconcile parts of that dream with the reality of once again living in a small town. Social media are instrumental in keeping up contact with those belonging to their 'old lives', including giving them access to 'first-hand' information and an expression of their distinctive tastes. Social media help to maintain their higher social status, but it also makes it all the more tantalising.

In this context, highly educated unemployed people were able to build on a reputation they could gain from social media to connect the legacy of their higher education to what is locally considered prestigious. Many use public-facing social media to show their particular skills and sensibilities, and sometimes they find temporary, low-paid jobs – some are regularly asked to organise cultural events and participate in educational workshops and tutorials for children and in tourist activities. Some set up small associations or vocational groups, or start to promote their own individual craftwork. Those with digital skills specialise in designing posters for the hundreds of cultural events that take place each year in the region, promoting these online, and in several cases they manage the online presence of local businesses. Despite being irregular and very underpaid, highly educated unemployed adults find these jobs quite prestigious and suited to them. This is because they contribute to the consolidation of that particular kind of cultural capital which is required by the social position for which they are aiming.

This survival on a minimal income is possible because in most cases their families provide for their basic economic needs. As one woman in her early forties who has never had a stable job commented, if she were not on Facebook she would feel she was completely dependent on her family: physically (she lives in a house owned by her family), educationally (her family supported her university studies for eight years) and economically. Instead Facebook was the easiest way to demonstrate to her family, and indeed to the entire community, that she was not worthless and also to express her autonomy.

This section has shown that the way formal education is set up, it often simply provides a visible way for people to maintain their cultural capital. But public-facing social media have come slightly to challenge this: they help the highly educated to gain or maintain cultural capital, and in general they drive people to show other kinds of values, such as social capital in the case of housewives or business capital in the case of entrepreneurs. This suggests that, while formal education gives people the skills to use the more broadcast-like social media quite well, most people use public-facing social media to show how their work contributes to their respective social positions. The notable exceptions are manual workers, farmers and state employees, who usually do not display their skills on social media no matter how good they are professionally.

Do work and education look in the same direction?

By the time of my field work, mainstream media were saturated by a general agreement that the education system needs to be adapted to the labour market, along with numerous disagreements on how this could actually be done. But let us first take a look at the official statistics: official data shows that the unemployment rate in the south of Italy drops dramatically with age and less dramatically with level of education. For example in 2014, the unemployment rate in the province of Lecce dropped from 62 per cent for people aged between 15 and 24 to 34 per cent for 25–34 year olds and 19 per cent for those over 35 years old. In the same year the total unemployment rate in the region of Puglia dropped from

26 per cent for those with lower or no education to 21 per cent for those with secondary education and 13 per cent for those with graduate or post-graduate studies.[18] So this data show that graduates above 35 years old have the highest chances of finding employment. However, only 12 per cent of young people from Grano go to university.[19]

We have seen that Grano society predisposes individuals from an early age to engage with distinct cultural paths, such as those of the high schools and those of the technical and vocational schools. Each of these trajectories corresponds to a very clear social position, making it extremely difficult for most people to change their course once they have started on the chosen educational path. Generally professional retraining can take several years and does not necessarily lead to permanent employment. This is reflected, for example, in the profound anxiety of the middle classes to put their children in the 'right' school or to engage in as many extra-curricular activities as possible.

In the affluent 1980s and 1990s, when employment in industry and consumption reached their absolute peaks, most people in southern Salento used to believe that formal education might lead to employment. In particular, the vocational schools acted to prepare the working classes who were required by the growing market. But now, with this economic boom ended, only the higher classes have retained the ideal of gaining a formal education as embodied by the theoretical high schools. Difficulties in finding employment after finishing school are shifted further off in time by sending their children to university, and they are compensated by the assurance that their children did attain the best possible schooling. In contrast vocational schools, which basically collect students who do not fit into the more prestigious schools, no longer seem to represent any ideal at all. We suggest that this lack of ideal is reflected in the insistence of students in vocational school on using social media during school hours.

All three head teachers in Grano and many other teachers confirm that the aspirations of parents for their children's future are always higher than the aspirations of the students themselves. In this society status is represented by the lawyer, the doctor, the intellectual and occasionally by the successful entrepreneur, and few families can afford to turn their children into any of these: they would need to support long and costly studies, and often would need to have useful personal connections as well as economic capital. In consequence there is a permanent sense that, despite the effort people make, they are hardly ever able to reach their aspirations. Not even parents who manage to send their children into graduate studies are very sure of what the outcome will be for their children. However, most of these parents simply feel obliged by their own status to follow this route.

In this context, many people in Grano see formal education as both a compulsory duty and a mirage.[20] They see that the education system should be made more flexible and adapted to the work market, but it feels little more than a catchphrase, an illusion offered by Italian politicians in recent years. At least five major reforms in the Italian labour system have been undertaken since 1995, two of them in just the four years before I wrote this book and these, according to left-wing observers, led to work being gradually seen as a product to be bought in a free market.[21] These reforms have included major changes in the pension system (from earnings-related to contributory pension), support for temporary work contracts and atypical work, a downsizing of the costs for redundancy and a restriction of employees' rights. They were intended to increase competiveness in the private sector and to re-ignite the national economy.[22]

Fig. 6.4   Meme shared on Facebook deriding the recent pension reform law known as 'Law Fornero,' after the name of the ex-Labor minister who raised the retirement age and hardened the requirements for retirement. The meme reads: 'Thank you Fornero!'

My research suggests that one reason why formal education is so separate from the labour market is that it overlooks the important local traditions of craftsmanship and apprenticeship. In Salento the traditional way to acquire working skills for adult life was through practice within the family and through apprenticeship. Traditionally people from all social classes would send their children, as young as 10 to 12 years old, to artisans or to help in commerce and agriculture in order for them to learn a profession and to learn the discipline of working. But this practice collapsed in the second part of the last century with the rise of massive industrialisation, mass consumption and fundamental changes in state education. Labour was increasingly pushed outside the family confines by the state and was instead tied to formal education, while the minimum age for compulsory education was raised. This series of reforms crushed in just a few decades not only the strong tradition of artisanship, but also any interest parents had in encouraging their children to learn practical skills outside the formal system.

The tradition of Italian artisan production challenges many of the requirements of a modern state, and public education is not designed to replace the disappearing artisanship. In this chapter we have discussed four social categories – entrepreneurs, people with liberal activities, women who work exclusively in their households and the higher educated unemployed – which each embody different artisanal practices. The people in these categories sense that their work is an essential part of themselves, and therefore should be invested with public visibility. So they use Facebook to show their individual attachment to a social and creative juxtaposition between education and work.

The role of social media

The previous chapter examined the public conformity of social media when we discussed how the entire society of Grano is driven by a specific set of ideals regarding visibility. This chapter shows that the education system and work are also seen as representing ideals, but that they vary significantly throughout the social structure and mark clearer social differentiation online.

We have seen that social media, and Facebook in particular, help people to display skills that are not necessarily labelled as work by society, but are recognised as work by their community, and why this move is critical for certain social groups. This also suggests that social media are part of the ideal of respecting the norms, as this is itself a manifestation of an ideal. People display their work or allude to their education online to the extent to which these correspond to certain traditions of visibility. So, online the intellectual is obligated to use rhetoric and be critical, the entrepreneur is inclined to combine business and personal charisma and networks, and many highly educated unemployed people will attempt to express their specialist skills and knowledge in what they see as the most desirable public space available in the oppressing confines of their town.

People know that in order to find a good job, one should attend a specific school in order to gain high 'culture', one should learn classical languages or the humanity subjects and, in order to have more opportunities in the future, children should learn English. But, in order to find employment in Grano you would normally need to know someone who can offer you a job or you need to have some sort of capital to start a business of your own. All these are not always very visible, and social media in their diversity cannot solve the taut relationships between public appearance and what people sense, think and do. Rather, the online public sphere is where people agree on showing their ideals, which often frame and justify their actions. As a result the Italian state and its institutions are portrayed as representing either the finest values (culture, history, religion, fine taste) or really annoying practices (politics, mafia, corruption). These are the frames in which most people see their lives. So, what people criticise on Facebook are essentially the ideals that education and work fail to represent.

Highly educated unemployed people stand apart because they position themselves slightly outside the requirement for consistency between the offline and online which characterises the social life of Grano. In many cases they are seen as young people who still have to demonstrate who they are, so they are allowed to use public-facing social media in more conspicuous ways. They use this opportunity to express their particular ideas and skills in the absence of a work environment suited to their training and knowledge that would make use of these. Many sense this enhanced visibility represents a true potential to be associated someday with the next local intelligentsia. It will be only in that distant and unsure future that they might recuperate the social confidence and social standing that has been shattered by the inconsistencies in their present society.

We have seen that the most successful areas for highly educated unemployed people are those related to creativity and which imply a strong visual component, such as in design, advertising, curatorship or maintaining social media sites. These resemble a new kind of artisanship, where local knowledge and practices are replaced by knowledge and skills learned in the north of Italy during their studies, and where permanent supervision and constraints from tutors are replaced by a relative freedom and autonomy. The new kind of craftwork is distributed rather than centralised; internationalised, rather than localised; and, in the absence of a skilled instructor, people use social media simply to try out different possibilities. Highly educated people have unmediated access to global flows of information and techniques, genuine knowledge of the local and a sympathetic audience for their work. They combine these not because they were trained to do so, but because they need to demonstrate the value of what they have learned. So these people could perhaps resolve 'the globalisation of locality', the modern paradox artisans in south Europe find themselves in, as a famous anthropologist suggested.[23]

The problem is that this entire new economy is completely ignored by schools. For example, people with relatively lower educational experience have little possibility of specialising online by themselves, because the formal education system prepares them for other types of work. Unlike the higher educated, they do not use public-facing social media to move up the cultural ladder. Instead, they use it to strengthen social relationships and to make differences between themselves and their peers less visible. So, in a way, both categories use Facebook to enhance the possibility of finding employment at some point.

Public-facing social media also make the discrepancy between work and education much more visible than before because more people now have the opportunity to see in one single place how these operate across different domains and in multiple situations. They can compare the work of people coming from humanistic education with those of people from a scientific background; they can contrast the working conditions of an average Italian worker with that of an average German one; or they can all admire different ways to craft things. So most people do not use Facebook, or Twitter and Instagram, to express random ideas or abstract reflections on society, but rather to try and fit themselves into the appropriate local ideal: be that a beautiful young teenager in search of a *fidanzato*, a beautiful housewife, a talented artist or an engaged public intellectual.

This represents a counterbalance to the much celebrated progress and fairness of social media, which in Grano is still subject to the continued power of normativity. It is particularly difficult to contradict, even online, the order and predictability of local social life, especially when it has a strong emphasis on the performative. This suggests that social media resemble the protective safety net built for centuries by people in

Grano into a dense web of informal practices which are based on conventional forms of reciprocity and kinship. Social media give people the assurance that their individual and group drives are in line with local ideals and norms. Education and work represent such crucial ideals which, unlike the ideals of family or beauty, are increasingly difficult to attain, especially because they do not always depend on the individual's capacity to craft themselves up to these ideals.

This suggests that new media have a huge potential, not simply because they allow for better communication and dissemination of ideas, but also because in smaller places they correspond to particular safety nets that are profoundly meaningful to people. Social media constitute the middle ground between personal and public; between traditional and innovative; between the transcendent and the transient; and between acquired skills and skills required by society. This is the place where people can scale their sociality, stress their particular skills and social positions, express their attachment to collective ideals, try out different notions of 'localness' and cultural differentiation and link up to the higher political economy of the state.

7
Conclusion

The central argument of this book is that social media use in Grano is related to the kind of individuals people see themselves as being. However, looking through the lens of anthropology it has become clear that these individual aspirations are only understandable in relation to very clear social and normative ideals in Grano about what individuals are supposed to do. People use conventional and new technologies to craft themselves according to these ideals. Digital technologies and the online environment have become important in emphasising the human capacity to conform to social expectations. We have seen that most people in Grano use Facebook pages, smartphones and WhatsApp not necessarily to invent or be creative for the sake of it, but to support and reflect their respective social positions and relationships. In particular, digital technologies help people solve many of the tensions and inconsistencies between strict social norms, collective ideals and the lives they actually live.

The various chapters of this book examine this process at different social levels. They all point to the dual nature of social relations in Grano: on the one hand, most people aim for their public appearance to be normative and to conform to the higher ideals that exist in their society, such as being the ideal *fidanzata*, the appropriate husband or the proper public figure. This points to the social roles people sense they have. On the other hand, the more intimate and personal relationships do not necessarily reflect these roles. They are governed by looser rules that might be renegotiated for each new situation inside nuclear families or between close friends. It is the permanent juxtaposition of these two ways of expressing social relations that define the actual person. The point of social media use in Grano is to try to explain to the self and to others what this social persona is.

This ethnography suggests that people use social media to craft and carry out ideal behaviours that are otherwise expressed through conventional institutions and practices. In particular, Facebook reflects the nature of people's public sociality. But Grano is a highly socialised place, so the perpetuation of the offline sociality on this platform is seen as nonsensical. Therefore Facebook is neither a reflection of a person's relationships nor of a person in his or her totality, but of one core element of what that person decides to be. However, this element is not random. It represents one personal comment on a series of social ideals which are related to the bigger cosmology. This can be seen in a myriad everyday gestures, in the insistence that the entire family reunites during lunch, dresses impeccably and gives their best formal education to their children, for example, but also in individuals carefully selecting and rejecting Facebook postings, defining degrees of interaction on social media and staying in permanent contact via mobile phone and WhatsApp.

Throughout southern Salento people start from a highly socialised familiarity with each other and, instead of repeating this on Facebook, they use social media to add additional components to this sociality. In consequence, many people do not really use Facebook to relate to their relatives or even their best friends from the town. Spouses rarely post on each other's Facebook Wall, but complement each other in their online postings in the same way that they complement each other offline. They do not need this platform to reflect, reproduce or strengthen their relationship because the whole of society is already doing this. So Facebook acts as a sort of smaller Grano, and posting very private things online would be like running out on to the streets shouting out your most private and personal thoughts.

This view of Facebook and privacy is also the result of most people in Grano trying not to stand out and impress too much. Yet, at the same time, these people are subject to high ideals and models that come from above, and to strict local conventions and practices pressed on them by their peers. The result is an extremely normative society with clear prescriptions for each social layer. So, generally, people have to express their personal relationships on Facebook in subtle ways, such as writing purposely ambiguous status updates or posting personal photos that only some of their online connections can decipher because they have privileged access to particular offline information. Also, by keeping to largely accepted genres, such as moral memes, people do not risk being criticised. Exceptions are usually articulated by individuals who are aiming for either a lower or higher social status than they actually have.

The place where social media does really help people with their personal relationships tends to be within more private and dyadic communication. In Chapter 4, we see how even in the apparent simplicity of these media people can build different layers of intimacy. WhatsApp became very popular in Grano in a relatively short period of time because people realised that this service is extremely versatile in expressing a multitude of intimate relationships: by promptly answering your mother at precise moments of the day, chatting continuously with your fiancée or having passionate discussions with your male friends each weekend about the Italian football championship. WhatsApp can be used in as complex or as delicate a way as the personal relationship requires. The fact that this service is free and easy to use reflects the informal character of these relationships, as opposed to the more elaborate visual content required on public-facing social media.

As a result, it quickly became characteristic for the nuclear family to be the key group using the medium of WhatsApp. In addition to other dyadic media such as phone calls, text messages or Skype, WhatsApp was seen as responding much better to the patterns of family life in Grano, partly because it gives people an opportunity to express in a new way how they think personal relationships should be conducted. Thus, WhatsApp is the epitome of what we call elsewhere the 'consistently on' domain, ushered in by mobile communication to create a constant sense of protection and comfort.[1] It is the well-defended, anxious and frequently tempestuous private-facing media that allow the calmer and more attractively arranged public-facing social media to exist.

In Chapter 5 we move from a concern with this dual nature of relationships in Grano to something that shows more consistency between the offline and the online. The crafting of the online persona is in keeping with a person's ability to craft an offline individual. It was found that, in Grano, the most popular notion of 'beauty' is intrinsically related to an immense burden to comply with a whole range of aesthetic and moral superlatives. Public-facing social media has a very precise role in expressing how individuals understand and embody these issues. People who can achieve glamour offline may find the addition of social media relatively inconsequential. But, generally, they still have to demonstrate this quality on Facebook in a manner that confirms beauty as being a civic duty and not a personal vanity. This is so because many people feel that the integrity of a person resides in the consistency between what they are offline and what they show online. This is one reason why most people use Facebook to focus on just a handful of elements which they consider characterise them and which they can manage well.

The dualism that has developed between the two most popular social media in Grano is also reflected in each of them relating to a separate set of ideals. While Facebook places people in relation to the higher ideals present in their community and Italian society at large, such as personal appearance, righteous behaviour and children's education, WhatsApp connects them with their aspiration for the ideal personal relationships that they want to have. The fact that many mother–child relationships are also significantly expressed on Facebook does not contradict this situation because this relationship relates to the mother's aim to appear to be the embodiment of a good mother. Close friendship between men is less visible online, while friendship and solidarity between women can sometimes be more conspicuous online than offline: an example is when 12 women and no men commented on a friend's video of her new haircut.

Looking upwards to the wider society, Chapter 6 discusses why people see education and work as ideal values bestowed by the higher forces of the state and local tradition. The chapter shows that people sense a duty to embody these values, and for some the best place to do this is on public-facing social media. However, if linking up to such ideals dominates Facebook, failures in the world of work or education are usually discussed by means of a critique of superior forces and institutions rather than by mentioning individuals, local teachers or employers. So, for example, people criticise the Italian state and especially its failure to create jobs. As such, Facebook represents an unprecedented opportunity for most people to reach out (for example, by quoting memes) to higher levels of society while respecting the local norms for public discretion and solidarity.

In particular, here as elsewhere, people with higher cultural capital want to do something that distinguishes them. The way this is done in Grano is through presenting their individual abilities to craft themselves intellectually, economically, artistically and as an artisan. While online most people are reticent about engaging with intellectual ideas (including political ideas), they might be quite enthusiastic about supporting other kinds of creativity. In particular, the online environment has made the work women do within the household more recognised as being a particularly sensitive and significant creativity that reflects their personal qualities. Married women use both people and objects with which they have been conventionally associated, such as their children, husbands, houses and home interiors, in order to craft an online presence that reflects the values they are expected to uphold.

Therefore a key point raised in Chapters 5 and 6 is that a very powerful and consistent consequence of social media has been the expansion of women's presence, especially of married women, into a public sphere that had previously been restricted to men. However, this has been done using more subtle and indirect techniques. For example, although married women are expected to keep up a certain standard of feminine beauty, such as having a strong body, elegant clothing and a particular kind of distinction, this could not be simply broadcast online since it would look like an individual rather than a social aspiration. Therefore married women focus on formulating a Facebook presence that will reflect with subtlety their personal values, which in turn need to subscribe to collective ideals.

This suggests that together with spelling out different ideals that come down from the higher levels of society into locally accepted genres, people also use public-facing social media to demonstrate their particular attachment to collective ideals. This contrasts with the older media such as television and newspapers which were authoritative, top-down and most of the time designed to follow the structure of society. Now, whereas those with 'high culture' can manipulate the larger political and economic ideas that circulate in Italian society, for most people in Grano new media constitute a more personal and enduring collection of what they decide is worthwhile in their society and also a living expression of how they want to be seen by it. By uploading different products of their work, posting beautiful photos of the sea, sharing moral memes and tagging friends after a birthday party, people express these collective values and reflect on their personal sense of worth.

How individualistic is social media?

The previous discussions raise a series of questions: why does social media represent such a normative and uniform environment if it is used by so many different people? Why do all these people become conformist and predictable exactly at the time and in relation to technologies that seem to give them new opportunities to escape from these rules? And where is the place of the individual in this context? This book suggests that the answers reside in the nature of social relations in Grano and in the ideas people have about the society they are living in, which can be understood from the way they use social media.

The last two chapters show that Facebook expresses conformity and social cohesion, but that this is also the key to understanding individualism. Facebook represents a space where many individuals feel obliged to express what kind of public figures, if any, they want to be: some choose to focus on a personal skill, such as being *artigiani*, being a local intellectual or demonstrating that they are highly educated. Only a few, such as a handful of feminists, liberals and social activists, use Facebook really to differentiate themselves from others in Grano. Rather, most people prefer to relate to different issues that are known as being socially acceptable. At the same time, when people join online groups, they usually adhere only partially to the ideas promoted by these groups. This is similar to the over 200 private associations in Grano which people follow to try out different personas until they find the group they really want to adhere to.[2] While for some local intelligentsia the phenomenon of *associazionismo*, the practice of setting up and being part of multiple associations, is an indicator of a lack of unity among people, many people insist that associations represent unique opportunities to express common values and similarity. Thus the numerous Facebook groups, events and business pages represent not only social obligations, but also opportunities for social differentiation. People act online to delineate their particular positions in the local society. This book suggests that the use of Facebook is for expressing a kind of individualism, which is socially determined and conformist.

This means that most individuals do not look for individual differentiation, but for collective differentiation. Social media help people express individuality as part of a collective effort. Local pressure towards conformity means that, whatever they do online, people do not try to be too different or to act in unpredictable ways. So if the average Facebook user worldwide is commonly portrayed as being driven by personal curiosity, a need to be lazy or simple personal vanity, the ethnographic material suggests that for most of the adult population in Grano this is simply not true. We have seen that people can spend much more time preparing and creating what they will post online than actually being online. Their postings also demonstrate an attachment to the collective values they share. All these preoccupations suggest that social media does not bring much liberty and autonomy to most people in Grano, but they rather grant the *possibility* of exercising liberties in different ways, through a subtle intervention online, in more private media, behind the screens or in private chats.

Social media provide the means for people to explore multiple versions of themselves, and to discuss ideas about these with close friends and family. People compare themselves with and relate to others and create communities with which to participate in the public sphere, with the integrity of each person resting in demonstrating online that they are not very different from how they appear offline. In doing this, they all contribute to crafting a particular social visibility that can be represented online.

If we were to name the social media that are most related to an ideology of less conformist individualism, these would be Twitter and Instagram. But, as we have seen, these media are regarded by locals as more complex constructions, quite transient, which few adult people in Grano feel they really need. They are used particularly by those who are less concerned about their relationship with their local society and would rather try to engage with the wider world. Thus a hardware shopkeeper can be in constant contact with French designers and trekkers from South America via Twitter, and a young woman who prefers to share her passion for photography on Instagram rather than Facebook might do so because she seeks objective appreciation and dialogue for her creativity. Both these people and some of their relatively few local followers will be aware that they are using these media in a nonconformist way, unlike those who use Facebook and WhatsApp to express social cohesion, even if in separate social groups.

We suggest that on Facebook and WhatsApp multiple versions of individuality are usually an expression of social conformity. People craft themselves online not in relation to some individual ideal, but in relation to a social one. Thus we have a multitude of groups where people express individuality online, but always in relation to the collective values shared within each particular group. These groups tend to relate to issues such as gender, class, social status and religion. We can have groups of female fiancées, groups of middle-class housewives, groups of working-class men, groups of artisans, and so on. In each case, whether they want to demonstrate they can look stylish or that their work reflects deeper moral values, people do this in conformity with local conventions rather than through expressing individual creativity.

Therefore, while new media is proclaimed to be a highly liberating technology, we see that in Grano it is characterised by conformity and normativity, only making people more similar to each other. The single domain where this is not true is in the domain of information.[3] In Grano social media and digital technology have not made people more distant and individualistic, but have offered them more choices in displaying and expressing core elements of their personalities. These elements have to be 'truthful' to the person and recognisable by the rest of community. So individuals can be creative and rebellious on Twitter and Instagram or atypical on Facebook when this is seen as an integral part of their respective social positions. But even in these cases, people use social media in order to enhance sociality.

How do we know if a revolution is going on?

Key literature describes the adoption of new technology and media as a process in which people become something different from what they were previously.[4] Some see recent modernity determined by a succession of technological revolutions, such as the social network revolution, the internet revolution and the mobile revolution, which might turn people into increasingly individualistic or 'networked individuals'.[5] At the same time mainstream discourses in media and social sciences agree that mass production, globalisation and digital technology have made goods and ideas increasingly accessible and affordable for the global population, and that this has resulted in increased homogenisation and standardisation. In particular, it is said that Facebook and social media at large grant an unprecedented autonomy and freedom to the individual.

In contrast, the rather conservative Italian town shows that essentially people do not think they are something other than they used to be 20 or 40 years ago; nor do they feel they socialise now in a radically different way than before the advent of social media or, for that matter, the internet and mobile phone. And this is true for the most passionate adopters of technology and social media as well as for those who resist it. The ethnographic evidence shows that social relationships in Grano did not change too much with the advent of the various successive media, such as television, computer, mobile phone and internet-based services. Rather, these technologies have always participated in social relations, for example, television acted as a pretext for enhanced discussions, the mobile phone balanced the decrease in physical presence, and now social media have rendered the dual nature of relationships neither more simple nor more sophisticated, but simply more visible.

This implies that most people in Grano allow new genres, such as personal photography, photography of local landscapes and moral memes to express something about them online, and many personal relationships are now inconceivable without constant visual and text materials. This is because in Grano visual images, such as tagged photographs or videos, seem to be judged as revealing deeper truths about people, which leads to a greater caution in the person deciding what to post. This indicates that social media do not transform relationships – people have to define new relationships by their own sense of truth and social visibility. Relationships might occupy different spaces, but the significance and characteristics of relationships remained largely unaltered.

So what social media does is to add nuances to social life and proffer new aspects to focus on. From this point of view, social media is not simply some kind of advance over previously existing technologies, even if it has complementary qualities to these.[6] Rather, as expressed by the concept of 'polymedia',[7] people use the expanded breadth and choice of communication technologies to continue relationships in new forms and in new social spaces. People in Grano use social media to fine-tune differences in the social hierarchy, age and gender: cultural elites prefer text-based intervention and fewer photos and memes; women's online visibility may decrease dramatically with later life stages; and men tend to be more restrained generally on Facebook than women. All these variations show how the concept of 'polymedia' could be analysed on a vertical dimension because people use each media to construct multiple layers of social visibility and intimacy that correspond to the various social relationships they want to express.

In this sense, this book cautions against too readily associating social media with either creativity or egalitarianism, when it could be so easily used predominantly for re-establishing conformity and extending hierarchy. Even the ideal of creativity is contested because it is associated with an elite group and helps to differentiate them from those lower down. By contrast, most people know they cannot compete in that field, and therefore they do not really bother trying. In this context, the multiple *possibilities* brought by social media in Grano have actually consolidated and not challenged the existing social structures.

Cohesion through social differentiation

We have seen that, in Grano, social conformity can mean different things at each level of society. Surprisingly for some, nobody is really interested in contesting online the social hierarchy. Most online postings represent a reflection of how people see society, thus making a subtle comment on the social hierarchy. Then there is a strong sense that society is characterised by a particular order and predictability that should not be contradicted, not even online, and this is expressed in the higher concern over what one should post, how one should behave or what one should 'like', with the constant stress being placed on the performative. As a result, most people engage on social media with people from the same social level and tend to express online the essence of their social visibility. For example, neither manual workers nor state employees upload their work on to Facebook if there is not a tradition of visibility for their work. In contrast, artisans, entrepreneurs and local intellectuals put their online presence at the core of their activity. Thus social media do not rewrite the rules of social visibility.

So, in effect, public-facing social media is used to mark an even clearer distinction between social categories. But we have seen that there are categories of people that have started to use social media to enhance their social visibility, such as the highly educated unemployed with digital skills and teenagers. Still, this varies significantly with age and the need for social differentiation: for example, women tend to post less about themselves on Facebook as they enter married life, whereas those with a higher education, who have returned to Grano because they could not find work commensurate with their education, can at least find their appropriate niche in the local hierarchy by using Facebook to demonstrate their acquired cultural capital. As in other respects, teenagers and many young people stand out as not yet demonstrating any particular cultural trajectory, but the need to network online is more dramatically manifested in the case of those in vocational school. Still, at some point in their early twenties most young people realise they should reduce the high number of their Facebook friends to just a few hundred. This marks the beginning of adult life when they start thinking in terms of the cultural paths with which they have engaged.

This suggests that, even if people now have more and concurrent audiences, the concern with the performative is still normative because most individuals try to present themselves online in the way they think society is expecting them to appear. So we can see social media as representing a frame that both lays out what the public sphere should be and the content of what private relationships and individuals are. It is a frame that standardises public display and sometimes justifies its practices. People use social media to give consistency to their relationships and explain to the outer world who they are as individuals and members of the community.

This means that social media constitute a forum for people to play out different ideas coming from local and national influences, from the traditional and the innovative to the transcendent and the transient, and to agree on what the balance between each of these forces should be. We have seen that social media reflect on the lack of synchronisation between the local and the higher levels of society which many times are seen as unpredictable. It could help people to reconcile the clash between the visibility they need on an everyday basis and the more obscure arenas of higher political and economic levels, or simply to scale their sociality and attach themselves to a particular social group. Social media help people to do all these things at once, and the result is the proliferation of a few online genres that reflect widely accepted ideas, such as the specific attributes of this region in relation to the rest of Italy, the undisputed beauty of the local landscape or social media itself being a place of morality and virtue.

The emphasis on morality is perhaps expressed most clearly in the massive use of internet memes discussed in Chapter 3. They do not simply point to universal values, but also to how individuals position themselves in relation to these. By sharing memes people also demonstrate complex ideas and critiques of higher levels of their society, without necessarily articulating them. For example, people can use memes to complain about higher structures of society that they see as having prevented them from gaining their expected social status, for instance by not delivering employment or a good education. Memes represent a huge stock of moralistic images that allow more people to express these issues much more publicly than they would have been able to otherwise.

The book suggests that what keeps people in order is their sense of morality, and social media is the perfect medium to express this. We have seen that moral life is not necessarily related to Catholicism or other spiritual engagement, but rather it consists in a way of life that reflects the bigger cosmology. It is a tradition in philosophy to argue that moral sense is more related to feeling than to logic, more to the heart than to the mind.[8] This points to a deeper discussion about what kind of feelings people derive from using social media platforms, which will be the subject of a separate work. Nevertheless, the insistence on displaying common values explains why social media do not represent simply a place where people delegate and work out different parts of their sociality. Rather, they choose to craft online that particular core element they sense will better attach them to collective values. So people feel that the safest thing to do is to craft themselves to emulate the ideals they commonly agree on, which can be more concrete and aspirational than reaching for morality.

However, the fact that common ideals bring social cohesion is not only true for the public-facing social media. We have seen that people use WhatsApp to build relationships that are seen as moral and normative. WhatsApp is overwhelmingly dominated by those in marital relationships and corresponds to a more dispersed household, which is a central aspect of society in southern Salento, as well as in many other Mediterranean communities. By the restrictive use of WhatsApp within just a few family groups and close friends, people attempt to restore some of the traditional kinship and familiar relations that used to be based on everyday practice, co-residence and vicinity. These relations declined with the social and economic progress the region experienced in the second half of the twentieth century that included major changes in residence rules and migration to work.

The fact that people choose to display online that which is seen as good, significant or beautiful, whether it is a personal photo, a relationship or a meme suggests that the constant recourse to morality as a source of common agreement makes postings on social media less problematic. This is more important in the online public sphere where people have to relate at the same time to many social categories, but also to the local, the national and the global. The unprecedented visibility requires complex rules and a recourse to local morality can be used to resolve any possible clashes. For example, the more things are local, the more people sense the duty to emphasise the positive and understate the negative. Therefore, alongside seeing affluence, glamour and eccentricity as belonging to distant spheres of society, people also sense that unwanted and unsolicited issues, such as poverty, social inequality and domestic violence, should be pushed out of Grano. At the same time people need constantly to demonstrate that what they post online is consistent with their social persona.

The sort of self-sustained ecology of moralistic memes along with many other socially normative genres, such as the burden of representing beauty, is a long way from writings that suggest that the internet is mainly about technology that drives a sense of individualism in current society. Rather, by fostering popular participation and by creating a conformism around how individualism can be expressed online, social media make sure that even the patterns of social differentiation demonstrate not social disarray and disorder, but unity and cohesion.[9] Whatever people do online, they aim to find ways to fit in at least one definition of normativity.

The conclusion from the evidence presented in this volume is that the primary emphasis on trying to not cause offence or distress, and instead to establish general and conformist codes that prevent major disruptions resulting from this new media, creates online practices that may seem straightforward and banal. But it is this banality that grants most people in Grano the confidence actually to use social media at all. In this context, social media does not work towards change – of society, notions of individuality, connectedness and so on – but rather as a conservative force that tends to strengthen conventional social relations and to reify society as Italians in southern Salento enjoy and recognise it. The requirement to craft an adequate online presence is one expression of this process in which people are obliged to display individual attachment to collective values and ideals. Crafting ideals is the way people look for the most appropriate ways to express the complexity of their own lives, while not really wanting to add any more complexity to them.

Notes

Chapter 1

1 This is a pseudonym to protect the anonymity of participants.
2 For details please see the project website https://www.ucl.ac.uk/why-we-post
3 See, for example, Castells, M. 2000. *The Rise of the Network Society.* Oxford: Blackwell 2nd edn.; and Rainie, L. and Wellman, B. 2012. *Networked: The new Social Operating System.* Cambridge, MA: MIT Press.
4 This cultural diversity also generated numerous stereotypes and prejudices on the social and economic differences between the south and north in Italy. For good critiques of these see, for example, Schneider, J. ed. 1998. *Italy's 'Southern Question:' Orientalism in One Country.* Oxford; New York: Berg; Galasso, G. 2009. *L'altra Europa. Per un'antropologia storica del Mezzogiorno d'Italia.* Naples: Alfredo Guida Editore. 3rd edn.; Daniele, V. and Malanima, P. 2011. *Il divario Nord-Sud in Italia 1861–2011.* Calabria: Rubbettino; and Barbagallo, F. 2013. *La questione italiana. Il Nord e il Sud al 1860 a oggi.* Bari: Laterza. For a wider perspective see, for example, Davis, J. 1977. *People of the Mediterranean. An Essay in Comparative Social Anthropology.* London: Routledge and Kegan Paul; and Ginsborg, F. 1990. *A History of Contemporary Italy: Society and Politics 1943–1988.* London: Penguin.
5 *Commune* is the administrative unit in Italy equivalent to a township or municipality in England and groups together several *frazioni* which are considered not to be large enough to be autonomous. In this book the name Grano will be used to name both the town itself and the *commune*, but the distinction will be specified when needed.
6 The map of Italy was modified under creative commons licence from https://commons.wikimedia.org/wiki/Maps_of_Italy by Bogdan Maran. The overview of Grano was photographed by the author.
7 They brought from the north of the province new materials and techniques such as the currently popular *pietra leccese* ('Lecce-style stone') used in construction.
8 There are more than 10,000 cars and 1,400 motorcycles registered in Grano alone.
9 This should not be confused with the oversimplified contrast between the so-called 'high culture' and 'popular culture' proposed by some authors. For a good critique of these issues see Galasso, G. 2009. *L'altra Europa. Per un'antropologia storica del Mezzogiorno d'Italia.* Naples: Alfredo Guida Editore. 3rd edn.
10 My household survey indicates that the rest are mainly agnostics or atheists, while the biggest religious group other than the Catholics was the Jehovah's Witnesses with a community that numbered fewer than 80 people.
11 Saturday is considered a working day.
12 The region was part of the Kingdom of Naples, which was predominantly ruled by Spanish kings from the Middle Ages to 1860.
13 The town obtained the title of 'principality' from the king of Spain in the seventeenth century. This was possible due to major changes in the structure of the nobility at that time; in this case the establishment of the 'nobility of the robe' (*nobilità del denaro*), who could buy feudal land and titles, as opposed to the 'nobility of the sword' (*nobilità di spade*) who owed their status mainly to military service for their prince. See Carducci, L. 2006. *Storia del Salento Vol. 2.* Galatina: Mario Congedo Editore. 115.
14 Such powers included, for example, guarding the strategic coast of the Adriatic Sea.

15 It was Joseph Bonaparte, brother of Napoleon I, who ruled for a short period of time as the King of the Two Sicilies, who abolished feudalism.

16 With the fall of Napoleon in 1815 the region was again ruled by the Bourbon family who restored the Italian princes (*principi*).

17 These were *mezzadri, coloni* and *braccianti. Braccianti* were the largest and most deprived group who were used as a basic labour force. *Coloni* were the lowest category of peasants who benefited from secured land on which to work. They possessed neither animals nor tools, and received 38 per cent from the products of their work. *Mezzadri* lived on the land that they worked and were half-owners of the animals and tools they used to work the land. They did not pay rent, but divided the costs and the products of their work with the owners of the land.

18 See, for example, the report of historian Ettore Ciccotti on the province of Lecce from February 1901 quoted in Zacchino, V. 2007. *Salento Migrante. Appunti per la storia dell'emigrazione Salentina (1861–1971)*. Rome: Edizioni Centro Studi Emigrazione. 25.

19 See, for example, Rossi-Doria, M. 1956 [1948]. *Riforma agraria e azione meridionalista.* Bologna: Edizioni Agricole; Rossi-Doria, M. 1982. *Scritti sul Mezzogiorno.* Turin: Einaudi; Barbagallo, F. 1980. *Mezzogiorno e questione meridionale (1860–1980).* Naples: Guida; Agus, M and Castellina, L. 2014. *Guardati dalla mia fame.* Rome: Nottetempo; or Zacchino, V. 2007. *Salento Migrante. Appunti per la storia dell'emigrazione Salentina (1861–1971).* Rome: Edizioni Centro Studi Emigrazione. The masses of unemployed people had to fight not only with landowners, but also with most of the state apparatus, represented by judges, prefects, police and military forces who, in many places, continued to support landowners and aristocracy well after the Second World War.

20 This is related to the transformation of agriculture, but mainly to cheap labour, which was increasingly provided by immigrants (for example Pugliese, E. 1984. B*raccianti agricoli in Italia: Tra mercato del lavoro e assistenza.* Milan: Franco Angeli; or Alò, P. 2010. *Il caporalato nella tarda modernità.* Bari: Wip Edizioni).

21 Romero, F. 2002. 'L'emigrazione operaia in Europa (1948–1973).' Bevilacqua, P., De Clementi, A. and Franzina, E., eds. *Storia dell'Emigrazione Italiana. Partenze.* 397–414. Rome: Donzelli Editore. 407–8. Romero shows that this was part of the significant migration of people from across the Mediterranean area to Central Europe that took place between 1950 and 1970 (398).

22 Zacchino, V. 2007. *Salento Migrante. Appunti per la storia dell'emigrazione Salentina (1861–1971).* Rome: Edizioni Centro Studi Emigrazione. 69.

23 As suggestively encompassed by the term *campanilismo* (coming from the term *campanile* meaning 'church bell'); see the use of the term in relation to Italian migrants in Australia in Baldassar, L. 2001. *Visits Home. Migration Experiences between Italy and Australia.* Melbourne: Melbourne University Press; or for Italian migrants in the USA in Bugiardini, S. 2002. 'L'associazionismo negli USA.' Bevilacqua, P., De Clementi, A. and Franzina, E., eds. *Storia dell'Emigrazione Italiana. Arrivi,* Rome: Donzelli Editore. 551–78.

24 In the newly emerging post-war society, the constant pendulum between on the one hand the social obligation to work and the need for money, and on the other hand family life was critical. See, for example, the description of 'territorial dualism' in Pugliese, E. 2006. *L'Italia tra migrazioni internazionali e migrazioni interne.* Bologna: Il Mulino.

25 As well as other major companies in the Toscana-Veneto region.

26 In many regions of southern Salento the tradition of processing and conserving leather goes back hundreds of years.

27 Namely, by Antonio Gramsci and Ernesto Di Martino, as suggested in Di Nola, A. 1998. 'How Critical Was De Martino's "Critical Ethnocentrism" in Southern Italy?' Schneider, J. ed. *Italy's 'Southern Question:' Orientalism in One Country.* Oxford; New York: Berg. 157–75). See also the discussion on how starting with the second part of the twentieth century in Puglia 'modernity' meant strong discontinuity from the past in Galt, Anthony. 1991. *Far from the Church Bells: Settlement and Society in an Apulian Town.* Cambridge: Cambridge University Press.

28 There have been many times when informal labour ('*lavoro nero*') and irregular work (*lavoro irregolare*) have been closely related: they could overlap or complement each other. However, in 2013 and 2014 unemployment in the province of Lecce was consistently a few percentage points higher than in the other provinces in Puglia for all age groups, which was in line with the rest of the south of Italy, that is, around 8 per cent higher than the national average.

29 Approximately £1,000.

30 There was no official data on poverty in Grano, but the general sense was that a few hundred people lived in what could be called 'absolute poverty'. The three local parishes distributed some 200 free parcels of food and clothes and a weekly free meal was offered by the Church for eight months of the year.

31 They are defined as *azienda agricola* – agricultural production units with more than 50 acres of land. Puglia has the second largest number of businesses active in the primary sector (*settore primario*) (this includes agriculture, fishing, woods, pasture land, but also some small production businesses such as homemade cheese and fish processing) among the Italian regions. The 86,000 businesses contribute 22.3 per cent to the local economy, which is almost 9 per cent more than for the rest of Italy (IPRES 2013: 162).

32 The estimates from the Department of Agriculture are that cereals are cultivated only on a little more than one-third of the agricultural land allocated to this kind of farming.

33 Another 13 units rear 160 cattle and 150 sheep, but declare an annual revenue of less than €7,500.

34 Artisanship has a distinctive role in the economy of Italy, with 24.7 artisanship units per 1,000 inhabitants delivering 12.5 per cent of the national GDP (Secondo Rapporto Nazionale sull'Artigianato 2006: 10–16).

35 For a critical discussion on the role of the nuclear family in southern Italy see for example Douglass, W. 1980. 'The South Italian Family: A Critique.' *Journal of Family History.* 5 (4): 338–57.; Barbagli, M. 1991. 'Marriage and the Family in Italy in the early Nineteenth Century,' Davis, J. and Ginsborg, P., eds. *Society and Politics in the Age of the Risorgimento. Essays in Honour of Denis Mack Smith.* Cambridge: Cambridge University Press. 92–127.; Gribaudi, G. 1993. 'Familismo e famiglia a Napoli e a Mezzogiorno.' Meridiane, Vol. 17: 13–42; Kertzer and Saller, eds. 1991. *The Family in Italy from Antiquity to the Present.* New Haven; London: Yale University Press, Viazzo, P. 2003. 'What's so special about the Mediterranean? Thirty years of research on household and family in Italy.' *Continuity and Change,* 18 (1): 111–37.; Fazio, I. 2004. 'The Family, Honour, and Gender in Sicily: Models and New Research.' *Modern Italy.* 9(2): 263–80, and Curtis, D. 2015. 'An Agro-Town Bias? Re-examining the Micro-Demographic Model for Southern Italy in the Eighteenth Century.' *Journal of Social History.* 1–29.

36 For a classic account of the role of women in a traditional Mediterranean context see, for example, Cole, S. 1991. *Women of the Praia: Work and Lives in a Portuguese Coastal Community.* Princeton (NJ): Princeton University Press. For discussions on the changes in the role of women within the family see, for example, Cutrufelli, M. R. 1975. *Disoccupata con onore: lavoro e condizione della dona.* Milano: Gabriele Mazzotta; and Rogers, S. C. 1975. 'Female Forms of Power and the Myth of Male Dominance: A Model of Female/Male Interaction in Peasant Society.' In *American Ethnologist* 2(4): 727–56.

37 Dirty laundry is washed inside the family' (Italian saying).

38 This is also reflected by the fact that family relations are omnipresent in Italian fiction and media (for example Vereni, P. 2008. *Identità catodiche. Rappresentazioni mediatiche di appartenenze collettive.* Roma: Meltemi Editore. 139).

39 The cheapest monthly subscription broadcasts 34 channels, which include the national channels (RAI), the main private networks owned by Mediaset and the channel LA7.

40 One argument was that even the national television network (RAI) was severely influenced by the media mogul Berlusconi who had appointed directors to this institution during his time as prime minister.

41 There is a tax on this type of advertising payable to the local council, but few people other than those who advertise on a regular basis pay this tax.

42 Similarly 60 per cent of respondents said they never 'liked' a national business and 80 per cent never 'liked' an international one. This perhaps reflects the majority view of the Italian business sector in 2015, which saw online promotion of brands as either difficult or unsatisfactory (E-commerce in Italia 2015: 19).

43 Local businesses could order online for their clients, but many saw this as annoying and time consuming. The volume of e-commerce in Italia for 2014 was €24 bn., which is one-tenth of the similar volume for the UK. However, this meant 8 per cent annual growth in a stagnating economy (E-commerce in Italia 2015: 11–12).

44 Many people from Grano described people from the region of Naples as being less restrained and less concerned with their appearance on Facebook.

45 Most respondents were aged 17 to 19 years old.
46 See https://www.futurelearn.com/courses/anthropology-social-media, accessed 26 July 2016.
47 This editorial effervescence is by no means unique; in any similarly sized town in the area you can find the same diversity.

Chapter 2

1   Religious instruction that explains the Catholic religion to believers.
2   Ask.fm (http://ask.fm/) is a social medium where users can post anonymous answers publicly. The site has been heavily criticised across Italy for facilitating bullying and paedophilia.
3   In my questionnaire on social media, 82 per cent of respondents declared that children should start using social media after reaching the age of 14.
4   For a discussion on the major differences between how teenagers from lower and higher classes in the north of Italy use Facebook, see Micheli, M. 2013. 'Facebook, adolescenti e differenze di classe.' *Mediascapes Journal*, 2: 91–105.
5   See the theories of Jean Piaget (for example Piaget, J. 1964. *The Early Growth of Logic in the Child: Classification and Seriation*. London: Routledge and Kegan Paul; and Piaget, J. 1973 [1929]. *The Child's Conception of the World*. London: Paladin).
6   There is a long list of reasons for this anxiety, including issues relating to paedophilia, inappropriate content and distraction from study.
7   See, for example, Aroldi, P. 2012. 'EU Parents Online. L'importanza del contesto familiare.' Mascheroni, G. ed. *I ragazzi e la rete. La ricerca EU Kids Online e il caso Italiano*. Brescia: La Scuola. 261–88.; and Clark, L. S. 2009. 'Digital Media and the Generation Gap.' *Information, Communication & Society* 12(3): 388–407.
8   Courses such as the European Computer Driving Licence (EDSL) courses. These represented supplementary sources of income for educational institutions.
9   Forty-six per cent of respondents said more than 70 per cent of their social media contacts were from their home town.
10 Eighty-three per cent of Twitter users, 71 per cent of Instagram users and 50 per cent of LinkedIn users access these services at least once a week, and 67 per cent of Google+ users accessed the service at least twice a week.
11 The relation between the use of the internet or social media and social capital has been extensively described in the literature (for example Wellman, B., Quan Haase, A., Witte, J. and Hampton, K. 2001. 'Does the Internet Increase, Decrease, or Supplement Social Capital? Social Networks, Participation, and Community Commitment.' *American Behavioral Scientist* 45: 436–55; Ellison, N., Steinfeld, C. and Lampe, C. 2007. 'The Benefits of Facebook "Friends": Social Capital and College Students' use of Online Social Network Sites,' Journal of Computer-Mediated Communication 12(4): 1143–68; and Gil de Zúñiga, J., Jung, N. and Valenzuela, S. 2012. 'Social Media Use for News and Individuals' Social Capital, Civic Engagement and Political Participation.' *Journal of Computer-Mediated Communication* 17: 319–36.
12 For a discussion of cultural capital, see Bourdieu, P. 1986. 'The Forms of Capital.' Richardson, J. ed. *Handbook of Theory and Research for the Sociology of Education*. New York: Greenwood. 241–58; or Bourdieu, P. 1996. *The State Nobility: Elite Schools in the Field of Power*. Cambridge: Polity Press.
13 In Goffman, E. 1990. *The Presentation of Self in Everyday Life*. London: Penguin.
14 Madianou, M. and Miller, D. 2012. *Migration and New Media: Transnational Families and Polymedia*. London and New York: Routledge.
15 Some couples might decide to re-join Facebook after several years, but with increased attention to managing their online presence.
16 See also Marylin Strathern's suggestion in Strathern, M. 1992. 'Foreword: The Mirror of Technology.' Silverstone, R. and Hirsch, E. eds. *Consuming Technologies: Media and Information in Domestic Spaces*. London and New York: Routledge. vi–xiii.
17 This could be related to the emergence of a new image of the South in the Italian media that started in early 2000. The aim is to move away from the stereotypical association with

criminality towards articulating the complex social and cultural traits of this region (for example Vereni, P. 2008. *Identità catodiche. Rappresentazioni mediatiche di appartenenze collettive*. Rome: Meltemi Editore. 136).

18　See also how anthropologist Daniel Miller suggested that, in Trinidad, Facebook can be seen as an omnipresent entity that supervises its users so that most Trinidadians are subjected to constant moral questioning and evaluation: Miller, Daniel. 2011. *Tales from Facebook*. Cambridge: Polity Press.

Chapter 3

1　Facebook page: https://www.facebook.com/Caffeinafestival and web page: http://www.caffeinamagazine.it, accessed 19 November 2015.

2　Facebook page: https://www.facebook.com/fanpage.it and web page: http://www.fanpage.it, accessed 19 November 2015.

3　Facebook page: https://travel.fanpage.it and web page: http://travel.fanpage.it, accessed 19 November 2015.

4　Facebook page: https://www.facebook.com/pages/Il-Pellegrino-di-Padre-Pio/31748533 1676880 and web page: http://www.pellegrinodipadrepio.it, accessed 19 November 2015.

5　Facebook page: https://www.facebook.com/DirettaNews and web page: http://www.direttanews.it, accessed 19 November 2015.

6　Shared from the Facebook page *Unimondo face2Facebook*, https://www.facebook.com/Unimondo.org/, accessed 19 November 2015. Non-Governmental Organization with more than 157,000 'Likes' in December 2015.

7　Shared from *La Stampa*, 14 December 2014.

8　Similar articles can be found in the national press, for example *La Stampa*, from 23 Decembre 2013 (http://www.lastampa.it/2013/12/23/societa/viaggi/notizie/la-puglia-la-pi-bella-del-mondo-XYC39UEBdhXKBC2avGXPLL/pagina.html), accessed 19 November 2015.

9　The applications could be found at http://www.pizap.com and http://ipiccy.com

10　Bourdieu, P. 1984. *Distinction: A Social Critique of the Judgement of Taste*. London: Routledge & Kegan Paul.

11　With important differences in gender, for example women prepare most of the food in the domestic spaces, while men specialise in cooking in public spaces (chefs, *pizzaiolo*).

12　For a comprehensive study that places these values at the core of the Slow Food movement, and its political implications, see Sassatelli, R. and Davolio, F. 2010. 'Consumption, Pleasure, and Politics: Slow Flood and the Politico-Aesthetic Problematization of Food.' In *Journal of Consumer Culture*. 10: 202–32.

13　Shared from the site: www.knitjapan.co.uk/features/c_zone/horiuchi/work.htm, accessed 19 November 2015.

14　See the official site of the Milan Expo at: http://www.expo2015.org, and for a brief description of how 'the immigrants crisis' was reflected in the local social media see http://blogs.ucl.ac.uk/global-social-media/2015/05/18/the-immigrants-crisis-and-the-limits-of-facebook/, accessed 19 November 2015.

15　In the general elections of 2013 they obtained the second largest number of votes for a single party in Italy.

16　See for example Papacharissi, Z. 2010. *A Private Sphere: Democracy in a Digital Age*. Cambridge: Polity Press. 153. In an Italian context see Sorice, M. 2014. *I media e la democrazia*. Roma: Carocci Editore; or De Blasio, E. 2014. *La democrazia digitale. Una piccola introduzione*. Roma: LUISS University Press.

Chapter 4

1　For example, Balbo, L. 1976. *Stato di famiglia. Bisogni, privato, collettivo*. Milano: ETAS; Brettell, C. 1991. 'Property, Kinship and Gender: A Mediterranean Perspective.' Kertzer, D. I. and Saller, R. P. eds. *The Family in Italy from Antiquity to the Present*. New Haven (CT): Yale University Press. 340–54.; Goddard, V. 1996. *Gender, Family, and Work in Naples*. Oxford: Berg; Meloni, B. ed. 1997. *Famiglia Meridionale senza familismo. Strategie*

economiche, reti di relazione e parentela. Roma: Donzelli Editore.; Fazio, I. 2004. 'The Family, Honour, and Gender in Sicily: Models and New Research'. *Modern Italy*. 9(2): 263–80; Barile, G. and L. Zanuso. 1980. *Lavoro femminile e condizione familiare*. Milano: Angeli.
2   His café is one of the few public places in Grano that does not close at lunchtime.
3   As some people in Grano observed, it is a trend especially among teenagers from lower economic and social backgrounds to form engagements at a very early age, corresponding less with their parents and more with their grandparents. This could represent a response to the relatively higher instability these teenagers see in their families.
4   Actually it was the regional train that goes to Lecce, where they changed to a national train to Milano, and then to an international one to Geneva.
5   As the Swiss system of pensions allows for the full pension equivalent for work on Swiss territory to be transferred overseas, many Italian men prefer to retire to their home towns where they can benefit from free housing, lower living expenses, the company of their family and relatively high pensions.
6   Anthropologists Daniel Miller and Jolynna Sinanan found that in Trinidad, too, some people are less inclined to use Skype for very intimate relationships. The authors suggest this is mainly because the webcam can contravene the rules of moderate visibility and adequate silence that constitute intimacy, and which in private spaces are taken for granted (in Miller, D. and Sinanan, J. 2014. *Webcam*. Cambridge: Polity Press, 60).
7   See also the role of radio sound in British homes (Tacchi, J. 1997. 'Radio Texture: Between Self and Others.' In Miller, D., ed. *Material Cultures: Why Some Things Matter*. Chicago: University Chicago Press. 25–45); or that of multiple media for a Philipino migrant in North Italy (Bonini, T. 2011. 'The Media as "Home-making" Tools: Life Story of a Filipino Migrant in Milan'. *Media, Culture & Society* 33(6): 869–83).
8   The information from *carabinieri* did not come as a denouncement, but rather as an informal suggestion.
9   See a detailed discussion of this concept in Wessendorf, S. 2013. *Second-generation Transnationalism and Roots Migration: Cross-border Lives*. Farnham: Ashgate.
10 Rita estimated the cost of Taekwondo lessons to be €80 a month, to which up to €100 could be added on a regular basis for equipment, passing from one clan level to another and participating in competitions that were held outside the town and were exhausting for the entire family.

Chapter 5

1   She corrected her nose and underwent laser surgery to her eyes to correct her sight.
2   Sassatelli, R. 2010. *Fitness Culture: Gyms and the Commercialisation of Discipline and Fun*. Basingstoke: Palgrave Macmillan.
3   Around €80–120 for the hairdresser, €40–80 for the beautician, €70 for the gym, €120 for petrol to go to classes in Lecce. In addition to this, she estimates another €40 on cosmetics and €80 on dietary products.
4   The importance of appearance for Italians, including in the most difficult economic conditions, was noted by scholars. See in particular the studies on the concept of *bella figura* ('good' or 'beautiful appearance') in Nardini, G. 1999. *Che Bella Figura! The Power of Performance in an Italian Ladies Club in Chicago*. Albany: State University of New York Press.; Pipyros, S. 2014. 'Cutting *Bella Figura*: Irony, Crisis, and Secondhand Clothes in South Italy.' *American Ethnologist*, 41(3): 532–46.
5   The famous *Cinecittà* studios in Rome and the numerous international productions made there during this period led to Rome being called the 'Hollywood of the Tiber'.
6   Pancino, C. 2003. 'Soffrire per ben comparire. Corpo e bellezza, natura e cura.' *Storia d'Italia. La Moda. Annali 19*. Turin: Giulio Einaudi editore. 5–42.
7   For an excellent account of the influence of television in Italian society throughout the second half of the twentieth century, with a particular focus on the role of female television stars, see Brancati, D. 2011. *Occhi di maschio. Le donne e la televisione in Italia. Una storia dal 1954 a oggi*. Rome: Donzelli.
8   By the end of the 1970s Milan started to become a centre for high fashion: in just two years, the fashion houses registered at the National Chamber for Italian Fashion (*Camera Nazionale*

della Moda Italiana) in Milan more than tripled in number from 14 to 52. In particular, Gianni Versace, who is considered the father of the superstar models and exporter of the 'Made in Italy' brand, used to pay fabulous sums to top models, organised spectacular advertising campaigns with top world photographers and used famous artists to promote his products.

9   Gianni Versace, who was the single most influential character of the Italian fashion industry, always called himself a tailor (*sarto*). He had worked from the age of nine with his two younger brothers as an apprentice at his mother's dressmaking boutique (*sartoria*) in Reggio Calabria in the south of Italy. He followed *liceo classico* where he was passionate about ancient Greek history and then studied architecture; as such his style was strongly influenced by classical art and the Cubist movement.

10   See, for example, Dei, F. 2011. 'Pop-politica. Le basi culturali del berlusconismo.' In *Studi Culturali,* 3: 471–89.

11   This was MediaSet's most popular satirical news review broadcast in prime time from Monday to Friday; the show invented the concept of *veline* in 1988.

12   This was a popular television show for teenagers, on air between 1991 and 1995, where 100 girls aged between 14 and 22 danced, sang and hosted talk shows.

13   For good accounts of this phenomenon see, for example, Brancati, D. 2011. *Occhi di maschio. Le donne e la televisione in Italia. Una storia dal 1954 a oggi.* Rome: Donzelli; Morvillo, C. 2003. *La repubblica delle veline.* Rizzoli; and Hipkins, D. 2012. 'Who Wants to be a TV Showgirl? Auditions, Talent and Taste in Contemporary Popular Italian Cinema.' In *The Italianist.* 32: 154–90. These also show how the figure of *veline* was used in popular Italian cinema.

14   For example Vereni, P. 2008. *Identità catodiche. Rappresentazioni mediatiche di appartenenze collettive.* Rome: Meltemi Editore. 49–68.

15   Designed by the scene designer Emanuela Trixie Zitkowsky, who also created the studios for the Italian version of Big Brother.

16   Fabio Fazio, the co-presenter of the festival, http://www.rainews.it/dl/rainews/articoli/Festival-di-Sanremo-2014-una-scenografia-da-Grande-bellezza-b4d93843-2846-4a9d-90ee-dea1c057b831.html, accessed 19 November 2015.

17   Fabio Fazio, the co-presenter of the festival.

18   *Stirare, piallare, segare.* She contrasts natural beauty with the products of aesthetic interventions and techniques women undergo: 'at 30 [years old] they look like the grandma of Silvan, at 50 they become the *velina* of Striscia [la Notizia],' in http://www.rai.tv/dl/RaiTV/programmi/media/ContentItem-395a507d-13b7-4f95-ae7a-f37500552f93.html, accessed 19 November 2015.

19   Each of these bags cost between €200 and €400.

20   For example, Simona hates the superficiality of the numerous encounters in the town or the lack of imagination in the organisation of public events.

21   Murray, M. 2009. 'Madrid: The Material Culture of City Life'. Unpublished PhD Thesis, UCL.

22   Famous Italian television star, model and actress of Argentinian origin who gained her glory by winning the Big Brother contest in 2010.

23   However, many young people in Grano approach this from the other way around: since these goods cost so much, they should save up for them or convince other people in their families to buy the goods for them.

24   This is one reason why many feminist women in Grano breach this rule as a gesture of opposition to the social conformity in their town.

25   Spending time with Giuliana and her friends made my female research assistant exclaim, in a puzzled and melancholy way: 'She is really happy!' Although she herself has lived in Grano for most of her life, she has never really thought that housewives could be so content and have a fulfilled life.

26   This might not be the case for the few women in second marriages who do tend to be much more active on Facebook and post relatively more about themselves.

27   See, for example, Sellers, M. 2009. 'The Influence of Marcus Tullius Cicero on Modern Legal and Political Ideas.' Ciceroniana, the Atti of Colloquium Tullianum Anni, MMVIII, 20 February 2009. Available online at Social Science Research Network: http://ssrn.com/abstract=1354102 (retrieved 14 November 2015); and Fishwick, M. 2006. *Cicero, Classicism, and Popular Culture.* New York; London: Routledge.

28   These techniques are called *captatio benevolentiae.* A famous radical example is when allegedly Elsa Fornero, the ex-Italian welfare minister, broke down in tears in front of

the assembled Italian Parliament when announcing a drastic austerity programme in December 2011.

29 In contrast, Instagram is dominated by personal photographs and Twitter with text and world photography.

30 This idea was used by different nationalistic forces in Italy, following the *Risorgimento* movement in the nineteenth century, to associate the unity of Italy with the Roman Empire.

31 See for example Simmel, G. 1971. 'Fashion,' In *On Individuality and Social Forms: Selected Writings*. Chicago; London: University of Chicago Press. 294–323.

32 Miler, D and Sinanan, J. 2014. *Webcam*. Cambridge: Polity Press.

33 In philosophical terms, this corresponds to the dialectical process of creative self-development described by Hegel as including self-understanding, self-actualisation and self-alteration. Because of the multiplicity of senses that act upon the self, Hegel called this process 'experience' (Hegel, G. 1977. *Phenomenology of Spirit*. Oxford: Clarendon Press, par. 86).

Chapter 6

1 It is also true that manual and agricultural workers use Facebook the least, relative to other occupational categories. This contrasts with other field sites in the 'Why We Post' project, such as Chile and China, where manual workers do post a lot on Facebook about their work.

2 Most women who do not hesitate to display their domestic work on Facebook are not married.

3 See also those who argue that children are an essential means to maintaining the division of labour and social spaces in Italian families (for example Dalla Costa, M. 1989. 'Stato, lavoro, rapporti di sesso nel femminismo marxista.' In Alisa Del Re, ed., *Stato e rapporti sociali di sesso*, 207–26. Milano: Franco Angeli.

4 See, for example, Rogers, S. C. 1975. 'Female Forms of Power and the Myth of Male Dominance: A Model of Female/Male Interaction in Peasant Society.' In *American Ethnologist* 2(4): 727–56; Strathern, M. 1988. *The Gender of the Gift: Problems with Women and Problems with Society in Melanesia*. Berkeley (CA); London: University of California Press; and for theoretical approaches see Moore, H. 1988. *Feminism and Anthropology*. Cambridge: Polity Press; or Lewin, E., ed. 2006. *Feminist Anthropology: A Reader*. Malden (MA); Oxford: Blackwell.

5 Interview in local press.

6 For example Granelli, A. 2013. 'Una via italiana alle 'smart specialization,' In IPRES, *Puglia in Cifre 2012. Annuario statistico e studi per le politiche regionali*, 159–71. Bari: Cacucci Editore.

7 Similar misunderstandings also applied to previous communication technology such as computers and mobiles (for example Livingstone, S. 2002. *Young People and New Media: Childhood and the Changing Media Environment*. London: Sage; Ito, M. and D. Okabe. 2005. 'Intimate Connections: Contextualizing Japanese Youth and Mobile Messaging.' In Richard Harper, Leysia Palen, and Alex Taylor, eds., *Inside the Text: Social Perspectives on SMS in the Mobile Age*. Dordrecht: Springer).

8 This is roughly the equivalent of years 10 to 13 in the UK education system, that is students aged 14 to 18.

9 Law No. 910 from 11 December 1969.

10 Ministerial Circulars No. 24 from 6 February 1991 and No. 615 from 27 September 1996.

11 The Ministerial Decree No. 30 from 15 March 2007 bans the use of mobile phones and other electronic devices in the classroom and the Ministerial Decree No. 104 from 30 November 2007 regulates the use of mobile phones in relation to the acquisition of personal data and privacy.

12 Ministerial Decree No. 362 from 25 August 1998.

13 Gesano, Giuseppe and Maura Misiti. 2011. 'La distribuzione territoriale della popolazione.' In Sveva Avveduto, ed., *Italia 150 anni. Popolazione, welfare, scienza e società*, 15–20. Roma: Gangemi Editore.

14 OECD Report. 2013. *Review of the Italian Strategy for Digital Schools*. The report shows that the average within the EU is 16 PCs for every 100 students.

15 The page has more than 1.4 million followers and this meme received more than 800 'Likes' and 686 shares in January 2014, much more than the average on that page.

16 This meme was shared from the same Facebook page as the previous one where it had 700 'Likes' and 622 shares in January 2014.

17 Such as *nepotismo* (nepotism) and *raccomandazione* (recommendation).

18 ISTAT, data available at: http://dati.istat.it/?queryid=298 accessed on 21 October 2015. For details, see data from the Ministry of Instruction, University and Research at http://statistica.miur.it/Data/uic2009_2010/capitolo_4.pdf, accessed 28 July 2016.

19 This is lower than the national average of 14 per cent.

20 The origins of the civic responsibility for formal education are much older and date to before the Second World War and the beginning of republican Italy.

21 In 1995 the Law 355/1995, in 1997 the Treu Package (Law196/1997), in 2003 the Biagi Law (Law 30/2003), in 2012 the Fornero Law (Law 92/2012) and in 2014 and 2015 the Jobs Act.

22 This series of reforms also weakened the once powerful Italian unions because the public trust in their scope and efficiency decreased considerably.

23 Herzfeld, M. 2004. *The Body Impolitic: Artisans and Artifice in the Global hierarchy of Value*. Chicago; London: The University of Chicago Press, 196.

Chapter 7

1 'Consistently on' implies that social media provides the sense that peers would always act in a predictable and self-assured way (Nicolescu, R. 2014. 'The Normativity of Boredom. The Use of Communication Media among Romanian Teenagers.' In Dalsgaard, A. et al., *Time Objectified: Ethnographies of Youth and Temporality*. Philadelphia (PA): Temple University Press. 150).

2 More than three-quarters of these associations are inactive. We should note a tradition for establishing professional associations (*leghe*) which have played a major political role in southern Salento since the turn of the twentieth century (for example Carducci, L. 2006: *Storia del Salento Vol. 2*. Mario Congedo Editore. 389–91).

3 This contrasts with many academic writings which, following Habermas, suggested that new public spheres tend to facilitate more liberal political discussions (Habermas, J. 1989. *The Structural Transformation of the Public Sphere: An Inquiry into a Category of Bourgeois Society*. Cambridge: Polity Press).

4 See, for example, Castells, M. 2000. *The Rise of the Network Society*. Oxford: Blackwell, 2nd edn. For a contrasting view on the social consequences of technology, see for example Baym, N. 2010. *Personal Connections in the Digital Age*. Cambridge: Polity Press.

5 Rainie, L. and Wellman, B. 2012. *Networked: The new Social Operating System*. Cambridge (MA): MIT Press.

6 See the discussion of new technologies as improved versions of the existing ones in Bolter, D. and Grusin, R. 1999. *Remediation: Understanding New Media*. Cambridge (MA); London: MIT Press.

7 Medianou, M. and Miller, D. 2012. *Migration and New Media: Transnational Families and Polymedia*. London; New York (NY): Routledge.

8 See Pascal, B. 1958. *The Pensées*. New York: E.P. Dutton & Co. 3, 274.; Hume, D. 1912 [1777]. *An Enquiry concerning the Principles of Morals*: Part 1.; or Bergson, H. 1977 [1935]. *The Two Sources of Morality and Religion*. Notre Dame (IN): University of Notre Dame Press. Ch.1.

9 This is akin to the 'structuralist' approach of Dumont, who saw hierarchy as a mode of social cohesion where each level is related to the larger whole (Dumont, L. 1980. *Homo Hierarchicus: The Caste System and Its Implications*. Chicago: University of Chicago Press).

References

Agus, M. and Castellina, L. 2014. *Guardati dalla mia fame*. Rome: Nottetempo.

Alò, P. 2010. *Il caporalato nella tarda modernità*. Bari: Wip Edizioni.

Althusser, L. 2001 [1971]. *Lenin and Philosophy, and other Essays*. New York: Monthly Review Press.

Aroldi, P. 2012. 'EU Parents Online L'importanza del contesto familiare.' Mascheroni, G. ed. *I ragazzi e la rete. La ricerca EU Kids Online e il caso Italia*. Brescia: La Scuola. 261–88.

Balbo, L. 1976. *Stato di famiglia: bisogni, privato, collettivo*. Milan: ETAS.

Baldassar, L. 2001. *Visits Home. Migration Experiences between Italy and Australia*. Carlton South (Victoria): Melbourne University Press.

Barbagallo, F. 2013. *La questione italiana. Il Nord e il Sud al 1860 a oggi*. Laterza.

Barbagallo, F. 1980. *Mezzogiorno e questione meridionale (1860–1980)*. Naples: Guida.

Barbagli, M. 1991. 'Three Household Formation Systems in Eighteenth- and Nineteenth-Century Italy.' Kertzer, D. and Saller, R. eds. *The Family in Italy from Antiquity to the Present*. New Haven (CT): Yale University Press. 250–70.

Barbagli, M. 1991. 'Marriage and the Family in Italy in the early Nineteenth Century.' Davis, J. and Ginsborg, P. eds. *Society and Politics in the Age of the Risorgimento: Essays in Honour of Denis Mack Smith*. Cambridge: Cambridge University Press. 92–127.

Barile, G. and Zanuso, L. 1980. *Lavoro femminile e condizione familiare*. Milan: Angeli.

Baym, N. 2010. *Personal connections in the digital age*. Cambridge: Polity Press.

Bergson, H. 1977 [1935]. *The Two Sources of Morality and Religion*. Translated by Ashley Audra and Cloudesley Brereton with the assistance of W. Horsfall Carter. Notre Dame (IN): University of Notre Dame Press.

Bolter, D. and Grusin, R. 1999. *Remediation: Understanding New Media*. Cambridge (MA); London: MIT Press.

Bonini, T. 2011. 'The Media as "Home-making" Tools: Life Story of a Filipino Migrant in Milan.' *Media, Culture & Society*, 33(6): 869–83.

Bourdieu, P. 1996. *The State Nobility: Elite Schools in the Field of Power*. Cambridge: Polity Press.

Bourdieu, P. 1986. 'The Forms of Capital.' Richardson, J. ed. *Handbook of Theory and Research for the Sociology of Education*. New York: Greenwood. 241–58.

Bourdieu, P. 1984. *Distinction: A Social Critique of the Judgement of Taste*. London: Routledge & Kegan Paul.

Brancati, D. 2011. *Occhi di maschio: le donne e la televisione in Italia. Una storia dal 1954 a oggi*. Rome: Donzelli.

Brettell, C. 1991. 'Property, Kinship and Gender: A Mediterranean Perspective.' Kertzer, D. and Saller, R. eds. *The Family in Italy from Antiquity to the Present*. New Haven (CT): Yale University Press. 340–54.

Bugiardini, S. 2002. 'L'associazionismo negli USA.' Bevilacqua, P., De Clementi, A. and Franzina, E. eds. *Storia dell'emigrazione Italiana. Arrivi*. Rome: Donzelli Editore. 551–78.

Carducci, L. 2006. *Storia del Salento Vol. 2*. Rome: Mario Congedo Editore.

Castells, M. 2000. *The Rise of the Network Society*. Oxford: Blackwell, 2nd edn.

Clark, L. 2009. 'Digital Media and the Generation Gap.' In *Information, Communication & Society*, 12(3): 388–407.

Curtis, D. 2015. 'An Agro-Town Bias? Re-examining the Micro-Demographic Model for Southern Italy in the Eighteenth Century.' *Journal of Social History*, 1–29.

Cutrufelli, M. 1975. *Disoccupata con onore: lavoro e condizione della dona*. Milan: Gabriele Mazzotta.

Dalla Costa, M. 1989. 'Stato, lavoro, rapporti di sesso nel femminismo marxista.' Del Re, A. ed. *Stato e rapporti sociali di sesso*. Milan: Franco Angeli. 207–26.

Daniele, V. and Malanima, P. 2011. *Il divario Nord-Sud in Italia 1861–2011*. Milan: Rubbettino.

Davis, J. 1977. *People of the Mediterranean: An Essay in Comparative Social Anthropology*. London: Routledge and Kegan Paul.

De Blasio, E. 2014. *La democrazia digitale. Una piccola introduzione*. Rome: LUISS University Press.

Dei, F. 2011. 'Pop-politica. Le basi culturali del berlusconismo.' *Studi Culturali*, 3: 471–89.

Di Nola, A. 1998. 'How Critical Was De Martino's "Critical Ethnocentrism" in Southern Italy?' Schneider, J. ed. *Italy's 'Southern Question': Orientalism in One Country*. 157–75. Oxford; New York: Berg.

Douglass, W. 1980. 'The South Italian Family: A Critique.' *Journal of Family History*, 5(4): 338–57.Dumont, L. 1980. *Homo Hierarchicus: The Caste System and its Implications*. Chicago: University of Chicago Press.

E-commerce in Italia 2015. 2015. Edited by Casaleggio Associati, accessed 19 November 2015. https://www.casaleggio.it/focus/rapporto-e-commerce-in-italia-2015

Ellison, N., Steinfield, C. and Lampe. C. 2007. 'The Benefits of Facebook "Friends": Social Capital and College Students' use of Online Social Network Sites', Journal of Computer-Mediated Communication, 12(4): 1,143–1,168.

Fazic, I. 2004. 'The Family, Honour, and Gender in Sicily: Models and New Research.' *Modern Italy*, 9(2): 263–80.

Fishwick, M. 2006. *Cicero, Classicism, and Popular Culture*. New York; London: Routledge.

Galasso, G.. 2009. *L'altra Europa. Per un'antropologia storica del Mezzogiorno d'Italia*. Naples: Alfredo Guida Editore, 3rd edn.

Galt, A. 1991. *Far from the Church Bells: Settlement and Society in an Apulian Town*. Cambridge: Cambridge University Press.

Gil de Zúñiga, Homero, Jung, N. and Valenzuela, S. 2012. 'Social Media Use for News and Individuals' Social Capital, Civic Engagement and Political Participation.' *Journal of Computer-Mediated Communication*, 17: 319–36.

Ginsborg, P. 1990. *A History of Contemporary Italy: Society and Politics 1943–1988*. London: Penguin.

Goddard, V. 1996. *Gender, Family, and Work in Naples*. Oxford: Berg.

Goffman, E. 1990. *The Presentation of Self in Everyday Life*. London: Penguin.

Gratelli, A. 2013. 'Una via italiana alle "smart specialization",' IPRES, *Puglia in Cifre 2012. Annuario statistico e studi per le politiche regionali*. Bari: Cacucci Editore. 159–71.

Gribaudi, G. 1993. 'Familismo e famiglia a Napoli e a Mezzogiorno.' *Meridiane*, 17: 13–42.

Habermas, J. 1989. *The Structural Transformation of the Public Sphere: An Inquiry into a Category of Bourgeois Society*. Cambridge: Polity Press.

Hegel, G. 1977. *Phenomenology of Spirit*. Translated by Miller, A.V. Oxford: Clarendon Press.

Herzfeld, M. 2004. *The Body Impolitic: Artisans and Artifice in the Global Hierarchy of Value*. Chicago; London: University of Chicago Press.

Hipkins, D. 2012. 'Who Wants to be a TV Showgirl? Auditions, Talent and Taste in Contemporary Popular Italian Cinema.' *The Italianist*, 32: 154–90.

Hume, D. 1912 [1777]. *An Enquiry concerning the Principles of Morals*. Available online at: http://www.gutenberg.org/files/4320/4320-h/4320-h.htm, accessed 19 November 2015.

IPRES, 2013. *Puglia in Cifre 2013. Annuario statistico e studi per le politiche regionali*. Edited by Istituto Pugliese di Ricerche Economiche e Sociali, ed. Bari: Cacucci Editore.

Ito, M. and Okabe, D. 2005. 'Intimate Connections: Contextualizing Japanese Youth and Mobile Messaging.' Harper, R., Palen, L. and Taylor, A. eds. *Inside the Text: Social Perspectives on SMS in the Mobile Age*. Dordrecht: Springer.

Kertzer, D and Saller, R. eds. 1991. *The Family in Italy from Antiquity to the Present*. New Haven; London: Yale University Press.

Lever-Tracy, C. and Holton, R. 2001. 'Social Exchange, Reciprocity and Amoral Familism: Aspects of Italian Chain Migration to Australia.' *Journal of Ethnic and Migration Studies*, 27(1): 81–99.

Lewin, E. ed. 2006. *Feminist Anthropology: A Reader*. Malden (MA); Oxford: Blackwell.

Livingstone, S. 2002. *Young People and New Media: Childhood and the Changing Media Environment*. London: Sage.

Madianou, M. and Miller, D. 2012. *Migration and New Media: Transnational Families and Polymedia*. London; New York (NY): Routledge.

Meloni, B. ed. 1997. *Famiglia Meridionale senza familismo. Strategie economiche, reti di relazione e parentela*. Rome: Donzelli Editore.

Meyer Sabino, G. 2002. 'In Svizzera'. Bevilacqua, P., De Clementi, A. and Franzina, E. eds. *Storia dell'Emigrazione Italiana. Arrivi*. Rome: Donzelli Editore. 147–51.

Micheli, M. 2013. 'Facebook, adolescenti e differenze di classe.' *Mediascapes Journal*, 2: 91–105.

Miller, D, Costa, E., Haynes, N., McDonald, T., Nicolescu, R., Sinanan, J., Spyer, J., Venkrataman, S. and Wang, X. 2016. *How the World Changed Social Media*. London: UCL Press.

Miller, D. 2011. *Tales from Facebook*. Cambridge: Polity Press.

Miller, D. and Sinanan, J. 2014. *Webcam*. Cambridge: Polity Press.

Moore, H. 1988. *Feminism and Anthropology*. Cambridge: Polity Press.

Morvillo, C. 2003. *La repubblica delle veline*. Rome: Rizzoli.

Murray, M. 2009. 'Madrid: The Material Culture of City Life.' Unpublished PhD Thesis, UCL.

Nardini, G. 1999. *Che Bella Figura! The Power of Performance in an Italian Ladies Club in Chicago*. Albany: State University of New York Press.

Nicolescu, R. 2014. 'The Normativity of Boredom. The Use of Communication Media among Romanian Teenagers.' Dalsgaard, A. et al. eds. *Time Objectified: Ethnographies of Youth and Temporality*. Philadelphia (PA): Temple University Press. 139–52.

OECD Report. 2013. *Review of the Italian Strategy for Digital Schools*. Edited by Francesco Avvisati, Sara Hennessy, Robert B. Kozma and Stéphan Vincent-Lancrin, accessed 19 November 2015, http://www.oecd.org/edu/ceri/Innovation%20Strategy%20Working%20Paper%2090.pdf

Pancino, C. 2003. 'Soffrire per ben comparire. Corpo e bellezza, natura e cura.' *Storia d'Italia. La Moda. Annali 19*. Turin: Giulio Einaudi editore. 5–42.

Papacharissi, Z. 2010. *A Private Sphere: Democracy in a Digital Age*. Cambridge: Polity Press.

Pascal, B. 1958. *The Pensées*. Introduction by T. S. Eliot. New York: E. P. Dutton & Co. Available online at: http://www.gutenberg.org/files/18269/18269-h/18269-h.htm#p_274, accessed 19 November 2015.

Piaget, J. 1973 [1929]. *The Child's Conception of the World*. London: Paladin.

Piaget, J. 1964. *The Early Growth of Logic in the Child: Classification and Seriation*. London: Routledge and Kegan Paul.

Pipyros, S. 2014. 'Cutting *bella figura*: Irony, Crisis, and Secondhand Clothes in South Italy.' In *American Ethnologist*, 41(3): 532–46.

Plato. 2015. *Platone. Dialoghi Socratici. Ippia Maggiore. Sul Bello*. Translated by Giovanni Reale. Milan: Bompiani.

Pugliese, E. 2006. *L'Italia tra migrazioni internazionali e migrazioni interne*. Bologna: Il Mulino.

Pugliese, E. 1984. *Braccianti agricoli in Italia. Tra mercato del lavoro e assistenza*. Milan: Franco Angeli.

Rainie, L. and Wellman, B. 2012. *Networked: The New Social Operating System*. Cambridge (MA): MIT Press.

Rogers, S. 1975. 'Female Forms of Power and the Myth of Male Dominance: A Model of Female/Male Interaction in Peasant Society.' *American Ethnologist*, 2(4): 727–56.

Romero, F. 2002. 'L'emigrazione operaia in Europa (1948–1973).' Bevilacqua, P., De Clementi, A. and Franzina, E. eds. *Storia dell'Emigrazione Italiana. Partenze*. Rome: Donzelli Editore. 397–414.

Rossi-Doria, M. 1982. *Scritti sul Mezzogiorno*. Turin: Einaudi.

Rossi-Doria, M. 1956 [1948]. *Riforma agraria e azione meridionalista*. Bologna: Edizioni Agricole, Bologna.

Sassatelli, R. 2010. *Fitness Culture: Gyms and the Commercialisation of Discipline and Fun*. Basingstoke: Palgrave Macmillan.

Sassatelli, R. and Davolio, F. 2010. 'Consumption, Pleasure, and Politics: Slow Flood and the Politico-Aesthetic Problematization of Food.' *Journal of Consumer Culture*, 10: 202–32.

Schneider, J. ed. 1998. *Italy's 'Southern Question:' Orientalism in One Country*. Oxford; New York: Berg.

Secondo Rapporto Nazionale sull'Artigianato. 2006. Edited by Giuseppe Capuano, Corardo Martone, and Daria Broglio. Istituto Guglielmo Tagliacarne. Unioncamere. Camere di Comercio d'Italia.

Sellers, M. 2009. 'The Influence on Marcus Tullius Cicero on Modern Legal and Political Ideas.' Ciceroniana, the Atti of Colloquium Tullianum Anni, MMVIII, 20 February 2009. Available online at Social Science Research Network: http://ssrn.com/abstract=1354102 retrieved 14 November 2015.

Simmel, G. 1971. 'Fashion,' On Individuality and Social Forms: Selected Writings. Chicago; London: University of Chicago Press. 294–323.

Sorice M. 2014. I media e la democrazia. Rome: Carocci Editore.

Strathern, M. 1992. 'Foreword: The Mirror of Technology.' Silverstone, R. and Hirsch, E. eds. Consuming Technologies: Media and Information in Domestic Spaces. London; New York (NY): Routledge. vi–xiii.

Strathern, M. 1988. The Gender of the Gift: Problems with Women and Problems with Society in Melanesia. Berkeley (CA); London: University of California Press.

Tacchi, J. 1997. 'Radio Texture: Between Self and Others.' Miller, D. ed., Material Cultures: Why Some Things Matter. Chicago: University Chicago Press. 25–45.

Verent, P. 2008. Identità catodiche. Rappresentazioni mediatiche di appartenenze collettive. Rome: Meltemi Editore.

Viazzo, P. 2003. 'What's So Special about the Mediterranean? Thirty Years of Research on Household and Family in Italy.' Continuity and Change, 18(1): 111–37.

Wellman, B., Quan Haase, A., Witte, J. and Hampton, K. 2001. 'Does the Internet Increase, Decrease, or Supplement Social Capital? Social Networks, Participation, and Community Commitment.' American Behavioral Scientist, 45: 436–55.

Wessendorf, S. 2013. Second-generation Transnationalism and Roots Migration: Cross-border Lives. Farnham: Ashgate.

Zacchino, V. 2007. Salento Migrante. Appunti per la storia dell'emigrazione Salentina (1861–1971). Rome: Edizioni Centro Studi Emigrazione.

Index

Illustrations are indicated in *italic*

abstract genres in images, appreciation by more educated people 82
adults, preference for television and the mobile phone 48
agriculture, as important area of employment 33
Alessandra
intimate new relationship via Twitter 116
return to Facebook 117, 118
Angela I, family Facebook page 41
Angela II, use of landscape photography on walks 71–2
anthropology, and social relationships 97
Antonio (18 year old) comment on self-promotion 39
Antonio (Maria Angela's husband) 156–7
aristocrats, use of social media 9–10
artisans
priority of Facebook page 154–5
reliance on social media 22–3

beauty
see also personal appearance
bellezza as an immense burden to the whole society but especially to women 138
as a craft, acceptability 144
cult of 1
demonstration on Facebook as a civic duty 179
as difficult social burden and obligation 137
not seen as a narcissistic selfish indulgence 137
Bianca (unemployed person), use of social media 168
building work, increase in Grano post Second World War 18
business
as most visible employment sector in Grano 22
owners, printing out of posters and leaflets, and asking retailers to display these for free 26
businesses, as repositories of social status 22

Catholicism 31, 64–5, 68, 124
'clever' memes *67*, 68

closeness, and use of smartphones 107
coffee, importance 12
collective values, Facebook 4
commerce *see* business
conformity 4, 54, 60, 145, 181–3
consistency between online and offline practices 3, 38, 54, 60, 125, 137, 179
crafting 86, 144, 147–8, 179, 183
cresima 31–2
gifts for 32, 59
cultural capital
and education 153
importance in Grano 56
and social media 46

digital technology
as coming-of-age for young people 34
use by teenagers 33
domestic goods, per household 44, *45*
domestic roles, present division 18
domestic worker, as critical to the moral and economic output of the family as a whole 157
Donatello, Mr (mayor), charm as speaker 140
dual nature of social relationships in Grano 177
duties, objectification of the local culture 145

e-reading device, unpopularity 27
economic crisis of, 2008
effect on Grano 20
invisibility 10
education
and constant contact with family 160
formal, limitations 170
as ideal value 180
impossibility of criticism of 164
and inequality 158–9
level of, and width of social contacts 41
social prestige and 56
as women's responsibility 23
elderly *see* older people
electronic devices, inventory within households 44, *45*
Elena (friend of Angela), photography of landscapes 72

203

barons stripped of their juridical powers, but keeping most of their privileges 16
commuters to and from 7
cultivation 22
current life 20
ending of prosperity in early 2000s 19
expensive local shops, mixed with butchers and general food shops 8–9
fiestas, spectacular firework displays after midnight 11–12
golden days 19
growth until 1960s 18
hierarchy, history of 16
highly socialised familiarity with each other 178
as important social and economic hub for a territory about 20–25 km wide 7
lack of change in character 184
lack of need for social media 2
lack of tradition of making something public 25
look to north after 2005 19–20
mass emigration post Second World War 17
middle-class, local, emergence 16
nature of place 5
normality 1
not typical of media use in rest of Italy 55
people trying not to stand out and impress too much 178
point of social media use 177
present-day, conspicuous consumption 20
prosperity and Asian competition 19
relationships, firmly established norms and conventions 97
residents' different indirect ways to express conformity to their respective social positions 146
seasons *see* seasons
social visibility reflects their social status 3
society highly hierarchical 16
traditional marital relationship in a modern setting 97–102
Grano Porto 14
groups, communicating in several concentric groups 24

high fashion brands, production in Grano 19
higher education, and Facebook as an asset to be protected 102
highly educated unemployed with digital skills, use of social media 23, 186
home education in Grano, importance over school 34, 161
home gaming
    popularity of devices 27
    still seen as a social activity 27
houses for newly-weds, need for 18
housewife, role of 111, 136, 157
housewives, use of social media online 48
'humorous' memes *66*
husband, role 23

ideals
    social ideals 10, 120, 146, 158, 178
    individual ideal 4, 129–30, 137, 183

striving for an ideal 114, 118–9, 132–4, 146–7
ideal of beauty 144–7
ideal of work 57, 136–8, 149–53, 155–8, 172–6
ideal of education 32–34, 149, 153, 159–62, 169–72
images, of pets and food 83–6, *83, 84*
information technology and social networking indicates a fall 4
Instagram 183
    teenagers' use 34
integration of Italian society ideals with local ideals 146
internet, use of 26
intimate relationships, restricted social visibility 119
Isabella, relationship with female friends in WhatsApp group 103–4
Isabella and Salvatore, use of WhatsApp 118–19

landline, frequency of use *45*
landscape 69, 73–5, 141–4
layers of intimacy, setting 117–19
liceu classico 159–60
liceu scientifico 159
lifestyles and ideas that co-exist in Grano 9
locality, globalisation of 175
locals stroll through the town (giro) 12
Luana, as beautiful woman 121–5, 145
Luigi (stone carver), use of Facebook 154

majesty of nature, in images 69–75
Maria Angela (housewife with 3 children) 155
    use of Facebook 156–7
Maria (ceramic artist), use of Facebook 154–5
marriage
    inability to finance 103
    and similarity of appearance of married couples 106
married couple with children
    sleepiness restricting time on Facebook 48–9
    use of social media 99–102
married women
    and beauty 123
    position in families 23
    use of social media 59
Matteo 167–8
memes 10, 62, 63, 68, 138
    see also 'clever' memes; 'humorous' memes; 'moral' memes; 'political' memes; 'romantic' memes
    for beliefs in Grano 62
    express complex ideas and critiques of higher levels of society 68
    as most popular Facebook posting genre in Grano 62
    shared by Grano residents *163*, 187
men, negligence of appearance 106
middle-classes
    formation 16
    use of social media 9–10